U.S. Marshals

Inside America's Most Storied
Law Enforcement Agency

Mike Earp

With David Fisher

HARPER **LUXE**

An Imprint of HarperCollins*Publishers*

WITHDRAWN

U.S. MARSHALS. Copyright © 2014 by David Fisher. All rights reserved. Printed in the United States of America. No part of this book may be used or reproduced in any manner whatsoever without written permission except in the case of brief quotations embodied in critical articles and reviews. For information address HarperCollins Publishers, 10 East 53rd Street, New York, NY 10022.

HarperCollins books may be purchased for educational, business, or sales promotional use. For information, please e-mail the Special Markets Department at SPsales@harpercollins.com.

FIRST HARPERLUXE EDITION

HarperLuxe™ is a trademark of HarperCollins Publishers

Library of Congress Cataloging-in-Publication Data is available upon request.

ISBN: 978-0-06-229864-5

14 ID/RRD 10 9 8 7 6 5 4 3 2 1

To my family, Chris, Mike, Joe, Kelly, and Joe G., thanks for putting up with me for so long. With much love.

To Duds, still missing you, bro.

And to the men and women of the U.S. Marshals Service and the hundreds of task force officers: Your dedication to your job, day and night, weekends and holidays, is truly inspirational. Without fanfare and with little recognition, you go through that door every single day making our world a safer place. I salute you, and may you continue to go home each night. Stay safe.

—Mike Earp

To Ingwald "Troop" Hicker, who for forty-two years served the public with great integrity as a New York state trooper and at the Division of Parole. He was a worthy representative of all the men and women of American law enforcement to whom we all owe so much, and was the proud father and father-in-law of George and Kathy Hicker, two of the finest people I have known in my life.

—David Fisher

"My friends think you're a rent-a-cop and I bet them you're for real. Are you?"

Raylan opened his coat to show his star hanging on the silver chain. "I'm a United States marshal . . . .

"I'm going to move the badge to my belt. Not get anymore remarks about it." Raylan told him, "In case you didn't know it, I'm one of the good guys. I've shot seven men in the line of duty, wanted fugitives, no women or students, and they all died." Raylan smiled at the defensive lineman. "You gonna have me telling marshal stories next."

—Elmore Leonard, *Raylan*

Contents

Foreword

By Chief Inspector Lenny DePaul, former commander of the New York/New Jersey Regional Fugitive Task Force, United States Marshals Service

In the late 1980s I was in the Secret Service, working in the Reagan White House, when a person with whom I'd gone through training told me, "You know what, Lenny, you really need to get into the Marshals Service."

My story was pretty much the same as everybody else's: I had no idea what he was talking about. "What the hell is a U.S. marshal?" I asked him.

"You know, like John Wayne," he said. "Or Matt Dillon. You travel around and lock people up. You get a case and you work it to death. Then you move on to the next case. You never have to wait for the phone to ring. You chase people, you're a manhunter. It's nonstop action."

"Where do I sign up?" I said. That was in 1989. I moved to Brooklyn, put a cot in the basement of one of my academy buddies' parents' house, and shared my space with the cockroaches.

It was about two years later that I first heard of this guy Mike Earp. That name, and the obvious connection to Marshal Wyatt Earp, was unforgettable. At that time he was coordinating the establishment of the Marshals Service's Puerto Rico Fugitive Task Force. That was a very tough place to work; for the marshals working there Puerto Rico was pretty much lawless. It was a difficult situation; there were a lot of people who didn't want us there. But as he was to do so many times after that, Mike Earp just persevered. He has always been a no-nonsense leader; his mantra was simple and direct: "Get 'er done." And that's what he did in Puerto Rico, he got the mission done without fuss, without drawing attention to himself, and without any sense of drama. Be aggressive, be smart, stay safe. But be aggressive. In many ways, maybe even without realizing it, that was the way we all learned to operate: get 'er done.

Mike Earp played a tremendous role in making that happen. I actually met him for the first time when he became the chief of the Investigative Services Division. When I started we weren't exactly on horseback but we certainly didn't have a lot of new equipment, we definitely didn't get a lot of respect, and no one knew too much about us. They thought we were the people who towed cars with too many unpaid parking tickets or evicted people out of their homes. Mike's ascension up the Washington ladder paralleled our growth as the nation's and maybe the world's best fugitive hunters. That's what Mike knows, fugitive hunting, and he did it as long and as well as anyone in our organization. I started getting close to him right around 2000, when he became deputy assistant director of the Investigative Operations Division, which is probably the toughest, most stringent, most stressful job in the entire organization. And then the assistant director, and finally the associate director of Investigative Operations, the number three guy in the agency. In that position he oversaw all operational missions. But he also helped shape the future. Working with Assistant Director Bob Finan, he convinced Congress of the value of the permanent regional task force structure, run from Washington, that has helped revolutionize American law enforcement. He has great people skills, and he has a manner about him that attracts dedicated, good people—then he tries to give them whatever support they need to get the job done without getting in their way. He has never been afraid to delegate authority—or to give praise—to the people he has worked with.

I learned the job on the streets. Two years after joining the Marshals I was assigned to the Eastern District Warrant Squad in New York, chasing fugitives. I did that for the rest of my career. When we started our first regional task force in May 2002 I had 25 investigators from ten different agencies; when I retired in 2013 the task force included 385 investigators from ninety different federal, state, and local law enforcement agencies. We were locking up about 120 violent fugitives every week, fifty-two weeks a year.

Reality programs started becoming popular while we were running that task force. I got several calls from a producer who wanted to speak to me. Basically I ignored him until Don Heinz, who was in charge of our Public Affairs Office, told me, "You know what, you're a brand-new congressionally funded task force. You're the flagship of the Marshals Service. Speak to them, see what they want."

Several days later two producers walked into my office. The first words that came out of their mouths were "Thanks for entertaining this idea. You guys are a parole office, right?"

I shook my head. "We have parole officers here, but we also have ninety other agencies as well. That's not what we do. We spend all of our time going after the worst of the worst, the most violent offenders, the murderers, rapists, terrorists." To explain it best I reminded them that Tommy Lee Jones played a relentless deputy marshal in the movie version of *The Fugitive*. Toward the end of that movie his character has finally cornered Dr. Richard Kimble, played by Harrison Ford, in a water tunnel. As Ford is getting ready to jump into the water, he has a long monologue in which he explains why he is innocent. It's a very compelling speech. You can't help feeling sorry for him. But when he finishes, Jones responds matter-of-factly: "I don't care." That's us; we don't care if you killed three people or are totally innocent. Our job is to find you and bring you back to the bar of justice. Hopefully, everybody goes home safely at the end of the day.

The producers' eyes lit up. By the time we were finished talking they knew they had hit the mother lode. Over the next three years we filmed sixty episodes of *Manhunters*, which became one of A&E's most popular shows. When A&E changed programming strategy and decided to move away from police shows, the project ended.

The production company's crews were with us day and night, wherever we went, whatever we did. They were with us in the dark of night when we were in the hills of Puerto Rico sneaking up on a fugitive, and they were with us running up the stairs in a Newark, New Jersey, drug den. A lot of the things they filmed never got on the air. One day, I remember, my guys were going after a parole violator whose underlying charge involved drugs. His apartment was on the fifth floor of a building in the Bronx projects. His brother told us he was in there, but that he was on the phone with his mother, saying good-bye. My people hit the door and found him straddling the window, threatening to jump if they came one step closer. They froze in place and began trying to talk him out of it. All of us have been through this same scenario numerous times. We have a pretty good idea of what to say. We're usually successful in talking them down.

The camera crew had climbed up the fire escape, they were on the ground, on the roof, they had cameras on him from every angle.

He jumped. He fell five stories and hit concrete. The cameras caught everything. Initially Steve Blando of our Public Affairs Office wanted to allow the producers to use this footage. "This is what happens with you guys every day. This is the reality of the job. The public should know about it."

We finally decided it should never be seen. It was a good thing the cameras were there, though, as one neighbor accused us of killing the man, claiming, "The cops pushed him out the window." The footage proved otherwise and everyone was exonerated.

Deputies are often mistaken for cops. We think that's a tremendous compliment. Nobody looks at us as agents with suits who carry guns; in the street they know us as cops. In fact, when we knock on a door or ram through it, we identify ourselves as "Police! Police!" Everybody recognizes that word in any one of the fifty different languages people speak in New York. We are not FBI, we are not DEA. We've learned from experience that if we told people we were marshals, we'd be there for twenty minutes trying to explain what a marshal is. Even after we do that, people don't believe we still exist. "Who are you, really? Why am I opening up my door? That's a fake badge, there's no such thing as the Marshals anymore."

Because we are a congressionally funded organization it would be nice to be better known. It might help us increase our budget. I think people still don't know what we do because we don't get the publicity other agencies get. We just don't get that media attention; most of the time we're happy to let the cooperating local law enforcement agency take the credit. That's just the reality of our job.

I like to think we do God's work; it's as simple as that. We do so much more with so much less; the statistics are staggering. The people we take off the streets are dangerous to the community; many of them have six or more prior arrests and they're out there living in the shadows, preying on the young and the elderly. When we take one of these guys off the streets we're not just arresting him for what he's already done, we're preventing the crimes that he is going to commit. Committing crimes is the only way these people can survive on the streets. When we arrest a murderer, for example, we've saved lives, we know it. Nobody knows he or she is alive because we did our job, but it's a fact.

I believe people are beginning to realize the Marshals Service is still around. *Manhunters* helped; the TV show *Justified* has helped, and people are beginning to get used to reading about us arresting another bad guy. We have cornered the market when it comes to fugitive investigations. What we need to continue being successful is additional congressional funding. The numbers don't lie. We've taken the pursuit of local fugitives national. It used to be that when a fugitive left his local jurisdiction, he was going to be hard to bring back. Even if a local agency found out where their guy had gone, they were dependent on another officer and his partner—people who had their own cases to work—to go out and get him. Too often that just didn't happen.

But that's what we do for a living: a deputy can call another Marshals office anywhere in the world and say, "I'm sending you a lead," and be confident that the men and women he's speaking with will know how to set up a perimeter, how to ask the right questions, how to put the case together, and will eventually make the arrest. If we didn't exist, fugitives would be having a field day, knowing that once they got out of town chances of them being caught were pretty slim. Now we track them wherever they go, and we're relentless. We don't give up until we put handcuffs on them. It may take a day, a week, or five years, but we will catch up with them.

My buddy from the academy was right. For twenty-four years my life was nonstop action. When I look back at my career there are so many fascinating cases I worked or my guys worked. But there was one night I will never forget. In 2006 Camden, New Jersey, was ranked the number one crime capital of America. It was a dangerous place to live. People didn't want to leave their homes at night. The attorney general told law enforcement to do something about it. My deputy commander, Bill Plitt, organized a joint effort and compiled a list of the top fifty fugitives in that area we intended to arrest. We arrested forty-nine out of that fifty, and I will never forget the night we locked up the forty-ninth guy. It was about 9 o'clock on a very, very hot summer night. As we brought him out of a house in handcuffs, all around us people were standing on their front porches watching us. And suddenly, like in a wonderful movie, one person started clapping, then a second and a third, until they were all clapping and cheering us for being in their neighborhood and trying to make it a safer place for them to live. That hit home. I thought, *I really like what I do for a living.*

Mike Earp was the driving force behind the creation of the modern Marshals Service. He was instrumental in the formation of the Sex Offender Investigative Operations Program, the Behavioral Analysis Unit, the Criminal Intelligence Branch, the Financial Surveillance Unit, expansion of the International Investigative Program, and the regional task force concept. When the New York/New Jersey Task Force celebrated our fifth anniversary, I sent him an e-mail telling him I would love for him to come up for our celebration. Mike told one of the people in Washington, "This is great. Lenny is inviting me to come up to New York for his anniversary and I don't know how long he's been married, but I'd love to make it if I can."

He called me several days later, laughing. Apparently someone had told him the real reason he had been invited—he had been so busy it hadn't even occurred to him that five years had passed since he helped put us in business. This book is the story of the new United States Marshals Service and how it has been transformed into the most productive law enforcement agency in the world. It is the story of Mike Earp and the thousands of courageous men and women working with him who risk their lives every day, too often in obscurity. I make you this promise: when you have finished this book you will never think of the world of law enforcement—or the U.S. Marshals Service—in the same way.

Introduction

Many years ago I remember sitting in the warden's office in a Tallahassee prison waiting anxiously as the helicopter set in motion by the man I'd allowed to escape approached. I had pretty much bet my career that this plan would work. And as we waited silently I started thinking, *Now how the heck did I get to this point?*

My name is Mike Earp, and on the last day of 2011, I retired from the United States Marshals Service as associate director for operations. I was in charge of the six operational divisions as well as all the domestic and international operations involving our 470-plus domestic and foreign offices. When I joined the Marshals Service in 1977, it was a very different organization. The days of the Old West, when legendary gunslingers like Wyatt Earp, Bat Masterson, and Bass Reeves enforced the law with a six-shooter, were long gone. The Marshals Service seemed to be a historical anachronism, a relic of America's lawless past. It had been founded by Congress two centuries earlier to be the enforcement arm of the judicial system, but rather than swearing in a posse and going after outlaws, deputies basically provided court security, handled juries, transported prisoners, managed seized property, and served federal court documents. It was a loosely structured organization; each of its ninety-four judicial districts was independently run by a presidential appointee who at that time often had no law enforcement experience.

Occasionally over the years, the public would be reminded that the Marshals Service still existed; for example, when deputies were ordered by the president to perform a special assignment like enforcing the Supreme Court order integrating schools by escorting young African Americans to class or guarding the Pentagon during anti–Vietnam War rioting. But essentially the organization was a relatively safe bureaucracy, a place where deputies went home every night at five P.M.

By the time I retired, more than three decades later, a revolutionary law enforcement strategy had put the agency right in the center of the bull's-eye.

Having become the enforcement arm of most federal agencies—including the DEA, the ATF, and a host of FBI cases—deputies were charged with tracking down and arresting the most violent criminals in America. By creating district and regional task forces, essentially modern-day posses, the Marshals Service brought together the best officers and resources of federal, state, city, and county law enforcement agencies to successfully bring America's most wanted criminals to justice. These days, when there's a really bad guy on the loose anywhere in America, deputies once again will be on his trail. The numbers are staggering; these district and regional task forces will arrest more violent criminals in a week than most other federal law enforcement agencies will arrest in a year. For example, during one week in June 2008, a massive task force known as Operation FALCON (Federal and Local Cops Organized Nationally) arrested 19,380 fugitives, among them 161 homicide suspects and more than 1,000 sex offenders.

Few people know about it, though. Most people still think of deputies as range-riding relics of the past—in fact, every deputy has been asked at one time in his or her career, "Where's your horse?" But every aspect of the organization has changed. While the ninety-four judicial districts still maintain some degree of independence, a relatively strong USMS headquarters leadership and structure has effectively standardized policies and directives, training, equipment, and strategies and provides oversight and support in both fiscal and human resource endeavors. I certainly couldn't have imagined any of that happening when I became a part-time deputy in sleepy ol' Tallahassee, Florida, in 1977.

While attending Florida State University's School of Criminology, I got the job through a family friend, Bobby Montgomery, then the supervisor of the Tallahassee office. As a special deputy U.S. marshal, I was restricted to working no more than thirty-nine hours a week; we had no overtime, only on-the-job training, and absolutely no benefits. It was a job. When I wasn't sitting in a courtroom, I often served as many as a hundred legal documents a day—which included criminal and civil summonses, complaints, and writs— to the various agencies that have business in the federal court system. Like each of the ninety-four districts, mine operated pretty much autonomously; just about the only function headquarters had was coordinating the movement of prisoners throughout the country. We worked in close concert with the surrounding districts and when necessary helped each other out. But it was essentially a local operation with very limited support.

Our communications equipment consisted of typewriters and an antiquated teletype machine, and we always carried a roll of dimes with us when we hit the street, in case we had to make a phone call.

Two years after being hired as a part-time deputy, I passed the official entrance exam to join the Marshals Service as a full-time employee and prepared myself to go off to basic training, but then the Carter administration put a freeze on hiring. I accepted a job with the Tallahassee Police Department. I was with them for three years, and it was there I learned how to be a law enforcement officer; we were a very active department, with some outstanding leadership. My supervisor, Sergeant David Frisby, was one of the finest cops I've ever met. I was on the SWAT team and was a field training officer. By the time I joined the U.S. Marshals Service full-time in 1983 I was an experienced police officer, trained by the fine men and women of the Tallahassee Police Department.

I knew when I became a deputy U.S. marshal that I would be required to perform a variety of assignments, including court security, witness security, and asset forfeitures, which were then our premier divisions, as well as having the chance to work fugitive investigations. But like a lot of my classmates at the Federal Law Enforcement Training Center (our academy), I wanted to continue chasing bad guys and locking them up, just as I'd been doing at the Tallahassee Police Department.

Fortunately for me, the Marshals Service mission had begun changing around that time. In 1979, the attorney general had given us responsibility for pursuing most federal fugitives. Essentially we became the nation's sheriff. In 1981, deputies successfully tracked down and arrested the infamous escaped spy Christopher "the Falcon" Boyce, a case that announced to the law enforcement world that the Marshals Service was back in the business of chasing bad guys and was surprisingly capable of catching them. But perhaps more important, that same year we initiated what became known as the FIST (Fugitive Investigative Strike Teams) program. It was a tremendously innovative concept: deputies would create a team of federal, state, and local law enforcement to work together for a brief period of time going after the most violent and wanted criminals in a given area. It was like forming a posse to clean up the town. Deputizing officers from other departments—force multipliers, as we described them—temporarily gave these officers the power to pursue fugitives beyond the borders of their own jurisdiction. A FIST operation was like a law enforcement storm blowing through a region, and when it had passed, hundreds of wanted criminals had been taken off the streets.

In about 1980, our associate director for operations, Howard Safir, created the Enforcement Division. Mr. Safir selected Chuck Kupferer to be the first division chief, and he, along with Debra Jenkins and Chad Allen, began to professionalize and standardize our fugitive investigations both domestically and throughout the world. While we were still tremendously underfunded, there was the emergence of an entirely new atmosphere. More and more directives were coming to us from Washington, new procedures were being implemented, we were just beginning to get the equipment we needed, and our training was becoming more intensified to meet our greatly expanded mission. The U.S. Marshals Service was slowly being transformed from a loose association of ninety-four district offices into a single unified, modern law enforcement agency. For example, we developed a national warrant information network (WIN), which became a repository for every outstanding warrant and served to knit our whole network of offices together; this meant that a deputy in Seattle could access information about a case in Miami. The files contained all the information we had, including license plate numbers, phone numbers, known associates, family members, and residences. It helped make us a truly national agency, and fugitives could no longer be confident of their safety by putting miles between themselves and their pursuers.

WIN served as the information backbone of the fugitive program for the next three decades, and continues to do so. The advent of WIN also signaled the beginning of the criminal intelligence capability that has transformed the Marshals Service.

By the end of my first year, I had taken over as the warrant coordinator of our Tallahassee office. As it did for so many other young deputies, that got me out of the courtroom and onto the streets, where I could go after bad guys working in Florida. Many of the people we were pursuing had committed drug crimes, but marijuana was the biggest drug at that time and people in that part of the drug trade were rarely dangerous. The violence that arrived with cocaine came later.

It was a very small office, so of necessity I was basically a one-man warrant squad. I would work with officers from various agencies; if I was pursuing a DEA fugitive, for example, that agency would assign an agent to work with me. There was tremendous cooperation among all the agencies throughout North Florida. When I showed up in a town, I knew I could count on every sheriff's department or local police department to provide the information and assistance I needed. In a lot of arrest situations, there would be just two of us to make the arrest. Legend has it—not that I ever witnessed it myself, of course—that on occasion one officer would stay in the front of a house while a second officer would go around back. When both officers were in place, the one in front would knock on the door and announce his presence: "Police!" The guy in back would yell, "Come in," and when the officer in front heard that invitation, he would do just that and make the arrest. In those days that type of behavior was condoned, if not encouraged.

Down in Florida we often found ourselves searching trailers for fugitives. That was a god-awful assignment. Trailers offer no protection: it's easy to shoot through the thin walls, and it's impossible to maintain silence. Everything in a trailer creaks and groans. Once my partner and I were searching a dimly lit trailer late one night and while clearing two bedrooms and the bathroom I walked right past a closet. I noticed a pile of clothes on the closet floor but didn't pay much attention to it—until my partner signaled to me that the fugitive might be hiding under those clothes. He didn't want to shine his flashlight there to alert the fugitive that he'd been spotted. I decided the quickest way into the closet was through the plywood wall. I slammed into it, and it collapsed right on top of the fugitive. He started groaning and we made the arrest. He had a little .380 in his pocket, but he never had the chance to get to it.

In the late 1980s, cocaine started flowing north from South and Central America, and with it came the cocaine cowboys; then the world of law enforcement changed quickly and forever. A new type of drug violence emerged that included rip-offs, armed robberies, and practically daily shootings over turf wars. It also meant that the stakes got a lot higher for the bad guys as prison terms got longer, and they no longer hesitated to try to shoot their way out of a jam. We marshals had to adjust on the trail, changing our training, our tactics, and our weaponry. We began carrying a lot more firepower and utilizing more manpower on arrests. No longer were two men sufficient to go into a house or take down a fugitive in a vehicle. We were at the point at which we couldn't be quite as confident as we had been that at the end of the day we were going home. We needed to have superior numbers and firepower.

In 1990, at the encouragement of my supervisor, Louie McKinney, and my mentor, Billy Joyce, I applied for and was promoted to the rank of inspector of the Enforcement Division. The structure of the Marshals Service is unlike that of any other federal law enforcement agency. We are all funded by Congress, but the Senate recommends for presidential approval not only our director (like all other agencies) but also ninety-four U.S. marshals, one in each of the ninety-four judicial districts. For the most part these people are not career Marshals Service employees (like in the other agencies), so there is a great learning curve to the agency. Today, most U.S. marshals have prior command-level experience with other law enforcement agencies, which has led to a more professional workforce and a better working relationship between headquarters and the field offices.

During the mid- to late nineties, several districts had formed multiagency task forces, but most districts just maintained their warrant squads without bringing on board other agencies. We realized even then with these district task forces that there was little continuity in the assignment of deputies; some were rotated quarterly, others semiannually, and others annually. So unlike detectives, who develop expertise with experience, our deputies continued to be rotated in and out of investigations—even as they became our best investigators.

While the organization was changing, there was still some tension between the old-school guys, who were not very supportive of the intensified investigative mission, and the younger personnel who wanted to hunt fugitives.

While I was working in Washington I began running both FIST operations as well as creating a task force for major cases. When we got involved in a major case, we would form a temporary task force and bring in our best people from all around the country; it was sort of a law enforcement all-star team consisting of experts in a variety of investigative specialties who would work that case—and only that case—until it was resolved. Many times these cases lasted for months and this team traveled all over the country tracking down bad guys on the run. The FBI used to refer to it as our Flying Squad because the task force included an extraordinary pilot and investigator named Jerry Lowery, who provided excellent aerial surveillance for those teams. Although initially I found myself calling on the same people all the time, as the warrant squad and task force concept took hold on the local level, I gradually found I had a much greater pool of really good and experienced people to choose from. In fact, after a while most of the local and regional operations were so good that they were entirely capable of handling those major cases without Washington's assistance.

In 1997, I was asked by the director to relocate and set up the Puerto Rico Fugitive Task Force. We moved into office space vacated by the FBI. We started with nothing, literally nothing: no phones, no air-conditioning, no chairs or desks, very little electrical power—did I mention no air-conditioning? There was very little cooperation with local authorities and no access to NCIC (National Crime Information Center) records, so we could have been talking to a three-time murderer without knowing it. We actually went over to the basement of the federal building and liberated furniture, including gray metal desks and squeaky chairs. But we quickly became operational. As we were moving in, an FBI agent had been taking down the Bureau's 10 Most Wanted in Puerto Rico list. We asked him to leave it right where it was. After he left I pointed to that list and told my people, "There's our first ten guys we're going after." Within a very short period of time, all the law enforcement agencies in the Commonwealth had agreed to participate in the task force. Within a year we had arrested nine of the ten men on that list. We could've had the tenth one too, who was wanted for domestic terrorism, but another agency was on him and asked us to stand down, which we did.

By the turn of the century there were as many as thirty district task forces, each of them with a different configuration, operating throughout the country and in American protectorates. The structure of law enforcement was evolving slowly. But it changed quickly and drastically after September 11, 2001, to meet the new and very real threat of terrorism. I remember attending a meeting with my FBI counterpart soon after that attack. He told me that the responsibilities of the FBI were changing, that going after fugitives and other criminal investigations were no longer going to be a priority mission; the FBI was prioritizing the antiterrorism business. The agent asked me which aspects of their anticrime activities we were capable of taking over. I suspect he thought I was going to tell him, "Fugitives." Instead I said, "Anything you guys aren't doing, we'll take over." Then I got up and left the meeting. Until that point the Marshals Service's relationship with the FBI had been somewhat competitive, as most agents did not want deputies infringing on what they considered their territory. This meeting told me that relationship was about to undergo a fundamental change.

We had earned it. This was all happening quickly and quietly, and the public simply wasn't aware that the role of the Marshals Service had changed so drastically or that we were capable of leading the national fight against crime. In fact, even now few people are aware of it; we often get confused with city marshals, whose primary job is to seize property over unpaid bills.

In response to our new mission, we decided to expand the very successful task force concept, with a plan to create eighteen permanent regional task forces that would be run directly from Washington and would cover the entire country. Each regional task force included multiple districts and would be funded directly by headquarters. The difficulty was always going to be funding. Just like the public, Congress was unaware of how successful we had been in fighting crime. We lobbied hard, even bringing out what was called a crime clock. It showed that every 23 seconds someone is a victim of a violent crime, every five minutes a woman is raped, and every six hours someone is murdered; it was a very sobering demonstration of reality. I explained, "We are 110 percent behind fighting terrorism, but this is terror within our borders that every one of us lives with every day." That got the attention of legislators. We had asked for $150 million—they granted us $5 million to initiate the program. To date we have obtained funding for seven regional task forces.

We went coast to coast, starting by setting up regional violent crime task forces in New York and Los Angeles. We had to sell the concept to both our own district offices and potential law enforcement partners, which took some time and some convincing before we got the buy-in we needed, but eventually the concept proved itself. Some district chiefs eventually put their entire warrant squads into their regional task force while others have chosen to maintain local control. The program has been tremendously successful; for example, in addition to our personnel, the New York/New Jersey Regional Fugitive Task Force includes force multipliers from eleven federal agencies, nine state agencies, and local law enforcement agencies ranging from the Atlantic City Police Department to the Westchester County Department of Probation and the Winslow Police Department. Coming at the same time that the Internet has enabled us to establish an extraordinary communications network, law enforcement has never before seen this level of cooperation between agencies on a permanent basis.

During the mid-2000s I realized that I was funding a handful of district task forces to conduct a weekly fugitive roundup in their local area. I generally supplied about $10,000 to each district to pay the overtime and administrative costs associated with the operation. I proposed to my boss, Bob Finan, that we conduct a nationwide old-style FIST operation that would take place during a specifically designated week. During that week every district would put complete emphasis on closing out fugitive warrants. I estimated it would cost us less than a million dollars to fund all ninety-four districts. When the concept was approved we selected Brad Miller, chief deputy of the Western District of Oklahoma, to run the operation. Brad came up with name FALCON as the 1981 capture of Chris "the Falcon" Boyce was generally accepted as a landmark in Marshals history. FALCON's objective was to target violent offenders across the nation, especially those involved with homicides, sex offenses, guns, gangs, and drugs. During this week we were going to go after the worst of the worst.

Getting FALCON up and running required tremendous cooperation. Brad Miller and his deputy commander Dave Dimmitt contacted every district chief—dialing and smiling, as they referred to it—and eventually got total buy-in. Working with state and local agencies was already part of the Marshals Service fabric, so almost all our traditional law enforcement partners, our force multipliers, agreed to participate. It marked the largest collaborative effort by law enforcement agencies in American history; including 25 federal agencies, 206 state agencies, 302 county sheriff's departments, and 366 city police departments. More than 3,000 law enforcement personnel were sworn in as special deputy marshals, giving them federal arrest authority, for the operation.

We asked each participating agency to give us a list of its biggest targets, and we started doing background research almost immediately. Incredibly, from concept to kickoff—or in this case kicking down doors—was less than two months. Initially we were hoping to make as many as 4,000 arrests, although we realized that probably was an optimistic target. Operation FALCON lasted from April 4 through April 10, 2005, which coincided with National Crime Victims' Rights Week.

We'd come in every morning and look at the reports and couldn't believe what was happening. In one week, 10,340 fugitives were tracked down and arrested, the largest number of arrests ever recorded in a single operation. In many ways it became a competition, which group could put the most bad guys in jail. Our people were pumped up, working day and night; we actually had to remind them to step down when necessary, because the last thing we wanted was exhausted people out in the streets chasing armed fugitives.

That was a tremendous beginning, and since then there have been five more FALCON operations. Even with some operational changes—for example, rather than pinpointing a single week, the district offices and task forces each pick the best week of a designated month—the success has been breathtaking; FALCON 2009 resulted in the capture of 35,190 fugitives, including 433 wanted for murder. As a group, the fugitives had a history of 138,200 prior arrests. These were career criminals taken off the streets—and we did it at a cost of $900,000. That's less than $30 a fugitive. That's about the best bargain possible in law enforcement.

For me, personally, it has been incredibly satisfying to be able to look back to the beginning of my career, when I was serving court documents for our small Tallahassee office. When I joined the Enforcement

Division in Washington in 1990, we had about thirty people assigned there; when I retired, there were more than three hundred administrative personnel and an additional one hundred contractors working there. I had watched the Marshals Service grow into an extraordinary nationwide crime fighting organization, the best manhunting force in the world. The Marshals Service's Technical Operations Group is recognized throughout the world as the best electronic surveillance manhunting organization that exists anywhere. The development of the Sex Offenders Investigative Branch in 2007 has resulted in the arrests of tens of thousands of sexual predators and the rescue of hundreds of kidnapped children.

The stories told in this book just barely scratch the surface of what we have accomplished in slightly more than three decades, but it has come at a cost. In 2011, the year I retired, two deputy marshals and three officers assigned to our task forces lost their lives, in addition to several others who were wounded doing their jobs.

Those are very high numbers. We spent a lot of time examining all our procedures, looking at our training, reassessing our tactics and our equipment to try to determine if and what we might be doing wrong, or could be doing better, and what steps we could take to protect our officers. We met with the personnel from local sheriffs and police departments investigating each shooting. And in the end we had to accept the reality that this is a very dangerous job and sometimes our people just get very unlucky. In most of these incidents, bad guys shot through a door, from inside a closet, or right through a wall; they didn't have eyes on a target but just took random shots.

We had a lot of professional people looking at us with apprehension, sometimes questioning the way we do our business. My response to them was to point out that we were averaging more than 120,000 arrests a year without incident, and sooner or later this type of tragedy was inevitable. These heroes—and they are heroes in the greatest sense of that word—paid the ultimate sacrifice to protect our citizens and our streets. I like to believe that all Americans can sleep a little easier knowing these manhunters are out there at all hours of the day and night, kicking down doors, stopping vehicles, and arresting heinous fugitives. As we have done since 1789, the United States Marshals Service makes this country a better place and makes every one of us safer and more secure.

That approaching helicopter I mentioned at the beginning of this introduction, by the way, was the final step in an elaborate plan to prevent an inmate's escape attempt from the Tallahassee Federal Correctional Institute. Another prisoner had offered information about the planned escape attempt in return for leniency. An especially violent felon, a German national who may have been involved with a European terror organization, had confided in him. People in Europe, he said, would pay to help him escape. We devised a plan to help us identify those people. The cooperator happened to be a helicopter pilot serving time for transporting drugs. With the assistance of the warden, and no one else, we arranged for the cooperating prisoner to "escape" while on a work detail outside the prison's fences. The "plan" was for the cooperating prisoner to contact individuals in Germany to facilitate a wire transfer so he could rent a helicopter, land it on the prison's baseball field, pick up the German prisoner, and transport him to safety.

The wire transfer was received and the plan was set in motion. We put the cooperating prisoner in a jail far away from Tallahassee. With the cooperation of the warden we had arranged for an unmarked law enforcement helicopter, flown by an experienced law enforcement pilot, to fly into the prison during a softball game the following weekend. The warden emphasized that he did not want that chopper coming anywhere near the ground, as we did not know what the other hundreds of prisoners in the rec yard might do. The guards in the towers were not armed, so we didn't have to worry about them shooting at the helicopter. Or so we hoped.

I was sitting with the warden looking out at the yard. An inmate baseball game was in progress and several hundred other prisoners were in the area. Suddenly the warden's radio cackled, and a guard in one of the towers reported a helicopter apparently heading straight for the institution. I sat there absolutely silent, watching my career unfold in front of me. The chopper came in low and hovered over second base. While most of the other prisoners scattered, we watched as the German national ran toward it. As he got closer the chopper suddenly moved over to first base. The prisoner followed. Then the pilot cut across the infield to third base. It might have been about this time when the prisoner, standing alone on the infield, began to realize that he had been set up. The helicopter suddenly rose straight up and took off. The prisoner was arrested. The cooperating prisoner eventually became a valuable informant, working for several federal agencies over the next decade and helping us put a substantial number of drug dealers and fugitives in prison.

Later that afternoon I met with the warden for a final assessment. He had a big grin on his face and I asked him why he was laughing. "Well," he said, "when I was coming back off the rec yard, one of the inmates came up to me and said, 'Warden, you not only gave us a beautiful afternoon out on the yard, with softball games and ice cream, but you also gave us a great air show. How you going to top that next weekend?'"

—M.E.

January 2014

U.S. Marhsals

1

The New Star of Law Enforcement

There is no hunting like the hunting of man. And those who have hunted armed men long enough and liked it never care for anything else thereafter.

—*Ernest Hemingway, "On the Blue Water,"* Esquire, *April 1936*

Deputy U.S. Marshal Harry Layne was tipped by one of his informants that a fugitive wanted for attempted murder was hiding in a building in the College Hill section of Tampa, Florida, although the informant did not know exactly which apartment. Just before dawn the next morning, Layne, his partner, and several officers from the Tampa Police Department were moving cautiously into the projects when a female officer screamed, "There he goes. There he goes. He's running."

Layne started chasing him into the night. He remembers,

I was running real hard, but in the dark I couldn't really see where I was going. That happens, but you don't think about it; the adrenaline kicks in and you keep going. The fugitive and the police officer ran through a backyard right under a metal clothesline, but I didn't even see it. I'm 6'3", much taller than them: that clothesline caught me right under my nose and snapped me backward; my legs went out from under me and I hit the ground hard. It almost took my head off; I was bleeding from both corners of my mouth and my gums, but I got up and kept going. We finally caught the guy—but he wasn't our suspect. He said he just saw people approaching the building with guns drawn and took off. He had his own reasons. But he did know exactly which apartment our fugitive was staying in.

Layne's team went to that apartment and knocked on the door. Hard.

A woman answered and told us he wasn't there. Okay, I told her, we'll just take a look. I found him fast asleep in a bedroom. I had my gun out and I nudged him with my flashlight and told him, "Wake your ass up."

He opened his eyes and looked up at me. Blood was dripping from the corners of my mouth onto my chin and vest. My face was probably bright red from running. His eyes opened wider with awe and fear as he realized what was going on. "Holy shit!" he said. "It's Dracula!"

I said to him, "If you don't want to start bleeding, motherf—er, show me your hands now!"

Deputy Marshals Mike Bunk and Jerry Lowery went to San Juan to help set up the Puerto Rican task force, which was run by the U.S. Marshals Service but was composed of personnel from a variety of participating federal and local law enforcement agencies. When the DEA learned Bunk was going to San Juan, they requested that he look for a fugitive who had fled there from Tallahassee, Florida. Bunk recalls:

We had an address, but when we hit the house he was gone. We knew where his girlfriend lived so Jerry Lowery and I went over there to take a look. When we got there, she was loading up her car like she was leaving. We knew that she had a daughter with the fugitive, and there was a young child in the car with her. We assumed this was the fugitive's child and suspected she was going to meet him. We started following her. I had never been to Puerto Rico before and had no idea where I was going—so I immediately got totally lost.

Losing her like that really irritated the two of us, so we started focusing on this case. We were determined to catch this guy. The girlfriend would come and go and we really believed she was visiting him, but we couldn't catch them together. Finally I had an idea. I was going to hit him in his macho. I was going to make him jealous. We got her pager number—at that time when you called a pager you spoke with an operator, who relayed your message. I called and sent this message to her in Spanish: "Where are you my love? I miss you." I didn't sign it.

If she actually was with him I knew that message was going to make him crazy. There was no way he could allow someone to flirt with his girlfriend. That's exactly what happened. Less than an hour after I called it in, my phone started ringing. And it just kept ringing. Between Saturday and Sunday he called my cell phone more than two hundred times.

I never answered it. Monday morning I decided it was time. When I answered it, he immediately started questioning me. I told him, "Buddy, you got the wrong number. I don't know what you're talking about." He didn't call again, but that didn't matter: I had his cell-phone number. We tracked it to a house, and when we hit the house he took off running out the back. We ended up chasing him into a deep gully, where he was arrested.

Everything you think you know about law enforcement in America has changed in the last two decades. There is a new sheriff in town.

For more than 220 years, since the founding of the federal judiciary system in 1789, the U.S. Marshals Service has been chasing fugitives across the country, tracking them down, and putting them in prison. Its success has been celebrated in both fact and fiction, in books and movies and innumerable TV shows, and famed marshals like Wyatt Earp, Wild Bill Hickok, Bat Masterson, and TV's Matt Dillon and Raylan Givens have become an important part of the popular culture. United States marshals fought at the O.K. Corral, escorted James Meredith to class when he integrated the University of Mississippi, and protected the Pentagon when anti–Vietnam War demonstrations threatened to overrun it. Deputies patrolled the streets of L.A. during the riots and the flooded neighborhoods of New Orleans after Katrina and have guarded the nation's airlines against hijackers. Despite the Marshals Service having a long and celebrated history, many people still think of it as a relic of the past.

The reality, though, is that there's a new deputy in town. That glorious history has about as much connection to today's Marshals Service as the Pony Express does to the Internet. Few people are aware of it, but in the last two decades the Marshals Service has become—by far—America's most effective law enforcement agency, taking more criminals off the street than all other federal agencies combined. Here's a test: In 2012, the bureau's almost four thousand deputy marshals tracked down and arrested a certain number of people. These were mostly career criminals, men and women who had an average of four felony convictions each, and more than half of them were classified as violent offenders, meaning they had committed at least one murder, rape, aggravated assault, or other potentially deadly crime—these weren't nice people. Many of these previously convicted felons knew if they were caught they were going to spend much of the rest of their lives in prison. Okay now, go ahead, take a guess: How many criminals fitting this description did the U.S. Marshals Service successfully put behind bars in 2012? Here's a hint: think of a high number.

No, higher.

Even higher.

Incredibly, in 2012 the Marshals Service tracked down and arrested 123,006 fugitives. That isn't a misprint: that's 123,006 really bad people, consisting of 86,704 state and local fugitives and 36,302 federal fugitives—as well as an additional 12,451 sex offenders. These are mostly career criminals, a whole stratum of society that gets up early every morning and survives by committing crimes; people who move relentlessly around the country, rarely staying anywhere too long, often living under an alias and always looking for the next payday—many of them armed and prepared to do whatever it takes to stay out of the system.

Working as a deputy marshal has become a very dangerous job: at a retirement party for an agent of another federal bureau, a U.S. deputy marshal asked the agent how often he had drawn his gun during his twenty-two-year career. This agent proudly told him that in twenty-two years he'd never had to draw his weapon. Then the agent asked the marshal how many times he'd had to rely on his gun. The deputy replied without even pausing to think about it, "When I'm out on the street I'll draw my weapon seven times—before lunch."

The Marshals Service was established by President George Washington in 1789 to be the enforcement agency for the federal court system. Marshals, Washington wrote to his attorney general, were to be "the fittest characters to expound the laws and dispense justice." These U.S. marshals were directly appointed by the president to execute all court orders in their district, and to do that each marshal was given the extraordinary power "to command all necessary assistance in the execution of his duty, and to appoint as there shall be occasion, one or more deputies." That meant a marshal could make anybody a deputy just by telling him to raise his right hand and repeat an oath, which is where the legendary American concept of putting together a posse and going after the outlaws was born. And unlike local and state law enforcement, deputy marshals have never been restricted by state borders; they always have had the power to make an arrest anywhere in the United States.

Since being created by America's first Congress in 1789, the U.S. Marshals Service has provided courtroom protection, escorted prisoners, guarded witnesses, served and enforced court-issued documents, seized and managed forfeited property, and carried out court orders. The Marshals Service has remained entirely nonpolitical and found itself right in the middle of many of the nation's most divisive issues; prior to the Civil War marshals were charged with pursuing escaped slaves, and a century later they enforced the Civil Rights Act. They've enforced Prohibition and protected abortion clinics. During the Vietnam War, marshals protected the Pentagon from demonstrators and then protected those antiwar protesters. And they did it without drawing much attention. In reality, for most of the service's history the job of a U.S. deputy marshal was defined by long stretches of tedium interrupted occasionally by several seconds of action. The Marshals Service certainly did not have the glamorous high profile of the FBI or the great respect of the DEA. For example, when Tony Perez got out of the Marine Corps in 1973, he joined the Los Angeles Police Department. While he was in the police academy a friend of his, a retired marine sergeant major, suggested Tony consider the Marshals Service. Perez says,

Until that time I didn't even know the Marshals still existed. All I knew about it was what I'd seen in Hollywood movies. It was all those good-guys-versus-bad-guys John Wayne pictures. Truthfully I thought it had died out with the Old West. When I first heard about it, like everybody else I confused it with the L.A. County marshals. I didn't know what the U.S. marshals did, how they did it, or how to become a marshal. At that time most of the re-cruiting was done by personal referral; one person who liked the job would bring another person in.

Donald Ward has a similar recollection:

When I took the test for the job in 1979, I didn't know a thing about the Marshals Service. A friend of mine from high school told me it was a decent job with good security. I was a Vietnam vet and I had nothing else working for me. Why not, I figured. I showed up for the test thinking there would be hundreds of people there to take it. Turned out it was just me.

It wasn't a job with a lot of action appeal. When Mike Bunk completed his military service in the early 1980s, he intended to become a Florida game warden, "But when I saw how little it paid I started looking for other jobs. The civilian personnel office on the base had a listing of government jobs and I saw the Marshals Service. Well, why not, I thought. Why not."

Although Perez, Ward, and Bunk couldn't know it, the Vietnam vets flooding into the Marshals Service were about to catch the wave of change. A century earlier the image of U.S. marshals had been very different: marshals had been the law of the Old West; they ran the towns and organized the posses; they tracked the bad guys into the brush and if possible brought them back alive—and when it became necessary, they shot them down. The iconic silver star pinned to their chest instantly commanded respect. But modern civilization had reduced their role to little more than dutiful civil servants.

With the suburbanization of America had come the rise of local law enforcement agencies—town, city, and state police departments—which practically eliminated the need for federal officers. With the occasional exception when their presence was needed to maintain civil order, the U.S. Marshals Service had become a comfortable relic, an agency with almost no function beyond maintaining courtroom security and with absolutely no public visibility; federal marshals were often confused with well-paid city marshals whose job it is to evict people from apartments. Deputy marshals didn't wear uniforms, and had little formal training. They were not issued any type of standard equipment—and just as in years past when their predecessors had been required to use their own horses, they were even required to use their own cars to fulfill their duties. The Marshals Service seemed to have outlived its usefulness. Americans knew all about Hoover's FBI and they were learning about the Drug Enforcement Agency and the Bureau of Alcohol, Tobacco and Firearms. But the Marshals Service?

Few people considered the Marshals Service a modern law enforcement agency; even presidents used their constitutional power to appoint ninety-four U.S. marshals to a four-year term as a means to reward political supporters rather than enhance law enforcement. Instead of appointing experienced law enforcement officers to the post, presidents and senators most often gave the job to their political and financial supporters. As a result, people from a wide range of professions were appointed U.S. marshals—among them public health nurses and even a bus driver. Those political appointees ran their districts without any real supervision; there was no central headquarters, no agency standards, and very little money. In fact, at times when deputies had to transport a prisoner across the country—handcuffed in a van or in the backseat of a deputy's own car—some of them would deputize their wives, who would then be paid to take the trip with them. "When I came in, it was sort of a Mayberry-type thing," Tony Perez recalls. "There was very little action; the image of the potbellied deputy falling asleep in court wasn't too far from reality."

All that began changing in 1969, when for the first time a central headquarters was established in Washington, D.C., to provide an organizational structure and to loosely supervise the activities of the district marshals. Within a couple of years, headquarters took control of all training and hiring decisions, and the framework for the modern Marshals Service was taking shape. In 1971, the Special Operations Group, a well-trained strike force set up to respond quickly anywhere in the country, was formed. Throughout the 1970s, newly recruited deputy marshals began stretching the assigned responsibilities of the service to actively pursue fugitives. The Marshals Service was slowly changing, and a lot of the veteran deputies weren't interested in embracing those changes. The young deputies had come out of the Vietnam War and wanted action, they wanted to go after bad guys; the veterans were satisfied to continue doing what they had been doing and, in many instances, were happy to let the newcomers take all the chances. "We used to refer to them as 'the old-school guys,'" Donald Ward remembers. "They were happy to go to court. They loved to take juries out to lunch and dinner. They looked at us like we were crazy. Why would we want to go out and chase people when we could stay inside?" Those veterans knew too well that there was no glory to be found—the Old West was comfortably settled—so the younger deputies set out to change the culture of the service.

Traditionally the Marshals Service had not had much of an investigative function—that was the FBI's job. But in July 1979, the Marshals Service assumed some of the FBI's responsibility for pursuing federal fugitives. In an agreement worked out by Attorney General Benjamin Civiletti, the FBI retained responsibility for pursuing high-profile criminals while the Marshals Service was given the job of tracking and arresting escaped federal prisoners and others who had committed lower-priority crimes. It didn't seem like much at the time, but this agreement allowing marshals to investigate crimes and to pursue fugitives and arrest them marked the beginning of the modern Marshals Service.

In January 1980, twenty-five-year-old Christopher John Boyce, who had been convicted of selling top-secret satellite technology to the Russians in 1977 and was serving a forty-year sentence for espionage, escaped from California's Lompac Correctional Institution. Boyce, the infamous "Falcon" featured in the best-selling book *The Falcon and the Snowman,* had used a handmade ladder and tin shears to cut his way through the perimeter to freedom. Boyce was the first high-profile fugitive covered under the new agreement between the FBI and the Marshals Service. And at that time he arguably was the most wanted man in the world. This was the case that began the transformation of the Marshals Service from a creaky old agency into one of the world's most successful crime-fighting organizations.

The timing was almost perfect. For decades, all deputy marshals had a government status of 082, a catchall for very low-level law enforcement work. That designation covered transporting prisoners, guarding courtrooms, and general supervisory work. But a couple of years earlier, the Department of Justice had approved a higher criminal investigator status for a limited number of deputies. About twenty-five men had completed the Criminal Investigation Training Program in Glynco, Georgia, the first time any member of the Marshals Service had received the 1811 classification signifying that they were qualified criminal investigators.

For Chuck Kupferer, the pursuit of the Falcon began when Howard Safir, the former assistant director of the DEA who had been appointed chief of the Marshals

Witness Security Division in 1979, called him into his office. Safir knew how important this case could be to the Marshals Service. Kupferer will never forget that meeting:

> The first thing he said to me when I sat down was, "From now on you have one thing to do, that's it. Catch Christopher Boyce."
>
> "Okay," I told him. "But who's Christopher Boyce?"
>
> "He's an escaped federal prisoner convicted of spying for the Soviet Union," Safir continued. "And you're the one that's on the dime. From this minute on I want to know everything you do, when you do it, and especially when you get this done."

This was at the height of the Cold War, so the pressure to find Boyce was enormous—and there was substantial doubt about the ability of the Marshals Service to do the job. In fact, when the CIA informed New York senator Daniel Patrick Moynihan that marshals were leading the investigation, Moynihan responded critically that if the Marshals Service was looking for the Falcon, he might as well just be gone.

"Safir reminded me of Moynihan's statement just about every day for eighteen months," Kupferer remembers. Kupferer began the investigation by putting together a team consisting of those twenty-five deputies who had been through Glynco. As a result of worldwide publicity, "We had hundreds of tips coming in. People claimed they saw Boyce anywhere you can think of. We sent teams all over the world. I had a team go to South Africa; another team went to Costa Rica, and I had teams in France, in Canada, Mexico. We couldn't ignore any bit of information; Boyce had the capability of being anywhere in the world. We even sent deputies on horseback deep into the California mountains. We thought there was a chance he was hiding up there and that was the best way to cover that terrain."

The investigators followed every lead. A former inmate at Lompac who had been especially close to Boyce claimed he knew where the Falcon was hiding. Kupferer recounts how they tried to confirm that tip:

We borrowed the DEA's best polygrapher and hooked up this guy. He told us Boyce was in the jungles of Costa Rica smuggling arms to Guatemalan guerrilla fighters. Supposedly he had cut out a landing strip in the jungle and had built himself a nice hooch there. It was a pretty detailed story. The polygraph expert told us, "This guy is gold."

Howard seemed to think we were onto something, until I said to him, "I hate to tell you this, boss, but this guy's full of shit. I asked him to describe the RPM required for a transport aircraft to lift off from a jungle airstrip and he had no freaking clue what I was talking about. This whole story's bullshit." As we discovered, there was nothing to it. Like many informers, this guy was trying to make something from nothing. But this type of investigative work was new to us; we had a lot to learn and within the next few years we would become very good at it. We eventually arrested this guy on another charge in New Jersey.

The investigation dragged on for months without any strong leads. Most fugitives eventually will make some type of contact with their former lives in order to get what they need to survive, but Boyce failed to show up on anyone's radar. During the investigation, deputies conducted more than eight hundred interviews, pursued hundreds of leads, and investigated numerous reported "sightings." Ironically, the first real break in the case came from an FBI agent in the bureau's Denver office. Kupferer explains, "That agent called Dave Neff, one of our inspectors in our Denver office, and said he had an informant who claimed he could put us on to Boyce and asked if he wanted to talk to him. 'Absolutely,' my guy said. 'Of course.'"

Given the growing competition between the two federal investigative agencies, that FBI agent never admitted that he had played a prominent role in the case. If Washington had found out that he had handed the keys to the case to the Marshals Service, his career certainly would have been affected. Kupferer says,

His informants were two brothers. They were bank robbers and they told us that Boyce was surviving by robbing banks up in the Northwest. They also informed us that a mutual friend of theirs and Boyce's was getting married in a place called Smith Falls, Idaho, and they were pretty sure Chris Boyce was going to be there.

I flew up there with a team consisting of nineteen Marshals Service inspectors and deputies, eight FBI agents, and someone from the Border Patrol. This joint task force was the very beginning of the strategy that we would eventually adopt. We moved into Smith Falls quietly, in small groups. At one point we decided to hike up into the mountains, so four of us got some fishing equipment and started hiking up a well-used trail that ran alongside a freshwater spring. I don't know if we really were undercover;

as we're going up that trail at seven thirty in the morning we ran into a fisherman coming down. "Where you boys going?" he asked. Fishing, we told him. He smiled. "Fish quit biting about an hour and a half ago." He knew something was going on.

We set up on the wedding, but Boyce never showed up. Our informers then told us that they believed Boyce was camped out in the Idaho badlands with a woman named Gloria White. We found her and leaned on her a little and found out that Boyce had been there—our informants were right—but he'd left and was living in the small city of Port Angeles, Washington. I set up a team of ten deputies and three FBI agents at the Redline Inn in Port Angeles. We started watching the various places around the city where we thought he might show up. For example, we sat on a local grocery store for a couple of days because we'd confirmed he had bought some beer there a couple of days before. We were being passive, just sitting back and waiting for something to happen, until Bob Dighera said to me, "Chief, this is not the way we should be doing this. This is the FBI way. Let's start shaking the trees."

If there is a single phrase that accurately describes the changing philosophy of the Marshals Service from passive to proactive, "shaking the trees" might well be it. Kupferer continues,

We set up four teams: one to cover the hotels and motels, two roving teams to search for a vehicle we believed he was using, and a mobile backup team for support. I was working with a female operative and we covered food stores. About seven thirty that night, Dighera and Dave Neff told us they wanted to go get something to eat, and I agreed we would cover for them. About ten minutes later Dave called back and said, really quietly, "Chief, he's in the goddamn hamburger place."

I asked him to repeat that.

"We pulled into the parking lot of this drive-in hamburger place and I looked over into the car right next to us and it's him. No question, it's him."

I didn't doubt that identification. Every one of us had spent the last year and a half looking at his picture. We knew what he looked like. The Pit Stop Restaurant and Drive-In was set up with a central walkway separating two rows of cars; a waitress would come out and take your order, then deliver it on a car tray. We put teams at the entrance and exit of the parking lot in case he took off. The plan was that I would walk down the center aisle and try to get his attention. "As soon as I'm alongside his car," I told Dighera and Neff, "you guys take him down."

I started walking down the aisle. At those moments your heart really starts beating. This really was the most wanted fugitive in America. When I was in front of his car, I casually glanced over at him. I had my pistol in an ankle holster. I kneeled down as if I were tying my shoelace. Boyce was looking right at me; suddenly car doors started flying open. People started running toward Boyce's car. Dighera ripped open the car door and I heard somebody shouting, "Drop that hamburger."

We all grabbed a piece of him. Dighera had hold of one arm, Neff had his other arm. A couple of other guys were behind him. I was right in front of him, and he looked at me and asked, "Who are you guys?" I'm sure he thought we were the FBI. I shook my head and told him proudly, "We're the U.S. Marshals, my friend."

That was the Marshals Service's first really significant arrest. Boyce had been living in that area under an alias for quite some time and had survived by robbing seventeen banks. When the team got back to Washington, they met with Howard Safir to determine what could be done to build on this success. The result of those meetings was the decision to create Fugitive Investigative Strike Teams.

The FIST concept was beautifully simple, although eventually it would change the basic strategy of law enforcement. Until this time, every law enforcement agency, whether it was local, state, or federal, acted pretty much independently, using its personnel to carry out its assigned mission within the borders of its jurisdiction. FIST operations were different: a team of deputies would move into an area for a prolonged length of time, for months sometimes, and form a task force consisting of members of all the federal, state, and local law enforcement agencies that elected to participate. Every member of the task force would be deputized, giving each of them the power to make arrests beyond their normal jurisdiction. It was in essence a modern posse. Each participating organization would bring its most important cases to the strike force, with the emphasis on high-profile and violent fugitives. In some ways it was like forming an all-star team of law enforcement officers, using their combined skills, contacts, and knowledge of their local jurisdiction to resolve their most difficult cases.

What made FIST operations unique was the level of cooperation among local, state, and federal law enforcement agencies on a continuing basis. Although the FBI decided not to participate, in addition to the Marshals Service, both the DEA and ATF agreed to get involved. This was a live test of a whole new type of law enforcement strategy. The first FIST operation took place in Miami in 1981, and based on its success, the concept was quickly expanded throughout the country. FIST 3 and FIST 4, for example, took place in New York City. In eleven weeks, a fifty-man team consisting primarily of NYPD detectives and deputy marshals made an astounding three thousand arrests, taking hundreds of violent felons off the street. Another FIST operation in the Southwest covered four American states and five major Mexican cities and included representatives from thirty-one different law enforcement agencies, including Border Patrol, Immigration and Naturalization, and the Mexican Federal Police. A Florida FIST operation brought together thirty-eight law enforcement agencies as well as personnel from twelve countries and resulted in the capture of 3,816 fugitives. Although the majority of people arrested were wanted on state and local warrants, these operations were set up and run by marshals. This was a huge step forward for the Marshals Service; prior to these operations, deputies rarely chased murderers, for example, because murder is a local crime. Joining forces with state and local agencies allowed marshals to go after the most violent criminals in America.

The forerunners of these FIST task forces were small, mobile warrant squads that would set up in a local district for an extended period of time to assist local authorities in carrying out warrants. It was obvious to the new, young deputies from the very beginning that the warrant squad was where the action was. Warrant squad personnel didn't post court orders on doorposts or spend countless hours in a courtroom; they tracked fugitives, and when the fugitives were located, the squads went into houses or apartments and brought them out. While FIST operations were conducted in major cities, almost all of the ninety-four Marshals Service districts set up their own warrant squads. And just as deputies had done a century earlier, deputy U.S. marshals began going into the wild to track down the bad guys—this time using the tools of modern technology—and bringing them home to American justice.

The success of the FIST operations, which by definition were intended to strike hard and fast and then pack up and leave, led the Marshals Service to form its first district fugitive task force in Philadelphia in 1983. That Violent Crimes Fugitive Task Force, which was created specifically to go after the most violent criminals on the loose—murderers, rapists, armed robbers—was initially funded by the Department of Justice for six months but has operated continuously since then. Eventually each of the ninety-four districts set up its own independent task force, run by the commander of that area. After 9/11, when the FBI began focusing more on terrorism than organized crime and criminal activity, it was decided to establish seven large regional task forces across the nation, which would be run directly from headquarters. Unlike a district task force, in which deputies can be removed and assigned to other jobs, investigators are assigned permanently to these regional violent felons task forces. Without most Americans even being aware that they were set up and operating, these task forces have radically changed the world of law enforcement. The New York/New Jersey Regional Fugitive Task Force, for example, has brought together 350 veteran officers from 11 federal agencies, 9 state agencies, and 77 local law enforcement agencies—all under the direction of the Marshals Service. Those officers bring their most difficult or violent cases from their local agencies in to the task force, which then focuses on those cases. Former task force commander Lenny DePaul explains the process:

Information sharing is paramount. Every agency brings something different to the table, whether it's the Department of Parole, which brings its databases of the people it has supervised, or the Nassau County Police Department. A contributing police department may have one murder in six months, and it is not really equipped to pursue the case. But the task force is able to put the most experienced manpower in law enforcement on that case. It makes life on the run very difficult.

Chasing fugitives may be the most exciting aspect of the job, but the Marshals Service also has continued to fulfill its historic responsibilities. U.S. marshals guard courtrooms and members of the judiciary; transport prisoners; seize, manage, and finally sell forfeited assets; and since 1970 have operated the renowned Witness Protection Program, under which cooperating witnesses—and often their entire families—are relocated to a secret, safe location where they live under new identities protected by deputies.

"Hooking and hauling" is the way deputies refer to working in the courts. The Marshals Service is in charge of the care, custody, and control of all federal prisoners, which entails moving prisoners back and forth during their trials, guarding witnesses, and providing protection for judges. "The courtroom is an excellent place to start," retired deputy marshal Vic Oboyski notes.

Nobody starts as an investigator. You have to work your way into it. In the courtroom you listen to court cases, you get to deal with prisoners and witnesses, you have some understanding of security and how to restrain prisoners; over time you get to know what's permissible, what judges will not allow, what defines probable cause or reasonable suspicion. It's the information you're going to need to know when you do get to go out after fugitives. But maybe most importantly, spending those long hours standing in the courtroom definitely makes every other thing you're going to do in your career seem a lot more exciting.

For many young deputies, the most difficult part of working in a courtroom is simply staying awake. "It gets real boring real fast," Bobby Sanchez remembers.

We would chew gum or candy, even though you're not supposed to, to stay awake. Eventually you get to know what the attorneys are going to say before the words come out, "Your Honor, my client has realized his mistake over the last few months and is determined that he'll never do it again." I remember listening to these guys and thinking, *What a racket: maybe they killed themselves studying in law school, but after that they get well paid for talking.* I thought, *I can talk pretty good too.*

There were marshals who didn't mind sitting in a courtroom for twenty-five years, but for me and the people I knew, we would dream about getting into fugitives. We wanted to start hunting.

Certainly the most interesting part of working in the courtroom was getting to know some of the prisoners. Deputy Phillip Matthews recalls transporting a prisoner accused of being a crack cocaine dealer to his initial pleading. Before going into court this accused felon met with his attorney, who told him the prosecution had offered him a deal: if he pleaded guilty, he would be sentenced to no more than twenty-five years in prison and a quarter-million-dollar fine.

They were really going at it in the interview room. I thought, *Wow, that's some fight they're having.* When it came time for this guy to go to court, I went and I got him. He told me very emphatically, "I ain't going to court. I ain't pleading guilty."

I corrected him. "Yes, you are going to court. You'll stand in front of the judge and be part of the hearing. Whether you plead or not is strictly up to you."

"Okay," he agreed. "I'll go into that courtroom, but no way I'm going to plead." He was really agitated and repeated several times, "My damn lawyer's lying to me."

Judge Royal Furgeson, a super-nice guy, was presiding. This judge was always very respectful of defendants and went through each count carefully and explained the options. Only when he was certain the defendant understood every aspect of the case pending against him would he ask him how he pleaded. In this case this defendant wouldn't even look at his lawyer. He was furious. But he answered all of Judge Furgeson's questions. "Do you understand you could go to prison for twenty-five years?" He did. But when the judge asked him, "Do you understand you can be fined up to $250,000?" he hesitated.

"Wait a second, Your Honor," he said. "You're telling me I could be fined up to $250,000?" When the judge assured him that was correct, he suddenly nodded his head. "Okay, okay, that's not a problem." And when Judge Furgeson finally asked him to make his plea, he didn't hesitate. "Guilty, Your Honor."

That definitely caught me by surprise. As I was escorting him back down the stairs to our cellblock he was kind of laughing, as if he had gotten away with something. I had to ask, "Dude, you got to tell me what's going on. A few minutes ago I thought I was going to have to separate you and your attorney; you were furious and you weren't going to plead to anything. Now you're all happy. How come?"

"Well, you were there," he said. "Did you hear the judge say I could only be fined up to $250,000?"

"I did. I heard that."

He gave me a big smile. "My lawyer was lying to me and I knew it. He told me the fine was going to be a quarter of a million!"

There really was nothing more I could say.

When you escort a prisoner back and forth for a while, superficial relationships do develop. "Learning how to handle people was a really important part of the job," observes Deputy Donald Ward.

When I started doing this, I had an old deputy tell me, you can come to work and fight it every day if you want to. And if you do, it's going to be a long twenty years. But if you come to work and figure these guys out, the time'll go a lot faster.

Some of these guys could be really funny when you got to know them. Fat Tony Salerno, the reputed head of the Genovese crime family, was always making jokes. He owned a farm in upstate New York that the government tried to seize, and his attorney successfully prevented that from happening. I was standing there when this attorney told him proudly that he had stopped the forfeiture. Then he asked Tony, "So what's my bonus?"

"I got a good one for ya," Tony told him. "Now I'm not going to get you whacked."

There was a time I sat with Salerno in his cellblock and talked about his situation. He knew he was never getting out of prison and accepted it. "I'm seventy-nine years old," he told me, and as we sat there he summed up his life. "They send me here for a hundred years; what do they get me for, five or six? Look, I went to the best places, I had the best booze, I screwed the prettiest women, so what are they going to do to me? They're going to feed me for a few years, give me my medical care. I can take that, I did real good." He paused and then repeated, "I did real good." And, in fact, he died in prison a year later.

Hooking and hauling gave marshals a backstage pass to some of the most significant criminal trials in the last several decades. Being there all the time, they became the shadow that was always present, allowing them to become spectators to history. Vic Oboyski remembers escorting several members of the Bonanno crime family to the courtroom after it had been revealed that family associate Donnie Brasco was actually an undercover FBI agent named Joe Pistone. "These guys absolutely refused to accept the fact that Donnie Brasco was an FBI agent. 'It's all bullshit,' one of them told me. 'That f—ing guy, he was with us. It was after we all got arrested that they made him an agent so they could get him on the stand to testify.' Throughout the whole trial they just refused to believe that he had fooled them."

In early 1992, then deputy marshal Lenny DePaul spent weeks escorting the "Teflon Don," legendary Gambino family boss John Gotti, back and forth from the Manhattan Correctional Center (MCC) to the federal courthouse. "I wouldn't say we got to be friends, but we did get to know each other very well," DePaul says.

John was quite the character; he always had something to say. When I picked him up in the morning, for example, as I put the handcuffs on him he'd ask casually, "Hey Lenny, got change for a hundred?"

After he had been convicted and sentenced, he was going to fly out to Marion Federal Penitentiary in Illinois on ConAir. We picked him up and took him to Stewart Air Force Base in Newburgh, New York. He was unusually quiet the whole trip, which didn't surprise me. He was going to prison for the rest of his life and I figured he was pretty depressed. I didn't say much to him; that wasn't my job.

We delivered him to the aircraft and I handed his medical records to the prison personnel. "This is it, John," I told him. "Good luck." What else do you say to a man knowing he will never have another second of freedom in his life? John didn't say anything for a few seconds, but he was literally shaking. I had never seen anything like that before from him. It was only later that I found out John Gotti hated to fly; apparently that was the one thing that scared him. He took about three steps up the stairway to the plane, then stopped; he turned to me and said with a kind of sad smile, "You think it's too late to say I'm sorry?"

In addition to the short trips back and forth to court, until recently, when private contractors took over much of the job, deputies also were responsible for transporting prisoners on much longer journeys, often spending several days driving felons across the country. "There were times I drove more than a thousand miles on one day," recalls Frank Anderson, who joined the Marshals Service in 1965 as Indiana's first African American deputy marshal.

> In those days they would set up a trip so you would be on the road for a week or more at a time. We'd pick up three prisoners in one city and drop them off in the next city and pick up two more and take them someplace else. We drove our own cars and they paid us ten cents a mile and eighteen dollars a day per diem. It was almost a requirement to be a deputy that you had a four-door car. We would customize these cars ourselves: we'd cut a hole in the glove compartment to install a radio, take the knobs off the inside of the doors and we were ready to go. Like a lot of other people, for our own protection we made a removable screen we could put between the front and back seats.
>
> People weren't used to seeing black deputy marshals in those days. We always had to have a guard ride with us and that would often be a city policeman or deputy sheriff, and sometimes I would have another black male with me. That was a very different time in America, and on more than one occasion we would be driving down a county road and turn a corner to see a

roadblock with state troopers and sheriffs pointing shotguns at us. The prisoners loved it; they
would be in the backseat screaming that we were
the prisoners and we'd escaped and handcuffed
the white marshals in the backseat. It's never fun
to have a shotgun pointed directly at you. In those
situations, I made sure I moved slowly until it was
sorted out.

"Those were memorable trips," Deputy Robert
Leschorn agrees.

There were times we would stick three prisoners in
the back of a Chevy Nova. They were belly-chained
and leg-ironed while you and your partner were in
the front seat with a pistol apiece and a shotgun.
And you didn't get three little guys who were being
good; more often you'd get three psychos who hated
each other. It was like putting three big, tough,
angry little kids in the backseat on a long trip and
having to listen to them fight. One time—I will
never forget this—we were hauling two black bank
robbers and one white racist. The white guy hated
the black guys, the black guys hated the white guy,
and we had to take them eleven hundred miles.
They were fighting every mile.

In situations like that we would change the seating arrangements. One of us would sit in the back without a gun—but they didn't know that.

Just like in the movies, during those long trips the deputies would get to know the people they were transporting. At times, as Deputy Bobby Sanchez explains, it was hard not to feel sympathy for some of these people.

When you first come on, the whole situation is new and you start to wonder if some of these people might be innocent or simply were in the wrong place at the wrong time. But then there was always something to remind you exactly why they were in this situation. I was escorting a stone cold killer back to the states from Puerto Rico and he started telling me how angry he was about his case. He had been hired by a man who owned a shoe company to take out his wife. They were going through a divorce or he had caught her cheating, but he wanted her dead. He hired this guy to do it. This guy intended to kill her after she'd left her office, but for some reason she had worked late that night. He got tired of waiting, so he went into the office and killed several people. The man who had hired him was devastated, and when he was questioned by police, he immediately flipped. As the hit man told me this story he started shaking his head, "He wanted her dead and now she's dead. I don't see no problem there. What's his problem with that?"

I remember thinking, *How can he be so cold?* That was something I learned: the people we were escorting didn't think like the people I knew; they had no remorse. They would kill somebody in a heartbeat and then go party. After you've been exposed to enough cold-blooded people, you believe they all deserve to be there. They're just killers.

Most of the conversations between deputies and their prisoners are just banter, two human beings making the best of an unusual situation. "They'll try to con you if possible," Frank Anderson says. "I had one guy tell me once, seriously, 'You know the last marshal I rode with let me drive the car.'" While there were stories of women prisoners offering more than conversation, usually when female prisoners were being transported, a matron was brought along. In the 1970s, there were very few female deputy marshals, so office workers—and some wives—were given eight-hour matron training and sent along on these trips. Geri Doody, who became a deputy marshal in 1980, reflects on those transports.

I had been working in the office as an assistant in the accounting department for about a week in 1971 when they told me I was going along to pick up a woman prisoner. And then they added, "And you're going to have to strip search her." I was horrified, scared to death. Oftentimes on these prisoner trips we would drive across the whole country. I didn't have any real training for that; I didn't even have a driver's license. I lived in New York, so I didn't need one. I didn't have a gun, I didn't have a badge; I would just get in the van and off we'd go.

The general unwritten rule that marshals followed was no matter how bad some of these prisoners were, they always had to be treated with respect. When stopping at McDonald's for a meal, for example, that meant buying the prisoner a Big Mac rather than just a Happy Meal. But the single most important rule was to never, ever, give a prisoner any personal information. There was a good reason for that—many of these prisoners were crazy.

Vic Oboyski was responsible for transporting a prisoner who had been writing threatening letters to the president of the United States, taking him back and forth from MCC to the psychiatric ward at Creedmoor Hospital. Oboyski's name and address appeared on the warrant and somehow this man got hold of it and started sending him bizarre and threatening letters in which he claimed to be a supreme Allied commander who was receiving his orders directly from NATO. Oboyski explains,

I was a supervisor in Brooklyn and the time came when this guy was being released from Creedmoor's psychiatric unit; we had to pick him up and take him to court. I sent a couple of deputies to go get him. When he got to the courthouse, our unit chief at the time, Dave O'Flaherty, and I went down to talk to him. He was a big guy who liked to dress in a complete Gurkha outfit, including the hat. Dave and I sat down with him to try to defuse the situation. I introduced myself and explained what was going to happen—that he was going to court—and he confirmed that he understood that. Then I said, "I understand that you've been in touch with the Allied Command?"

"Oh yes," he confirmed and then confided in us, "That's where I get my instructions." I asked him if he had his instructions at that time. "I do," he said. "They transmit them to me. I have a receiver."

A receiver? Dave and I had dealt with situations just like this one several times before; that's part of the job and we had it down to a routine. We usually confronted these people with reality; we asked them where this receiver was located and explained that we had to check it for security purposes. Almost always they told us that it was implanted in their fillings. We would make them open their mouth, then make a big deal of pretending to look inside. We'd shine a flashlight in there and discuss what we saw and eventually we would agree that wow, there actually was a receiver hidden there. In this instance Dave asked him the usual question: "Where's your receiver?"

The Gurkha didn't hesitate: "It's in my anus," he said.

"Put the flashlight away, Dave," I said firmly. Then I told this guy, "Lemme be honest with you here. We really don't care if you have a receiver in your anus." Dave immediately agreed; we would not be checking that particular story.

In fact, being threatened was not at all unusual. Dave O'Flaherty recalls the time he escorted Puerto Rican terrorist Willie Morales back and forth to his hearings. Morales had lost both his hands when a bomb he was making exploded prematurely.

After you've been with a prisoner on a regular basis for any length of time, you do get to know each other a little. I gave him the nickname Stumpy, because he liked to poke me with his stumps. We would be on an elevator and he would push me with his stump and warn me, "This is a gun, you know. When I get out of here, I'm going to kill you."

I'd always respond, "Want to shake on that?" Morales actually escaped from the third floor of the Bellevue Prison ward. Somehow he managed to cut through chicken wire covering the window and shimmied down to the ground on a sheet. After a shoot-out in Mexico City, he made his way to Cuba and has lived there ever since.

Not every prisoner could be cuffed and put into the back of a car. At times it took some ingenuity to figure out how to transport a prisoner. One of the first felons Jimmy Bankston arrested was a Harris County, Texas, man charged with counterfeiting immigration resident alien cards. Bankston remembers,

He wasn't violent, and we knew for sure he wasn't going to run because he literally weighed eight hundred pounds. Run? He could barely waddle. The difficult part wasn't finding him—in fact, you couldn't miss him—the problem was figuring out how we were going to transport him from his apartment to the infirmary at the Harris County

Jail. We ended up renting a U-Haul open trailer, which had what was called an easy-loader dock. We tried everything, but we couldn't get him in it. He was cooperative; otherwise, there was no way we could have done this, but eventually we set him on the back and he kind of rolled into the trailer, then sat up like Buddha. The worst part of the whole experience was feeding him after we got him to the jail. I remember bringing him four or five trays of food and watching him eat; food was just rolling down his body. There are many things I've seen in my career that I've forgotten, but, unfortunately, watching food roll down his stomach into his belly button isn't one of them.

In addition to the car trips, at times it is necessary to transport prisoners by airplane. When a prisoner is being transported on a commercial flight, several deputies will sit around that person in the rear of the airplane. The airlines insist that the prisoner wear handcuffs, and that his cuffed hands are covered with a coat or blanket. But in certain situations small private planes have been used. In the 1990s, Dominican American citizen Melissa Polonio and her husband, Jorge "Chi Chi" Garcia, ran a $4,000-a-day crack empire in the South Bronx section of New York City. They had used their profits to buy several buildings and owned numerous expensive cars. In April 1995, apparently in a jealous rage, Polonio walked into a Communion party in Washington Heights and stabbed a beautiful young woman in the heart, killing her instantly. Then she took her two children, two boys, and fled. Eventually she became one of the first women named to the U.S. Marshals Service's 15 Most Wanted Fugitives list.

"We tracked her for several years," Deputy Marshal Joseph Lobue says.

We kept developing information from sources that she was somewhere in the Dominican Republic, but we couldn't find her. Working with the Dominicans and the DEA, we ran down at least twenty different leads but we kept coming up empty. Always empty. One of the things we learn in the Marshals Service is tenacity. It's part of the job description. We all take tremendous pride in the fact that we never give up; at different times every one of us would become obsessed with a case and just not let go. For me, this was one of them.

I went down to the Dominican several times to follow leads. Eventually we got information she was living on a farm in a very rural area. The problem with that is that everyone in that area knew each other and any stranger who came anywhere near there got made immediately. It was impossible to penetrate it. I got to see a lot of the Dominican countryside; but deputies weren't allowed to carry a weapon so there were times I found myself in some pretty uncomfortable places and felt very vulnerable. We chased Melissa Polonio for more than five years and still couldn't find her.

We only had a few things we absolutely knew were true, one of them being she was desperate to see her two kids, who were living in New York with her mother. Her mother was on public assistance, and I was able to get a photograph of her. We continued to monitor flights from New York to the Dominican, and lo and behold, we found out the mother had booked a flight to go down there with the two boys. Purely coincidentally, two Dominican policemen who happened to be in the city for training were booked to go home on precisely the same flight. It was one of those great breaks that you get if you work hard enough.

I drove those policemen to the airport. We blended in with the crowd, and finally the mother came walking into the terminal with the two children. The two officers flew down there with her. For the next few days Dominican police tailed the mother everywhere she went. She made moves to lose the tail that made everyone believe she knew she was being watched. But ultimately she led them to her daughter's new boyfriend. They thought they had her in his house, but once again came up empty. The new boyfriend was detained, and the Dominicans did the type of interview they do to gather information. The boyfriend agreed to cooperate. He took them to a location, crying the whole time, but she was there and finally they captured her.

I was thrilled. As soon as I found out they had her in custody I made preparations to fly down there. I'd been working on that case for five years, and I intended to bring her back. A colonel met my flight and told me we had six hours to get her out of the Dominican before it became a diplomatic problem. We were in a real jam. The American embassy made arrangements for a small U.S. Customs plane to fly over from Puerto Rico to get us. The weather forecast was bad, but we didn't have a choice; we had to get her off Dominican territory. There were five of us, the two pilots, myself and my partner, and Melissa Polonio on that small airplane. I'm claustrophobic, and I hated flying on these small planes even when the sun was shining, but there was no option. Every deputy has learned that when transporting a prisoner, there are going to be times when you're going to have to do something really uncomfortable. For me, this was the most memorable of all those times.

Unlike a lot of prisoners, Melissa Polonio was very talkative. She had gotten out of the narcotics business, she told me, and had been earning a living making calls for a phone sex company. Okay, it's a living. We had started talking about that when we flew into the storm.

It very quickly became the worst flight of my life. Lightning was flashing all around us, driving rain was pounding against the windows, and we were being tossed up and down, right and left. I was scared, but Melissa Polonio was terrified. She started screaming in this guttural voice, praying to God that she didn't want to go to jail and begging him to knock the plane out of the sky.

Meanwhile, I was also talking to God; the difference was that I was asking him, "Please don't listen to her, she doesn't know what she's talking about. Please don't answer this one, God. Please!"

We landed safely in Miami and eventually I took her up to New York. She was convicted of manslaughter and sentenced to between twelve and twenty-five years in prison.

Marshals who have transported prisoners point out that perhaps the most difficult part of these trips, especially the long drives, is not becoming complacent. Almost all transfers go as planned, without incident, so at times it is easy to forget that the person being transported is a bad guy looking desperately for any opportunity to escape. Many of these people are going back to prison for a second or third time and are facing long stretches; for some of them the trip is their last chance to escape before being locked up behind bars for the rest of their lives.

It is very rare for a suspect to make a break for it during his or her trial, and prisoners almost never get away with it, but felons do make escape attempts while they're being moved. When Deputy Marshal David Dimmitt was transferred from an office in Nebraska to Albany, New York, one of the first things he did was inspect the prisoner transport vehicles. "Part of the problem with the Marshals Service at that time was that there wasn't a strong set of regulations enforced at the national level," Dimmitt remembers.

Local people pretty much ran their districts the way they wanted to; in Nebraska, all the windows in these vehicles had been covered with wire cages that were actually made by prisoners in Leavenworth. When I got to Albany, I asked the chief why his vehicles did not have those protective cages. His exact words were, "Not required, can't afford it, don't do it."

A month after that, we were transporting a man named Gary Evans, who was the primary suspect in at least three murders. He had been housed in a local jail in Rensselaer County and we were taking him into federal custody. I was the supervisor of a small suboffice and we had five people in the office that day. We felt he was at risk from other members of a large burglary ring, who believed he might become an informer, so I put two deputies in the Chevy Astro van with him and a third deputy in a follow-up car. I watched them leave; by the time I got back to the office someone was on the radio reporting an escape in progress.

They were going over a bridge when the deputy in the follow car suddenly saw the van window explode. A microsecond later, a pair of Chuck Taylor sneakers popped out of the window. Evans had kicked out the window. Then he came out of the window. He was still restrained in handcuffs, a belly chain, and ankle cuffs, but he actually managed to twist his body out the window. He got caught on a window latch and was hung up and riding on the side of the van for a few seconds, then he dropped onto the road. A lady in a car behind the van managed to stop before hitting him.

Evans got up; one of the handcuffs and the belly chain had broken free, but he still was bound by the ankle restraints. You can't run in ankle cuffs, but with a little practice you can move pretty fast. He took off straight into traffic so the van couldn't turn around to pursue him. The deputy in the follow car was a former Navy SEAL, so he left his car there and took off after him on foot. He caught up to him pretty quickly. Evans stopped and looked directly at him. They stood there that way for a few seconds. They were only a few feet apart, and Evans must have realized there was no way out for him— suddenly he leaped backward over the low railing of the bridge. The deputy lunged to try to grab hold of him but didn't get there in time. He looked over the side; it was about eighty feet to the ground, and as Evans was falling toward what he probably thought was the Hudson River he was flipping off the deputy. But he didn't land in the river. At the place he jumped the land extends out into the river. It's covered with some large rocks. Instead of landing in the water, Evans smashed onto the rocks.

It was over by the time I got to the scene. I went down there to confirm that he was dead or if there was any chance to help him. He had landed on his back with one arm behind him. He was dead. I rolled him over—and he still had his middle finger extended up.

While I was still under the bridge, looking at his body, I got a call from a state trooper who told me Evans had been talking about committing suicide rather than going back to prison. I was pretty upset that we hadn't been warned about that. By the time I got back to my office Evans's lawyer was waiting for me. He showed me a picture Evans had drawn on the back of a legal document during his hearing—it was a butterfly, and underneath he had written a few words that could lead you to believe he was going to take his own life. I thanked the lawyer for sharing that. Later the local newspaper accused some of my people of conspiring to kill Evans, which made me furious; that discussion got real ugly. Personally, I don't believe Evans was suicidal—but I do believe he was willing to die trying to escape. He wasn't the first person to feel that way. And that's exactly what ended up happening.

The reality is that prisoners have escaped from custody, and certainly among the most infamous events in Marshals Service history is the escape of bank robbers

Terry Lee Conner and Joseph William Dougherty. In 1985, two deputies were transporting Conner and Dougherty from the federal prison in El Reno to Oklahoma City, where Conner, who had already been sentenced to twenty-five years for a 1982 robbery, was going to testify at Dougherty's trial for the same crime. Before leaving prison, one of them managed to get hold of a handcuff key and while en route used it to free their hands. Both deputies were riding up front, a violation of service policy. "And common sense," Tony Perez points out. "We didn't have caged cars in those days so there was nothing separating the prisoners from the deputies. They overpowered the deputies and forced them to pull over. Supposedly Dougherty wanted to kill them, but Conner talked him out of it. They left the deputies handcuffed to each other around a tree, took their guns, and drove off in the car. Then they disappeared."

Conner and Dougherty were among the most successful bank robbers in history; it's estimated they stole more than $2 million in a series of heists. They became known for breaking into the homes of bank executives the night before the robbery—in at least one instance posing as U.S. deputy marshals—then forcing them to assist in the crime by threatening their families. They were known to make their hostages put on so-called explosive vests, warning them that they would blow them up if they did not cooperate. In several instances they took the executive's family to the bank before it opened, then forced arriving bank employees into a room. In the year following their escape, Conner and Dougherty robbed at least four additional banks all over the country. Perez remembers,

At that time the FBI did not play well with others, and they definitely did not like to share information.

We followed endless leads, we did a lot of phone monitoring, and we conducted countless interviews. The FBI put these people on its 10 Most Wanted and we put them on our 15 Most Wanted. Eventually I personally went to the Bureau of Prisons with a really unusual request. I asked two wardens to each release one inmate from their respective prisons because we believed these people would lead us to Conner and Dougherty. These were serious criminals, convicted bank robbers who had worked with Conner and Dougherty. We wanted them to let them go as if they had received an early parole or there was some kind of administrative error or they got an early release because of overcrowding; the reason didn't matter, whatever worked for them and seemed believable. I gave both wardens my assurance we were going to put deputies on them and watch them wherever they went. We were confident that as soon as they got loose, they would be in contact with Conner or Dougherty.

It definitely was a labor-intensive surveillance, but we really wanted these guys. One of these "parolees" got on a Greyhound bus, and we saw that every time the bus stopped he would make a call from a pay phone. As soon as he got back on the bus we'd contact the phone company and get the records of that specific phone at that specific time. We had developed good relationships with local phone companies across the country, and the technicians were beginning to know who we were. We also discovered an American Express card that had been dormant for a long time was suddenly being used. Eventually we found that phone calls had been made to an Imperial 400 Motel at a motel in Arlington Heights, Illinois.

By that time Conner and Dougherty had been running for almost eighteen months. That's a long time to be tracking people, but they had gotten away from us and we wanted to get them back. As we were surveilling the place, Terry Lee Conner came out of room 110, a bottom-floor room, and went into the front office to pay for an additional night. On the way back he stopped to get a complimentary cup of coffee and we confronted him. "You know what to do," we told him. He got down on his knees very slowly and gingerly put the cup of coffee down on the sidewalk.

Dougherty happened to be away from the motel when Conner was arrested. Apparently he saw all the activity in the parking lot and took off. He had vowed publicly that he would not go back to prison. But two weeks later, the FBI arrested him as he did his laundry in a small California town. Both Conner and Dougherty eventually were sentenced to several hundred years in prison, and one of the very few successful escapes in the history of the Marshals Service was resolved.

Bringing fugitives back from foreign countries always carries with it additional risk. By May 1996, Deputy Phillip Matthews had been tracking Roland Campbell, the leader of an infamous gang of bank robbers known as "the Forty Thieves," since his escape from Baltimore Prison five years earlier. Campbell, who was also wanted for murder and narcotics trafficking, was known to have used twenty-four false identities, nine social security numbers, and eleven different birth certificates. He was considered violent enough to earn a spot on the Marshals Service's 15 Most Wanted list. When Campbell was captured in the city of Cuatro Reinas de Tibás, Costa Rica, in July 1996, U.S. Marshal Lenny DePaul, who had been working in Puerto Rico, flew down there to bring him back to the United States.

Unlike Dimmitt in the Evans case, DePaul had been briefed about Campbell's history. He knew Campbell was a violent man who headed a violent gang and that while he was doing time in San Diego he had supposedly suffered a serious asthma attack and was rushed to the hospital. That turned out to be his escape plan. Members of his gang had been waiting for the ambulance; they shot one of the guards, allowing Campbell to make his getaway. DePaul knew that Campbell wasn't coming back from Costa Rica easily.

DePaul's five-man team picked up Campbell at the jail and drove in a convoy to the airport. Then, he recalls,

We walked into a back room where several people were waiting for us. One of them was a very beautiful Spanish woman who seemed to be trying to take control of the situation. "Who's that?" I asked one of our embassy people. "A court officer," I was told. Then they warned me, "Be careful. We're not quite sure who's on which side." With that, one of the officer's colleagues came over to me and said, "Campbell is not feeling well. His asthma is making him have trouble breathing. He needs to be taken to the hospital right away."

Bells started going off in my mind. I turned to my partner and said, "He isn't going anywhere. He's definitely not going to any hospital." A minute later we got word from our pilot that we were going. "Let's go," I said. "Let's get him out of here." People were starting to stir; whatever was about to happen, it wasn't going to be good for us. This wasn't our country. We gave Campbell a quick search and discovered he was wearing two layers of clothes and carrying cash in dollars and pesos. When we ordered him to get up, he refused. We didn't have time to screw around with him; this situation was going downhill quickly. We cuffed his hands to the arms of an office chair on rollers and started wheeling him out of the room onto the tarmac. "Thank you for your hospitality," I said. "We're leaving." And we were leaving quickly.

DePaul's team wheeled Campbell out to the plane. When the prisoner still refused to get up, his hands were cuffed behind his back, and two deputies each took a leg and dragged him up the steps, his head banging on each step.

We didn't have time to be gentle; there were a lot of soldiers armed with AK-47s standing on the tarmac, and we couldn't be sure whose side anybody was on. We knew one thing for sure, Campbell could afford to pay any one of them a lot more than their salary.

We were able to confirm later on that if we had left the airport, we would have been driving into an ambush. Everybody had already been paid. They were waiting for us along the different routes from the airport to the hospital. We never would have made it.

Taking prisoners out of other countries has rarely been simple. In the past, diplomats had to get clearance and there were often political ramifications. Many felons, like Campbell, claimed to be a citizen of a particular country and demanded their rights. It often would take a considerable amount of time to get everything straightened out. During that time anti-American activists would be trying to prevent deputy marshals from leaving the country. A team of deputies including Tony Perez actually accompanied American combat troops into Panama in 1989 to arrest dictator Manuel Noriega on drug charges and bring him back to America for trial. Howard Safir had told Perez not to bother coming back empty-handed, whatever it took. Noriega had taken refuge in a church but eventually came out and was arrested by Perez. Deputy Dan Stoltz, who was on Perez's team, recollects how tense the situation became.

Once we had him, we took control of the airport. Nothing was going in or out without our permission, and there was a Swiss diplomat who didn't like that at all. He waved his diplomatic passport and started making all types of demands. Mike Carnivale was our supervisor, and when this diplomat started making a racket, loudly reminding us how important he was, Mike walked over to him. I saw a look on Mike's face that made me think we were going to have some problems. Mike grabbed the guy by his arm and spun him around, took him over to a chair, and forced him to sit down. Then he picked up a bright orange traffic cone that happened to be there, slapped it on the guy's head, turned the chair into the corner, and told him he had to sit there for fifteen minutes.

I thought, *Well, there's an international incident.* Once I stopped laughing, I went over to the guy and took the cone off his head, apologized to him, and put him on an airplane. But with everything that was going on in that country at that time, we just weren't in a situation to allow anyone to cause any problems. We never knew what could set off some serious problems.

More than a century ago, deputies had to bring their prisoners to justice on horseback or by stagecoach, and they had to be continuously looking out for an ambush. When moving a prisoner today, deputies are still taught to watch continually to see if they are being tailed—and warned not to stop for any reason. The more infamous a prisoner is, the more people there are who don't want to see that person behind bars. Consider Joanne Chesimard, who was a member of the radical Black Liberation Army. She had been charged with numerous crimes, including murder, kidnapping, and armed robbery and eventually was convicted of murder. When she was moved from the Manhattan Correctional Center in lower Manhattan over the Brooklyn Bridge to the federal courthouse, it was always in a convoy of at least six vehicles. One afternoon, Dave O'Flaherty was driving the transport van on the return trip from court. At the base of the Brooklyn Bridge in Manhattan there is an exit ramp leading directly to the back entrance of the MCC. As O'Flaherty started down that ramp, a car suddenly cut him off, forcing him against a low curb on the bridge. When the van hit that curb, it began flipping over onto its side. Chesimard smashed her nose against the metal screen. The deputies weren't hurt, and Chesimard was quickly hustled back into the prison. The car raced away. It was never determined if this was an accident or, more likely, an attempt to free Chesimard.

But maybe the most unusual "transportation" assignment requires a deputy to remain with a federal prisoner throughout his execution. Deputy Frank Anderson served as one of two witnesses to the June 2001 execution of Oklahoma City bomber Timothy McVeigh, who had murdered 168 people, including 19 children, when he blew up the Alfred P. Murrah Federal Building.

Obviously it was a very sobering situation. My own feelings about it never came into the process. When I first became a law enforcement officer, my father told me, "Son, I don't care who it is; if someone violates the law, you've got a responsibility to enforce it." That's what I did.

I had a conversation with McVeigh. He knew a little about me. I had been in charge of seizing the Indianapolis Baptist Church for nonpayment of $6 million in back taxes, for refusing to withhold income taxes and social security taxes from employee paychecks. That was the first time in history the government had seized a church and we'd had a three-month standoff when church members refused to leave the building. Rather than confronting them, we'd just waited them out and as a result we'd had a peaceful resolution. Apparently McVeigh knew all about that. He claimed he had bombed the federal building in Oklahoma City to retaliate for the shoot-out in Waco, Texas, in which David Koresh and seventy-five members of a Christian sect known as the Branch Davidians had been killed. In fact, McVeigh said to me something like, "If you'd have been at Waco, that wouldn't have happened."

I don't know if he meant he wouldn't have been on death row if the government had simply waited out the people at Waco. McVeigh was calm the whole time. His execution was being shown on closed circuit to 232 survivors and relatives of the Oklahoma City bombing. The one thing he wanted to know was where the camera that went to

Oklahoma City was located. He just fixed his eyes on that camera and continued glaring into it as they gave him that lethal injection.

In the Old West, deputies would place dead fugitives in an upright wooden coffin and take a photo to prove they were dead. After McVeigh's execution, Anderson was required to remove McVeigh's clothing so his body could be photographed, providing visual proof that he had not been abused. In more than two centuries, some aspects of a marshal's job hadn't changed at all.

2

"Take No Guff, Give No Slack, Hook 'Em, Book 'Em, and Don't Look Back."

Deputy Marshal Bobby Biggs: Sam, are you out of your mind? He's dead.
Deputy Marshal Samuel Gerard: That ought to make him easier to catch.

—The Fugitive (*1993*)

In 1982, the U.S. Customs Agency broke up a smuggling ring known to have brought at least twenty-seven tons of marijuana into the country. Customs had arrested several members of the operation, who were convicted and received long sentences, but the head of the gang, Steven Jenks, had disappeared literally without a trace. The wife of one of the members of his sailboat crew had fled with him. Twelve years later, the Customs agent who had been working the case for more than a decade brought it to the Marshals Service. He was getting ready to retire, he said, but before he did, more than anything else he wanted to see Steven Jenks behind bars. And he needed help.

Deputy Mike Bunk, working in Tampa, got the case. He began by talking to the crew member whose wife had fled with Jenks, figuring he might be pretty angry about that.

It turned out that he actually was okay with it.

Bunk then began focusing on the woman herself. Her father had passed away four years earlier, he discovered, but her mother was still alive and living in Florida. "I started researching all of her family members," Bunk explains.

I wanted to see where they were going, who they were talking to. When nothing came up, I started doing trash pulls on the mother's house. That means instead of the sanitation department picking up her garbage, I did it. I brought it back with me to our office and dumped it out on a bench we had in the squad room. It was about the most disgusting thing I've ever done.

After the first week, people were suggesting I give it up—some people were suggesting it pretty strongly—but on about the tenth trash day I came across an Ann Landers column, an advice column that had been cut out of a newspaper. Someone had written the words, *Thought you'd like this. Love, me* on it. Love, me? That caught my attention. I wondered who would send this without signing their name. In the files I found a letter that the woman who had fled with Jenks had written many years earlier. I'm not a handwriting expert, but to me it looked like the same handwriting. I contacted Ann Landers—actually, the person who distributed her articles—and asked if the same column runs in all the papers that carry this feature on the same day nationwide. It does, I was told. Then I asked, "Do you decide on the format? You know, how many lines it'll be, how many paragraphs?" That answer was they did not; each newspaper would format it in its own typeface to fit its own needs.

They gave me the date that particular column appeared in the papers. I went down to the Tampa library and started pulling all the newspapers throughout the state of Florida published on that date. In about the tenth newspaper I looked at, I found what I was looking for. The column I got out of the garbage had been published in the Naples

Sun. It matched perfectly—the format, the words at the end of each sentence, the typeface, a slight misprint. That made me believe this woman—and maybe Jenks—were in the Naples area.

I tried to figure out what to do next. I kept doing trash pulls, hoping for another lead, but I didn't find anything. I also continued to interview people, trying to develop an informant, one person to give me just that thread of information I needed. Finally an informant who knew the mother told me she was very sick, probably getting ready to pass away. I hoped her daughter would try to get in contact with her.

About two months later, this informant called again. The mother was in the hospital in Brandon, Florida, he told me, and the woman's estranged husband, the member of the drug crew who had recently gotten out of prison, had visited his former mother-in-law a day earlier. He'd promised her that he was going to try to get in touch with her daughter, his wife, to let her know what was going on. Then he'd left the hospital, stopped at a row of pay phones and made at least one phone call.

There were three pay phones outside the hospital. The informant told me about what time the call had been made. I got those phone numbers and subpoenaed the phone company's records for all calls made within that time frame. Only one call had been made; someone had called a number in Pahrump, Nevada. Pahrump, Nevada? I got the address and had a deputy working in Nevada go out to take a look at it. It turned out to be a telephone message center. People would call there and leave a message, and someone calling from an entirely different place could call and retrieve it. We needed to know where the person who had retrieved the message had been calling from. The owner of the message center was able to provide a name and address: it was a name we'd never heard—but it was a phone number and address in Fort Myers, Florida. I had to smile when I heard that—Fort Myers is just north of Naples.

Bunk discovered that number belonged to a Mail Boxes Etc. call center. People would have to come in to pick up their messages. Somebody was being extremely careful about receiving messages. Bunk feared this was going to require a long stakeout, so "before going there I called the retiring Customs agent and asked if he wanted to go with me and my partner. He did, very much. The two of them stayed in the parking lot picking out the best locations to set up surveillance while

I went inside to ask a few questions. An employee immediately identified a photograph of the girlfriend, but said she had never seen Jenks. Unfortunately, she said, this woman came in irregularly, sometimes once a week, sometimes once every three months. The owner of the store agreed to let us set up surveillance; he even offered to let us pose as employees."

Bunk sat down, getting ready for a long stay. There was no way of knowing when, or even if, the woman would ever come back. At the least, he figured, they might be stuck there for weeks. An hour later she walked into the store. Literally, an hour later. Bunk was amazed.

I'm never this lucky. But it was her. We tailed her to a trailer park and watched as she went into a twenty-foot trailer. It was a nice trailer, but it wasn't very luxurious. We decided not to wait, and the three of us hit it. Steven Jenks was inside and the Customs agent was able to close his career by arresting him.

Jenks and his girlfriend decided to cooperate. I mean, really cooperate. They handed over several million dollars' worth of assets, a yacht, a Piper Cub, and diamonds. The woman came into our office with her attorney. The attorney looked at her and asked, "Do you have it?" With that she started pulling threads from the hem of her dress, and about forty diamonds fell onto my desk. Blue diamonds, gold diamonds, as much as $3 million in diamonds. The Customs agent took possession of them. Eventually Jenks was sentenced to three years in prison, while his girlfriend, whom he later married, was not charged.

There is no typical case for a deputy marshal. Because of the unique responsibilities given to the Marshals Service, the range of cases deputies work extends to just about anything imaginable, from chasing a serial killer into the hills of Puerto Rico to patrolling the streets during the L.A. riots, from running a championship horse farm seized because the owner stole the money to support it to chasing down a smuggler who has vanished for Customs. "Every day is different," David O'Flaherty says. "I just loved the rush. Every day we went out knowing we were facing danger, knowing what could happen. Over the years I've told people I would've done that job for free and I wasn't kidding."

Although few people are aware of it, U.S. marshals have the broadest arrest authority of any American law enforcement agency. While other federal agencies have specific statutory authority—Customs, for example, controls our borders; the DEA focuses on drugs; and the FBI has emphasized stopping terrorism and investigating cybercrimes—the Marshals Service has a hand in every aspect of federal law enforcement. In addition, the power of state and local law enforcement to make arrests ends at their borders. "We are able to make the amount of arrests we do," explains Deputy Marshal Jimmy Bankston, "because we have a different job. We don't get involved until a warrant is issued, and by that time another agency may have put in a tremendous amount of really good work. By the time we go to work the investigation is over. For example, a local police department may have spent months solving a difficult murder case and their suspect has left their jurisdiction. Local law enforcement doesn't have the resources to pursue that suspect. In the vast majority of arrests we make, we track down suspects, put on the handcuffs, and walk away." Or as a popular slogan once defined it: Take no guff, give no slack, hook 'em, book 'em, and don't look back.

Following the 1979 agreement with the FBI, several of the larger districts set up what were called "warrant squads," whose only function was to pursue fugitives. Because each of the ninety-four districts operated pretty much independently, there was no coordinated national program. The initial warrant squads went into operation in the larger cities, where more manpower was available. Generally deputies were assigned to these warrant squads as part of their normal rotation, but many people discovered how much they enjoyed those teams. As Deputy Bobby Sanchez says, "I fell in love with it. Once you started working fugitives you never wanted to work anything else."

Robert Leschorn agrees.

All we did was hunt fugitives day and night. We loved the thrill, we thrived on it. We were finally out of the cellblocks and on the streets. There weren't many rules to follow; those first few years of the fugitive program were absolutely the Wild West. We'd have one guy in the front of the house and one guy in the back of the house and a bank robber in between who didn't plan on going back to prison. These were bare-bones operations; if we had a really difficult arrest, we could get a third man. Maybe we didn't have the proper support, and we were working with the minimal gear, but we had a lot of guts and we had a lot of fun.

We'd start banging on doors as early as five A.M., figuring we would catch people in bed. We referred to ourselves as "the wake-up police." We'd make a collar and take them in, go have some breakfast, then start running prisoners to court. Doing our assigned jobs in the courtroom was still our priority, but as soon as we got done with that, we'd put on jeans, grab our street gear, and go hunt fugitives.

Harry Layne, who had spent a year working in the Witness Protection Program, says, "I'm glad I did it because I learned how much I hated it. I wanted to do the same thing we all wanted to do, kick in doors and bring in fugitives."

It was that possibility of real action that initially attracted a lot of young people to the job. Deputy Tony Burke said he joined the Marshals Service in the early 1990s for the same reason he previously had joined the U.S. Marines.

To me, being a United States marshal was the purest form of law enforcement. In the movies I'd seen growing up, the marshals were always the guys wearing the white hats. It seemed pretty obvious to me that there would be more action, more freedom, and a much wider type of cases than any other law enforcement job. Deputies didn't spend two years on an investigation that resulted in three arrests; there wasn't a lot of politics. It was simply:

here's a bad guy, go find that f—k and bring him back. Then go get me another one.

Most deputy marshals spend the first few years of their careers rotating in and out of different assignments. That is how they learn to handle the various responsibilities the job entails. But Burke wanted to chase bad guys, and the very casual organizational structure of the Marshals Service made it possible. He finished his training and reported to the Los Angeles office in late December 1995.

When I showed up, all the supervisors were out on leave for the holidays, so there really was nobody running the place. I looked on the assignment board and saw something called fugitive operations. I thought, *Yeah, that's where I need to be.*

Normally when you first get in, you get stuck in court and driving prisoners around on a bus. I got the phone number of a senior deputy marshal named Sam Donavet, who was working out in Compton. I called him and introduced myself, telling him I was supposed to be assigned to him. Admittedly that wasn't exactly true, but only one of us knew that. "Great," he said. "I need some help. Can you be out here at oh six hundred? We're going to do a caper with a murder suspect."

I got there early. This was my third day on the job, but that was another fact that I failed to mention. I couldn't have been more excited. We had the suspect's apartment surrounded. I was sitting in the car with Sam, waiting for him to give the word to move in, when the suspect walked out of the front door. Everybody immediately reacted; doors flew open, people started running, and the suspect took off like a rabbit. He literally ran right over the top of one of the cars. I didn't stop to think about anything; I jumped out of the car and took off after him. I had never been in Compton in my life, and I didn't have any idea where I was going. I was just running blindly. One other deputy was with me, but he got left behind when we went over a fence. The suspect ran across the four lanes of Long Beach Boulevard and I went right after him, I didn't even slow down. Only after I'd crossed the first two lanes of traffic did it occur to me that this was a seriously bad idea.

Burke followed the suspect into a dilapidated squatter house.

The place was a mess, and at least I was smart enough not to start searching for him myself. This is how bad this place was: I leaned against a wall to catch my breath—and the whole wall collapsed into an alley. It almost landed on several other deputies who had caught up with us. We surrounded the house and the experienced guys went through it very methodically. When they found him he started fighting; they had to Tase him and I almost got to put the cuffs on him. But that was my first arrest.

For some reason Sam was under the impression that I had already completed my six months' rotation through courts, transportation, and the other assignments. I was able to maintain that deception for almost three months. I would come into the office early and find out who was on leave, then I'd borrow their assigned cell phone and vehicle. That lasted until a morning in early March when I was walking down the hall with all my equipment—I had six duffel bags, a shotgun, and a cell phone hanging off my belt—when I ran into the supervisor I actually had been assigned to. He had never seen me before, so he stopped and asked me who I was. When I told him my name, it sort of registered with him and he asked, "What are you doing with all that shit in your hand?"

I told him the truth, "I'm supposed to meet Sam. We're doing a hit."

He shook his head in disbelief, "A hit my ass. You're the f—ing new guy, you're supposed to be in court. How long have you been here?"

"Since December twentieth," I admitted.

He exploded. "What!" I told him most of the whole story, then handed over all my equipment. After that, I started doing the assigned tasks, escorting prisoners to court, listening to the same procedures day after day, counting the seconds. But at night, after court was adjourned, I would meet up with the guys on the warrant squad. We'd be out till after midnight chasing fugitives, and then again the next morning I'd be right back in court. My supervisor didn't really know how to handle this. When he asked me to slow down, I told him I didn't need to sleep.

Nine months after reporting to the office Burke was assigned to the warrant squad as part of the normal rotation.

I was finally where I wanted to be. I wanted to prove that I belonged there. I went ballistic. I was relentless, always out on the street making arrests. I had great interviewing skills so I developed a large group of informants. Even after my rotation ended and I had to go back to the courts, I kept hitting the streets at night. The supervisors tried to slow me down by taking away the fugitive cases I was working. So I'd go around and look on other deputies' desks to find other open cases. I'd find that fugitive and arrest him, then leave a little yellow sticky note on the deputy's desk that his case had been closed.

In those days you could get away with that kind of stuff. They tried everything to stop me. I had an assigned car, so they took that away from me. I didn't have a vehicle. I started going around making arrests in my personal car, an '89 Nissan Sentra, a piece of crap with a baby seat in the back. When my supervisor heard about that, he freaked out, telling me, "You can't use your personal vehicle. What if you get in an accident?"

"Well, that's what I got insurance for," I told him. There was an afternoon I didn't even have that car when one of my snitches called to tell me a fugitive I was looking for had shown up and that I'd better get right over there. There was an old Nissan pickup that we used to carry supplies parked out in the back. I grabbed the keys to it and told two football-player-sized deputies to come with me. We all squeezed into the only seat. Then we went and arrested the guy. The problem was we had no place to put him. There were three of us and one seat. So we handcuffed him to one of the tie-downs in the open bed of the truck and drove him to the correctional facility. He was screaming at us the whole time, "You motherf—ers, f—k you guys."

I think it's pretty accurate to say that by this time my supervisors did not appreciate my sense of humor. They were tired of dealing with me and sent me in to see the marshal, the presidential appointee who ran the whole district, a man named Tony Perez. Tony Perez was already a legend in the Marshals Service. Tony used to ride around Los Angeles on his motorcycle. One of the stories I'd heard about Tony Perez was that he had arrested a guy in East L.A., about a mile from the federal building, chained the fugitive to the back of the motorcycle, and made him walk behind him the whole way. It was the way deputies in the Old West walked prisoners behind their horses.

But when Tony Perez heard what I'd done he was all over me. "What the f—k are you doing, you crazy motherf—er? Your supervisors effin' hate you. What the f—k were you doing out there?" I pointed out that I'd made the arrest without anybody getting hurt, but that just set him off some more. "What the f—k do you think this is, the Old West? What the . . ."

When he finally slowed down, I said, "Well, you know, I heard that story about you chaining a guy to the back of your bike, so I figured what's so wrong with the bed of a truck? He's a crook." Tony glared at me and shook his head, and then he turned around. He didn't realize I could see his reflection in the glass, and he was laughing his ass off. Finally we made a deal: if I calmed down for the next six months, if I gave the supervisors a break, he would guarantee that on the next rotation I'd get on warrants. I agreed immediately, and truthfully, when I did, I really believed I could do it. If I just kept my head down and my mouth shut, I would get on the warrant squad. For six months? I knew I could do it. But then there was this one guy . . .

His name was James George Brummer. This guy was wanted by everybody. He was a former biker, a member of a Hells Angels affiliate called the Galloping Gooses. The DEA wanted him for selling cocaine, ATF wanted him for dealing automatic weapons, we wanted him for escape, and the State of Montana wanted him for kidnapping and sexual assault on two women. The Marshals Service's Montana office believed he might be in California because his ex-wife and his only son lived in

a little town way out in the desert named Victorville. They thought he might be in contact with his
son. But when I spoke with a deputy in the
Montana office, after giving me some of the details
he very quietly warned me to be careful. There's
something real strange going on around this case,
he said; there were whispers that somebody in his
office might be hiding something. "Just be careful
who you talk to about this," he said.

Victorville was a two-hour drive from L.A., but
whenever I had some spare time I would go up
there. Brummer's wife lived in a gated community.
When I tried to interview her, she told me, "Good
luck finding him, he's out of my life," and slammed
the door in my face.

I was getting more and more frustrated. I had
some leave time saved up from my prior government service so I started taking a few days off.
Then I took several weeks off. I pissed off my supervisors by making two arrests while I was supposed to be on leave. When they confronted me
about it, I told them, "It's my leave. Can't I do what
I want? It's like my hobby."

After my leave ended, I continued going up to
Victorville on weekends. On one of those trips, I
noticed Brummer's teenage son was carrying a

pager. *Man,* I thought, *I've got to get that pager number; that's probably how he's communicating with his son.* I went to his junior high school and recruited a kid to get me that number. Once I got it, I obtained a court order allowing me to access all calls to that pager, to the ex-wife's cell phone, and to their home phone. I went through the records for the previous month, but I didn't find anything unusual. But I did discover that the boy's birthday was coming up; kids' birthdays are a big deal, so if Brummer was ever going to contact his son, I figured this would be the time. So I took another week of leave and camped out in the local post office. I went through every piece of mail. And the Wednesday before his birthday, like clockwork, there was an envelope addressed to the son with no return address. When I held it up to the light, I could see the word "birthday." I didn't have a search warrant so I couldn't open it, but the stamp had been canceled in Las Vegas. I smiled, thinking, *I got you.* Victorville was about two hours in the other direction from Vegas.

Las Vegas is a big city and Brummer could have been anywhere—or nowhere. The problem was how to narrow down the search.

I was running out of leave time so I stepped it up. Since Brummer was a biker, I went to several biker bars in Vegas and showed his picture around. I was right, he'd been to several of those places, although no one really knew anything about him and he didn't come in regularly or often. I developed a few leads about places he might be living and sent them to our Vegas office. At that time the Vegas office was totally lame. They all wore suits to work, everybody drove Crown Vics, and at 5:01 that office was empty. I'd dealt with them before so I knew from experience that they never followed up a lead, so when I'd needed something done I would literally drive over there and make the arrest myself. The head of that office didn't like me at all and had told Perez, "Keep that mother out of my state. I don't want him anywhere near here." Nice.

The Brummer case was huge for the Marshals; it was a nationwide case, and the Vegas office didn't do a thing to follow up on my questions. Nothing. So what I did was get copies of all of the wife's phone records for the previous six months. I learned that out of all those hundreds of calls, only two of them, one to her cell phone and one to the pager, had come from the 702—Vegas—area code. I traced one of those numbers to a Howard Johnson motel and the other to an address just outside the city. I sent that information to our Vegas office and, once again, they didn't do a thing. The Marshals Service was changing rapidly, but not in that office.

Burke recently had become a member of the L.A. office SWAT team. Purely coincidentally a seminar on SWAT tactics was being held in Las Vegas. He received permission to attend, but just before he left Tony Perez insisted he take a new deputy named Joe Extron with him. Maybe Tony Perez believed having a new man tagging along with Burke might slow him down. If so, it didn't have the desired effect. Burke remembers,

Joe Extron had graduated the academy about four months earlier. When we broke for lunch the first day I took him aside and said, "Joe, f—k this seminar, here's why I'm really here. I'm not supposed to even be in Nevada, the marshal here hates me, the supervisor of warrants hates me, but I f—in' know this guy is here and I'm going to get him."

Joe looked at me, his eyes opened wide, he smiled and said, "This is f—in' awesome!"

"Let's go to the Howard Johnson's," I said. "Maybe we'll get lucky and they'll have a record of who made the phone call. Even if it's a fake name, there's a chance we can associate it with an address. We'll go over there and look around, and if we see him, we'll call in the f—in' local warrant squad and let them arrest him."

Joe was right with me. I don't think he could believe what he had fallen into. The motel was kind of a dive in North Las Vegas. It looked like a real hole. But to my surprise the office was fully computerized and automated; it was amazing. And the manager could not have been more helpful. I told him the time and date the call was made and as he was pulling up the records, I said, "Let me show you his picture."

The manager took a look at it and stopped what he was doing. " 'Jeez," he said, "jeez. Are you sure that's him?"

"Dude, I've been chasing this guy for eight months. This is him."

The manager shook his head. "He's our maintenance guy. He's been working here for almost eight months. He's living in one of our rooms." I started freaking out, but it got better. "He's painting the room right above us right now." Brummer was no more than twenty feet away from us.

"This room he's in," I asked. "Can he see the parking lot out the window from there?" I'd left

my Marshals Service placard on the dashboard. Joe
and I went outside and I casually glanced up at the
room. I could see him through the window, standing on a ladder. I popped open the trunk, and Joe
and I hunched down behind it. "F—k this, Joe," I
said. "I've been chasing this guy for a long time.
We're just going to storm that room and knock that
f—er off that ladder."

Joe was all enthusiastic, "All right, let's do this."

We ran upstairs and ran right into the room. He
was on the ladder holding a paint roller. I pointed
my gun at him and ordered, "Drop the brush." He
had this look of rage on his face that I read as *I'm
gonna kill you, motherf—er.* So I put my gun away
and went for him. We got in a huge fight and I was
beating the crap out of him. Joe was pointing his
gun at the two of us, yelling over and over, "Holy
shit! Holy shit!" I pummeled Brummer pretty good
and got the cuffs on him, then we dragged him
down the steps. I draped him over the front counter and told the manager, "You better call the local
police because I don't even know where the jails are
in this town."

I called the Marshals Service office, but it was
almost six o'clock and everybody was gone for the
day. I left a message on their answering machine,

"This is Tony Burke and I know you don't like me. But I'm in Las Vegas for a seminar and I was doing the Brummer case and I caught him. I was wondering if I could get some deputies to help me transport him." I got a call back maybe ten minutes later. Before I said one word their warrant supervisor said, "You c—sucker, what the f—k are you doing here?"

I explained what happened and even apologized, but I told him that Brummer was there and we had to take him somewhere. He didn't want to know anything about it. "Good luck booking him, and you take him to court."

"F—k you," I told him and hung up the phone. We booked him at the local police station on a state warrant, rather than a federal warrant. I called Tony Perez at home. I had to tell somebody that we'd caught this guy while we were supposed to be at a seminar. When I got Tony on the phone, he was pleasant and wanted to know what was going on. "I'm in Las Vegas at that seminar, you know. And you know that case with James George Brummer? Well, like, I caught him."

He was thrilled, ecstatic. Then I continued, "But then I had to tell the warrants supervisor to f—k off." After a brief pause to let that sink in, I told him the whole story. He assured me I'd be okay. Later we found out that rumors claiming someone inside the Montana Marshals office were credible when U.S. marshal Bill Strizich pleaded guilty in federal court to a charge of lying under oath about buying and distributing cocaine. Both Brummer and Strizich went to prison. And from that day forward, I was on the warrant squad; I got to spend the rest of my career hunting fugitives.

With the proliferation of warrant squads throughout the nation's ninety-four districts, the fundamental mission of the Marshals Service had begun changing. The initial training was improving, and as part of that training, deputies were being taught investigative techniques. In addition to the FBI, other federal agencies began handing over fugitive cases to the service so they could focus on their primary mission. Traditionally, for example, the FBI had been responsible for pursuing DEA fugitives, but after the Marshals Service had proven its ability to hunt them down, Attorney General Ed Meese issued a memorandum of understanding officially handing over that responsibility. Eventually similar memorandums were signed with ATF, IRS, NCIS, even the Department of Agriculture, effectively turning the Marshals Service into the fugitive hunter for all federal agencies with the exception of the FBI. In 1983, Deputy Chiefs Bob Leschorn and Debbie Jenkins and Chief Chuck Kupferer met in Washington to figure out how to improve public recognition of the changing organization. Leschorn explains:

> We looked at the notoriety the FBI got from its Top 10 Most Wanted list, and I suggested we make our own Top 15. I wanted to go above the FBI. I wanted our Top 15 to be the most incorrigible, rotten, nastiest killers in the country. I got permission to make it work.
>
> I got 150 cases from our best fugitive hunters and picked the worst criminals on the loose in this country. Debbie Jenkins put the package together, and Chuck took it to Howard Safir. After several rewrites, the Top 15 was created. Getting those people became our priority.

While the Marshals Service continued to operate officially as a collection of mostly independent local districts, training, equipment, and objectives and procedures were becoming more centralized. The success of the warrant squads had led to the creation of the FIST operations beginning in Miami in 1981, when

761 fugitives who had been convicted of committing 491 crimes were arrested in five weeks. As mentioned, FIST operations were designed by the Marshals Service to forge a working relationship with state and local authorities to use all available resources to take primarily violent criminals and drug traffickers off the streets. Creating FIST helped establish the Marshals Service's standing as the team agency willing to work alongside local and state law enforcement agencies, sharing information and, even more important to those departments dependent on budgets for their operations, the credit.

"The rules we worked under were very different then," retired marshal Donald Ward says.

In one of the first FIST operations in New York, I worked with a Hispanic deputy out of Texas and a black NYPD officer. In New York in those days, we used what we called "jacks"; in fact they were wooden billy clubs with a leather handle. Our Hispanic deputy had never seen one of these things, so I bought one for him. He learned how to use it, and eventually earned the nickname "Jackman." I could eat—I could eat anything—so I became known as Pacman. And politically correct or not, that NYPD officer was Blackman. So we became known as Jackman, Pacman, and Blackman. In those days we could get away with a lot of things that would cause problems today. For example, there was an old ten-dollar-a-night fleabag hotel up in Harlem, a well-known drug den that we nicknamed the Kennedy Arms because one of the Kennedys had been mugged in the lobby. One night we walked in there and lined up all the tenants in front of the check-in booth in the lobby. When their turn came, they'd step to the front and hand us their ID. We would call in to the office to see if there was a warrant out on them. If we got a hit, whichever one of us was working the phone would start flashing the lights on and off. "We got a winner!" And that fugitive would be sent to another room. The guys at the back of the line were shaking their heads and saying, "Man, I hope that light don't flash for me!"

Heroin was big back then and if we were looking for a fugitive known to be involved in drugs, we'd sit on a block and watch to see which building the junkies were going in. Eventually we'd follow them into the place, then put them in a corner and tell them we weren't interested in their stash, we just wanted a little help. We'd show them pictures of the people we were after. "You know this guy? How 'bout this guy?" We could get away with being tougher in our line of work.

The challenge facing the Marshals Service at that time was how to squeeze the most production out of its limited manpower and a small budget. Accomplishing that required some very creative thinking—which is how its well-known sting operations developed. The program began in Brooklyn based on a single belief: the people deputies were pursuing were not the smartest kids on the block. On any block. "We started with a thing called Gem Tours," remembers David O'Flaherty.

It was a joint operation with the NYPD. We sent out flyers addressed to wanted felons at their last known address—it might have been the address of a close relative, their mother for instance, or an address they'd given when being paroled—informing them that they had won a free trip to Atlantic City and twenty-five dollars in quarters for the slots; we also told them when and from where the bus to the casino was leaving. We set up a table on a corner and when a fugitive showed up with his letter, we'd get on the radio with our people on the bus and tell them, "We got a winning number here, 567." They would check their list to see which fugitive got that numbered letter and the reason he was wanted.

"Okay, confirmed," I'd tell them, and a female deputy would escort that fugitive to the bus. When the bus door opened, the deputy sitting in the driver's seat would reach out to shake the guy's hand, and when he grasped it, the deputy would hold on tight and put him down on the floor, then pull his gun and arrest him. Then search him. The best part of it was that as the bus filled up, the guys we'd already arrested would be laughing at each newcomer. We arrested thirty men that day. And incredibly, even after we'd arrested these guys and read them their rights, some of them actually asked, "Do I still get my twenty-five dollars in quarters?"

After the marshals proved the concept would work, these stings became an essential part of most FIST operations—and even were portrayed in the opening scene of Al Pacino's movie *Sea of Love*. In each sting, hundreds of letters were sent to a variety of addresses that were associated with the fugitive. The bait had to be something so desirable that it just couldn't be ignored. In one of the largest and most successful stings in history, that lure turned out to be tickets to a Washington Redskins game. At that time few things were more valuable in the Washington, D.C., area than tickets to Redskins football games. In December 1985, more than three thousand letters were sent to the last known addresses of fugitives believed to be in that region announcing that as part of a promotion for a new cable television network, Flagship International Sports Television, they had been awarded two free tickets to the upcoming Redskins–Cincinnati Bengals game. There was one catch: These nontransferable tickets had to be picked up at a pregame brunch hosted by Flagship at the D.C. Convention Center. Identification was required. Additionally, at that brunch ten people would win season tickets for the 1986 season and even more exciting, the grand prize winner would be awarded an all-expenses paid trip to Super Bowl XX in New Orleans!

Robert Leschorn was in charge of setting up the trap.

We decorated the place nicely. We had signs reading LET'S PARTY and LET'S ALL BE THERE, and our guests were greeted by Santa Claus, the Redskins mascot wearing a full headdress, and a yellow chicken with oversized red shoes who was concealing his weapon under his right wing. The one hundred fugitives who showed up were escorted into the room by beautiful female officers who held them close enough to pat them down. The room was filled with 166 law enforcement officers, including deputies and officers from

Washington Metro PD, many of them dressed as ushers and usherettes, cleaning personnel, and caterers. "Officials" of Flagship International Sports Television wore tuxedoes. Everything was filmed.

One of the very excited fugitives who showed up told David O'Flaherty, "This is my lucky day. I never won nothing." To which Flaherty responded, "You don't know how lucky you are." He continues the story.

Eventually the fugitives were taken upstairs in groups of twelve to a small room where the chief of enforcement, Louie McKinney, announced we had a big surprise for them. With that the SWAT team came out from behind a curtain, put them on the ground, and placed them under arrest. Some of the fugitives were more upset at being fooled than being arrested. One of them complained to a reporter as he was being escorted to the bus that would transport him directly to jail, "They said we were going to a football game. That's false advertising."

An incredible 101 arrests were made that day, including 2 people wanted for murder, 5 for robbery, 15 for assault, 6 for burglary, 18 for narcotics violations, 1 for rape, 1 for arson, and another for forgery. Two of them were on the D.C. Metro PD's 10 Most Wanted list. The whole operation cost $22,500, or about $225 for each arrest. There was no better bargain in law enforcement; the biggest cost was stamps.

Sting operations were inexpensive to run, often provided great results as well as a lot of positive publicity, and were a lot of fun to plan and execute. It was a strategy that brought in a lot of fugitives for a little bit of money. In Los Angeles, for example, the 102 fugitives arrested had a combined 865 felony arrests. In addition to taking criminals off the streets, these operations helped build desperately needed organizational pride.

Another New York sting featured the FIST Bonded Delivery Service, which was created solely to deliver bait to fugitives. Several trucks were outfitted with fancy logos and stick-on signage, and deputies were dressed in the appropriate deliveryman uniforms. Invoices were sent to the last known address for each fugitive announcing that his or her name had been selected in a random drawing to receive a prize worth up to $2,000; the offered prize had been specifically selected to fit that individual's mentality, ranging from a big-screen TV to a box of sex toys or X-rated movies, which were sent primarily to sexual offenders. The prize was whatever might prove irresistible to that person. FIST Delivery Service offered to deliver the prize to the location selected by the recipient, but he or she had to show up in person with identification to pick it up. Fugitives were given a phone number to call to arrange for the delivery, and an operator was standing by waiting for that call. If the bad guy smelled a scam and was reluctant to provide an address, the operator explained that the courier would make one attempt to deliver the package then send it back to the company. If the fugitive continued to hesitate, our operator would tell him, don't worry about it, we'll keep it ourselves.

Greed is a fascinating emotion. Greed is what makes most criminals tick. That threat—we'll keep it—usually caused the reluctant fugitive to dive in. You're not keeping my TV! Eventually even the most hardened criminals were showing up on street corners to pick up their prizes or making plans to accept the delivery at a relative's home. No one expected a wary fugitive to walk up to a truck before sizing up the situation, so generally the smallest and most vulnerable-looking deputy would play the role of the deliveryman. He'd stand outside his truck, glancing anxiously at his watch until the fugitive finally decided the scam was not a scam. After that fugitive handed over the invoice and showed his ID, the deputy would explain that he'd hurt his back and ask the fugitive to help him get the box of the truck. The box contained a heavy object, and when the fugitive bent down to pick it up, the deputy would pull out his weapon and arrest him as his backup moved in. As in other stings one fugitive was irate when he was arrested—because the marshals refused to let him claim his prize. He was dragged away screaming at them, "You don't have to be so mean!" The FIST Bonded Delivery service was responsible for the arrests of 303 felons who had committed more than 3,000 prior offenses.

There were all types of creative stings. The Hartford, Connecticut, office invited fugitives to attend a special luncheon hosted by pop singer Boy George—even offering to pick them up. Fifteen fugitives accepted the offer, got in the chauffeured limousine, and were driven directly to jail. Ninety fugitives were arrested in New York when they showed up to apply for lucrative jobs at the Prior Offenders Employment Opportunities. The Miami office created "Puño Airlines" and informed fugitives by letter that they had won a weekend in the Bahamas, which included a free flight and $350 in spending money. A ticket counter was set up at the airport, and those fugitives too wary to be picked up by a limo were arrested at the bogus counter.

When Texas inmates won a lawsuit against the state for keeping them in overcrowded prisons, the Marshals Service district office sent letters from a fictitious law firm to fugitives who previously had been imprisoned, informing them they were entitled to a payment. They were instructed to show up at the law firm's address on a Saturday morning to receive a settlement check. Almost a hundred fugitives actually showed up. Only one of them had a no-bail warrant issued against him and, ironically, he was the only one bailed out. But rather than disappearing after being released, he returned to the "law firm" demanding his payment.

While the Marshals Service continued to compile an impressive number of arrests, its low public profile deprived it of the funding it needed to grow. Deputy Jimmy Bankston recalls once meeting with a key congressional staff member who informed him that the request for additional funding had been turned down. Again.

> Finally I asked him the question, What is the intent of Congress? Do they just want to see people indicted and then be allowed to roam free around the country to commit more crimes? Or do they want to see those people behind bars? Because if they do, they could give all the money in the world to investigative agencies like the FBI and DEA and ATF, but when those people indicted become fugitives, that isn't going to stop anything. He looked at

me and he was just speechless. Next thing I know we started getting substantial increases in our annual budget.

Once Congress appropriated additional funds, the Marshals Service had to determine how best to use them. The FIST operations had proved that the innovative concept of numerous law enforcement agencies working together was viable. It was an entirely new way of attacking the criminal population. In fact, it was so successful that some of the larger districts set up their own permanent task forces in cooperation with state and local law enforcement. The productivity of these district task forces led to the 1999 creation of five regional fugitive task forces commanded from Washington. In addition to providing funding for these new organizations, the Presidential Threat Protection Act of 2000 directed the U.S. attorney general to "establish permanent fugitive apprehension task forces consisting of federal, state and local law enforcement authorities . . . to be directed and coordinated by the United States Marshals Service." As retired assistant director Robert Finan of the Investigative Services Division points out, the Marshals Service finally had gained recognition for its ability to track down fugitives.

And then the question came up, How can we design a task force for the sole purpose of capturing the violent and dangerous of all the country's federal, state, and local fugitives?

This was the opportunity to bring together the assets of multiple police departments and multiple Marshals Service districts to go after the worst of the worst . . . The regional fugitive task forces restrict our focus and assets to getting murderers, rapists, arsonists, child molesters, and kidnappers. These are not white-collar criminals. We go after people who hurt people.

Unlike a district task force in which deputies may be rotated in and out, these regional task forces have permanently assigned personnel and report to headquarters in Washington, D.C., rather than a district supervisor. The creation acknowledged publicly what had already been true for a long time—the Marshals Service had come full circle: just as deputies had done a century earlier, their primary mission was once again tracking down and arresting outlaws.

The methods and the tools used to go after those fugitives had also changed drastically after deputies had started doing warrants. In the early days of the service's fugitive-hunting program, everything was low-tech.

"When I first started working the warrant program in Los Angeles," Chuck Kupferer remembers, "we drove a hand-me-down Nash Rambler Matador that we'd gotten from the FBI. Two of us would go out with a roll of dimes for the pay phone in case we had to make a call, and we used our own sidearms. Even the radios we got were hand-me-downs from the FBI." The training, which some new deputies didn't get until they already had been working for months, was still focused on the service's traditional jobs. "Our most advanced technology in those days was a pair of binoculars and a phone book," says Donald Ward. "We didn't have any support. If we had a license plate number, we'd go over to the parking violations bureau to see if there was a parking ticket on record that might give us an address. If we had a really hot case and we wanted to send a photo to another office, we'd go out to the airport, find a pilot who was flying to that city and hand him that photo, then alert a deputy there to meet the flight."

It wasn't just the lack of state-of-the-art equipment. Great manhunters are made, not born. Deputies had to learn how to pursue fugitives who desperately did not want to be caught. A lot of the early training was trial and error. New Yorker Vic Oboyski starting chasing fugitives his third year on the job, "although only part-time. That's the way we got started. All the people in the office had at least one or two cases, but initially it's mostly probation violations, failure to appear, cases that are not that difficult. From that you learn how to shake the bushes a little, how to get rap sheets, interview people, find the necessary paperwork, and use whatever internal resources we had available."

Deputy Geri Doody recollects:

It was all pretty basic in the early days. We relied on phone records, informants, and footwork. We would have to subpoena phone records, wait a few weeks to get them, and make notes on index cards. The whole thing was pretty loosely run. One day, for example, I was making out the daily report about one of our Top 15, a guy named John Matthew Boston, who had just been profiled on *America's Most Wanted*. As I began looking through the phone records I saw quite a few calls had been made to people we could associate with him from Montego Bay, Jamaica. When I made my report, they told me, okay, go ahead, take a trip.

I got down there right after Hurricane Gilbert had hit the island and the whole place was a mess. Everything was topsy-turvy. I met with the Jamaican PD, which was a real ragtag organization. Their police station was in an old hotel. There was one phone in the station and it had a lock on it so the cops couldn't use it to make personal calls, but that probably wasn't necessary; not too many people on the island had working phones so there weren't too many people to call anyway.

The phone records put Boston on the island, so we paid informants and gathered some records and developed a good idea where he was. My partner, Art Roderick, and I were not allowed to carry guns so we had to depend on the Jamaican cops. We decided we were going to do an early morning raid, which meant that the night before we physically had to go to each cop's house and knock on their front door—they didn't have doorbells—and tell them to meet us in the town square just after dawn. When we finally got to John Boston's location, we were afraid the chickens in the front yard were going to give away our presence. Art and I stayed behind the cops who went into the house and made the arrest. In those days, that was about the level of technology we had.

Deputies used everything available to them to gather information. Mike Bunk was not the only deputy to pick up garbage. One fugitive was able to walk out of a Metro Washington prison when a female correctional officer who had become infatuated with him smuggled him out in a guard's uniform. Deputies felt certain the prison guard and the fugitive remained in touch, so they mounted a camera on a telephone pole across from the correctional officer's home. A deputy was assigned to go through the camera footage every day just to make sure the fugitive hadn't shown up at the house in the middle of the night. In addition, deputies regularly collected her garbage, dumped it out on the floor of the office, and went through it, scrap by scrap by scrap. By checking her phone bills they discovered she had been sending Western Union Moneygrams to various places. At that time a Moneygram was the highest-tech way to discreetly transfer money. All the intended recipient had to do to pick up the cash was present the proper ID. Deputies checking the records at the local Western Union office discovered that a relative of this woman had sent a Moneygram to Richmond, Virginia, and the money was scheduled to be picked up the following day. When the escaped con walked into the Western Union office to collect his money, deputies were waiting there to arrest him.

Perhaps the only thing that hasn't changed in the decades since the Marshals Service got into the fugitive business is the reality that there is no substitute for hard work, for poring through endless details searching for the one clue that might make a difference, for talking to countless people and putting bits of information together, for going through all the garbage. Infamous Boston mob boss Whitey Bulger, who was indicted for participating in nineteen murders—although sources claimed he had killed as many as forty men—had disappeared after supposedly being tipped off by an FBI agent in December 1994 that he was about to be indicted on a RICO charge. The situation was tremendously embarrassing to the bureau: one of its agents had allowed a killer to escape, and for sixteen years agents were unable to find any trace of Bulger or the woman who had fled with him, Cathy Greig. Finally, in 2010, the Boston office of the FBI asked the Marshals Service for assistance in finding Bulger, although bureau officials insisted that the FBI had to remain the lead agency. Deputy Marshal Neil Sullivan was assigned to the Bulger Task Force.

The small task force used all the impressive techniques of modern crime fighting, including the best technological resources available to law enforcement anywhere in the world—some of these capabilities still generally unknown to the public. In June 2011, the task force began a large media effort in fourteen cities. Thirty-second TV ads featuring age-enhanced photographs of Bulger and

Cathy Greig were shown on programs like *Live with Regis and Kelly* and *The View*, displayed on billboards, and distributed to news stations with the announcement that the reward for information leading to Bulger's arrest was $2 million, more than any other fugitive on the bureau's Most Wanted list. The reward for information leading to Greig's arrest was doubled to $100,000.

Within hours of the beginning of the campaign, the task force received more than two hundred tips. Sullivan went through them one by one, and finally, on the third day, one of the calls caught his attention. A woman calling from Europe claimed she had lived in an apartment complex near Bulger and Greig in Santa Monica, California. She gave the precise address and the names by which she knew the couple, Charlie and Carol Gasko, the type of details most informants don't provide. Intrigued, Sullivan got in contact with this woman, Anna Bjornsdottir and listened to her story. She correctly described the couple's basic appearance, their mannerisms, even their regional accents, and explained that she and Greig had shared a love of dogs and cats, especially a stray cat named Tiger.

After hanging up the phone, Sullivan began doing a background check on both Charlie and Carol Gasko on a variety of databases—but nothing came up. Literally, nothing. No dates of birth, no California driver's licenses, no credit card history. It was as if these two identities had been created out of thin air—which in fact they had. In this case it was the complete lack of basic information that is generally available about anybody, rather than any specific details, that convinced Sullivan he had a strong lead.

The Boston task force contacted FBI agents in Santa Monica and asked them to track down this lead. Bulger was a killer and presumably was well armed. He was eighty-one years old and obviously knew that if he was caught, he'd spend the remainder of his life locked up. So there was good reason to believe he might fight back if he realized he was being arrested. FBI agents convinced the manager of the residence, who had been casual friends with Charlie Gasko for four years, to call him and tell him the storage lockers in the basement had been broken into and that he was asking all the residents to take a look to see if anything was missing. When Bulger came downstairs, forty FBI agents were waiting for him and made the arrest. In his apartment, deputies found thirty weapons, some of them hidden in hollowed-out books, as well as more than $800,000 in cash stored in the walls.

As this case proved again, in the thirty-two years since taking over some of the minor fugitive-hunting work from the FBI, the Marshals Service had established itself as the best manhunting force in the world.

3

On the Right Side of the Tracks: Finding Fugitives

Voucher 1, $375.00, is for the subsistence of my deputies, and posse, and hire of horses with forage for the same. This expense was incurred in the arrest of William Bonny [*sic*], known as "Billy the Kid," charged with murder and passing counterfeit money; also for the arrest of an accomplice by the name of Rudebaugh. This man Bonny was a most notorious character. Large rewards had been offered for his arrest by the Territorial authorities, and frequent attempts made to capture him. He was finally captured by my deputy, lodged in jail, and afterwards shot by Deputy Garrett in attempting to escape. The whole expense in making this arrest was $1,072.00.

—*U.S. Marshal John Sherman Jr.,*
November 20, 1882

In the early 1990s New York, Deputy Marshal Vic Oboyski received a notice from the Royal Canadian Mounted Police (RCMP) that a psychotic killer had fled Montreal and was believed to be hiding somewhere in the heavily Orthodox Jewish Borough Park neighborhood of Brooklyn. According to the memo, this man previously had been convicted and had served time for killing his mother's maid with a baseball bat and, after being released, had committed another murder. "I spoke to the people up in Canada and they told me he was wearing a Jewish-style beard," Oboyski says. "I'm thinking, a Jewish-style beard? What's a Jewish-style beard versus a Mexican-style beard? Apparently this guy wasn't Orthodox himself, but he was a person of faith. I had searched for literally thousands of fugitives, but this was a new experience for me."

Deputies have gone into just about every city and town and every social and cultural group in America while tracking fugitives. Every case is different and requires its own approach. As Oboyski explains,

> You take what information you've got to start with, then you run with it. We had an address in Brooklyn. We watched it for a while and eventually saw an old Hasid walking out very slowly and followed him to a local synagogue. That turned out to be

the rabbi and I decided to go and talk to him. His wife brought me into his office. The rabbi looked like he was about ninety-two years old. When I identified myself as a U.S. marshal, he looked at me quizzically and asked, "Vut's a U.S. marshal?"

I told him, "You know, law enforcement. Like the Old West."

"The old vest?"

"Yeah, yeah, like *Gunsmoke*."

"Gunsmoke? Vut's a gunsmoke?"

Oboyski handed the rabbi his badge. The rabbi examined it, nodded his head, and said, "Okay, you're a U.S. marshal. Well, God bless you, you're a good one."

Oboyski realized this was the first time in his career that his investigation had been blessed by a rabbi. He told him about the man he was looking for and the rabbi tried to be helpful, basically telling Oboyski not to expect too much cooperation from the Orthodox community. "Look, the basic tenet for a Jew is to protect another Jew. That goes back centuries. What can you do?"

"But this guy's wanted for murder," Oboyski said.

The rabbi waved his hands like he was shrugging it off. "They don't care. I'm telling you, it's not going to be easy." The Hasidic community is very insular, he explained. They don't feel comfortable with outsiders, and unless Oboyski suddenly grew a beard and started speaking Yiddish, they would know instantly he was an outsider.

In addition to spending time in the area, Oboyski began filing the usual requests for information through the numerous databases available to deputies. Marshals usually begin each search by gathering as much background information as possible, knowing somewhere in all of it there is going to be a thread that eventually will lead to that person's location. But very few of the regular databases contained any information about this very private, closed community. Oboyski continues the story.

But among the things I found out was that this guy had gone to a dentist who was Orthodox, although not a Hasid. When I interviewed this dentist, I showed him an illustration an NYPD sketch artist had done for us showing what this guy might look like with a full beard. The artist had done an outstanding job and I had found some people who identified him. There was no question he had been in Borough Park. The dentist looked at it, then asked me why we were looking for him. When I told him he had murdered somebody, he said, "Allegedly."

"He's murdered before," I told him. "He was convicted of killing his mother's maid with a baseball bat."

The dentist asked Oboyski if the fugitive had served time. He had, Oboyski told him, and he had recently been released. "Okay then," the dentist said. "He served his debt to society."

Oboyski realized it was a big game to the dentist, as if he were playing a role in a TV detective show rather than protecting a violent killer. The marshal replied: "Maybe, but now he's wanted for another murder."

"Allegedly," the dentist said, then asked, "Did he kill a Jew?"

"I admitted I didn't know," Oboyski recalls.

And then I told him it didn't really matter. But he was adamant that he wasn't going to tell me a thing. This wasn't that unusual, mostly it was just as the rabbi had warned me it would be. So I made another appointment to go back and see the rabbi; unfortunately, I got there almost two hours late. The rabbi's wife opened the door and scolded me for being late. "We got tied up on other things," I said.

"You couldn't call? You didn't have a phone?" I apologized again, and she sighed and said, "You should've called."

When I walked into the rabbi's office he shrugged. "So you couldn't stop and make a call? You make an appointment, you keep the appointment. If you're going to be late, you call."

After Oboyski had apologized once more, the rabbi enthusiastically began discussing the investigation. Had Oboyski checked all the utilities? In fact, that was one of the first things he'd done. There were no accounts in this man's name. Did Oboyski check with the post office? Yes, he'd spoken with the postmaster. The postal system had no address for him. As they continued the discussion, the rabbi wouldn't provide direct information, but he did try to be helpful, and through the leads he provided Oboyski confirmed that the Hasidic community was hiding this man. A particular synagogue owned a building with several apartments that were used regularly to hide people that needed to be hidden. It was essentially a safe house that was used mostly to house people traveling through the country illegally.

Oboyski says,

I took that information to the late Charlie Rose, a really good assistant district attorney, and told him we knew the fugitive was around the neighborhood, that we had found the safe house, but no one would talk to us. At my request, Charlie issued subpoenas to five rabbis and the dentist, directing them to appear in front of a grand jury. They showed up in the courthouse with a small army of thirty or forty people, all of the men—except the dentist—dressed in the same long black coats and hats and wearing beards; the wives were there pushing baby carriages and holding little children by their hands. The whole lobby was jammed full. The judge was not pleased at all. Charlie Rose had warned these men that he would prosecute them if they lied, so none of them wanted to go before the grand jury where they would be required to give sworn testimony. To avoid that they began cooperating with Charlie. We got the alias the killer was using, and the suddenly cooperative dentist told us that he had been moved from Borough Park to a safe house in the upstate Orthodox community of Monsey, New York.

When you start working on a case, there is no good way of predicting how long you might be working on it. I've closed cases in a day. This one would take about a year. I spent a lot of time bumping into the bureaucracy. I had to get phone records, medical records; I had to get subpoenas and a court order to bring in my hostile witnesses. Sometimes there is nothing to do except wait for the information you need to come back and meanwhile work on the other cases piling up on your desk. The Canadians had told us that the fugitive was taking medication for his mental problems so I contacted a pharmacy in Monsey and asked if they had filled a prescription for a person using his alias. The pharmacist's technician was reluctant to help until I told her that this was a murder investigation. Then she looked it right up; the pharmacy had filled a prescription for Haldol, a powerful antipsychotic drug; she gave me the name of the psychiatrist who had written the prescription. I got him on the phone.

There are always people who will talk to you, people who can be convinced that talking to you is the right thing to do, and other people who have to be made to understand that it is in their own best interest to talk to you. This psychiatrist was reluctant at first, telling me he had never actually seen this patient. Oh, that was interesting, this guy was prescribing a pretty strong drug to a patient he had never seen? I said to him, "Look, Doc, I'm not looking to get you in trouble, but you know you're not supposed to give meds to unknown persons." I pointed out that there are strict laws against what he did, but added that I really didn't want to get involved with all that unless he made it necessary.

He became very cooperative. "What do you want to know? I haven't spoken to him in months."

"Tell me the last thing you know about this guy."

The last thing the psychiatrist remembered hearing was that this man was going to spend time at his grandmother's house somewhere in California. Oboyski had the grandmother's address in Los Angeles. The RCMP had pulled his records and found that collect calls had been made to her number from a mental hospital where he had been getting shock treatments. Oboyski immediately contacted the Marshals Service office in L.A. and gave its deputies all the details. He faxed the sketch to them. The fugitive's grandmother lived in a small apartment building. Deputies found him there, still dressed in his Hasidic clothing, staring aimlessly over the third-floor balcony. They made the arrest and he was sent back to Canada to be prosecuted for murder.

The Marshals Service doesn't show up at a crime scene and collect evidence. In most cases it doesn't even investigate a crime or develop suspects. It simply tracks down people who are wanted by a law enforcement organization and brings them back. Often marshals are looking for people who don't want to be found and try to disappear or, as Oboyski says, "They know there are people out there who want to put handcuffs on them, so they're on the run."

There is an entire substratum of fugitives continuously moving around this country, trying hard to stay under the law enforcement radar. Many fugitives being pursued by local law enforcement leave that jurisdiction, knowing that it may well become too time consuming and expensive for those local officers to pursue them. But when a serious crime has been committed, or the fugitive remains a danger to society, the Marshals Service gets involved. Every deputy has a deep pile of cases on his desk and, in most instances, it is entirely his or her decision which fugitives to go after. Deputies work numerous cases simultaneously; some of them will go on for years, while others might be resolved in a day.

If there is one criterion that determines how to prioritize cases, it is simply: How dangerous is this person to society? Basically, deputies usually start with the most violent fugitives and work their way down from homicides to rapists to other sex offenders to high-profile drug crimes. Fugitives listed on the Marshals Service 15 Most Wanted Fugitives list are always at the top of the list. Marshals chase DEA fugitives, so major drug traffickers become priority cases. And while tracking and arresting federal fugitives has become the core mission, in many situations local law enforcement agencies take advantage of the skills the Marshals Service has developed and bring deputies in to help them solve crimes. From major national crimes like the hunt for the D.C. Sniper to local homicides, when a crime has been committed by an unknown subject, an unsub, local law enforcement will often invite deputies into their investigation.

"I might be working on a case and I'll get a call that a homicide has been committed in some town and they're requesting assistance," explains Deputy Marshal Bill Noble. "When we know the fugitive might still be in the area, time becomes very important, so I'll take that case and run with it until we catch the person. But sometimes a lead grows a little bit cold, then I might move back a little more into other cases."

John Bolen, the chief deputy of the Capitol Area Regional Fugitive Task Force, which includes about thirty-three different participating law enforcement agencies, discusses the problem.

Sometimes I'll have a stack of homicides on my desk and a stack of rapes and a stack of child pornography cases. Trying to prioritize those cases is a very difficult thing to do. When we were just getting into the fugitive business in southern Ohio, we didn't have a whole lot of those cases to work, so we just worked the cases as they showed up on our desks. It's way different now. Now we put kids first; we prioritize cases involving children. Whether it's child pornography, child molestation, child abduction—we place those cases first. Then we prioritize based on our law enforcement partners' needs. We work very hard to create close relationships with our state and local partners. When a police chief or a detective or a sheriff calls me and tells me, "John, I need your help on this one," it goes right to the top of the pile.

Tracking down a fugitive or a suspect requires the application of a great variety of investigative techniques, world-class technology, and often creative strategies. But basically, for most fugitives it comes down to what is known as "snitches, bitches, phones, and riches." According to James Benjamin, "There are three things every fugitive needs: a way to communicate, money to eat and travel, and a place to stay." When fugitives take action to fulfill any one of those needs, they show up on the grid and it's possible to find them. Deputies use informers, which include relatives, friends, associates, and often former lovers (there are no better informers than spurned or abused lovers who want to get even); tap into databases that track most forms of communication from the U.S. mail to social media; and follow the money trail.

Each case presents its own unique facts and problems. Joseph Lobue works a case "as if it were a spiral. You start on the outside of the perimeter and keep trying to narrow it, keep spinning, keep spinning till you get to the bull's-eye, and that's your target. I always started with the peripheral information and just kept narrowing things down. The one thing most cases do have in common is that they require dedication, hard work, and a lot of patience. You just can't give up. If you keep going, eventually that person is going to turn up somewhere." Lobue had earned a reputation in law enforcement for closing cases involving suspects from the Dominican Republic, so when the ATF and NYPD were unable to track down Bartolome Moya, who was known as the "Shadow Kingpin," the leader of a brutal New York City drug gang that posed as police officers to kidnap and murder their competition while stealing their drugs, they brought Lobue into the case.

"This guy was unbelievable," Lobue remembers.

He was believed to have been involved in everything from murder to bombings. I got involved when a New York City detective asked me to help out. It was one of the strangest cases of my career. Like I always did, I gathered as much material as possible and started with the peripheral information. I interviewed his family, friends, and associates; I ran his driver's license and his aliases through our databases; and I started getting hits on those documents in Camden, New Jersey. We didn't find him in Camden, but we did find people who knew him and they helped us track him to Philadelphia, where in the summer of 1993 we placed him under arrest.

Until that point it was a relatively simple case—but then it began twisting into the most bizarre case of Lobue's career. It turned out that Moya was dying of congestive heart failure. He could barely walk and had been hiding in a family member's house, essentially waiting to die. The Marshals Service took him back to New York in an ambulance and put him in Beekman Hospital. At his trial three members of his gang were convicted and sentenced to life without parole, but after a doctor testified Moya had only six months to live, the judge sent him home to die. As far as Lobue was concerned the case was over.

But early the following spring, Lobue got a call from the NYPD detective.

"You're not going to believe this," he told me, "but Moya got a heart transplant. He's not dying." It was incredible; he had gotten a taxpayer-funded $400,000 heart transplant at Philadelphia's Temple University Hospital. The U.S. attorney had gone back into the grand jury and got him reindicted.

They asked me to go find him again. I knew he had to go for regular medical checkups, and after doing our research, we found out when he had an appointment to see his doctor. I hung out in the waiting area, just mingling with the crowd until he walked in. He was easy to recognize; he was the guy wearing a face mask to protect himself against infection. He had gained some weight, and he had a spring in his step so obviously the transplant was working. We had a Spanish-speaking officer with us and we identified ourselves, and I thought his transplant was going to fail right then and there. We stayed with him throughout the entire checkup, then put him in an ambulance and took him back to Beekman. For the second time I thought I was through with this case.

Once again Lobue was certain this case was closed. The judge released Moya to house arrest with a $250,000 bond and ordered him to wear an ankle bracelet. Apparently the judge figured that because Moya needed to take drugs every day to fight infection, he couldn't run very far. And he figured wrong. As Lobue recalls,

I was at home recuperating from a minor knee operation when I got a call telling me Moya had cut off the ankle monitor and disappeared. We went to all his old places in New York, Camden, and Philly, but he was gone. We put the case on *America's Most Wanted* and *Dateline* and eventually got some pretty hard information that he had gotten out of the country and had gone to Santo Domingo in the Dominican.

I flew down there and started all over again by identifying and locating his family members. We also knew he had to be getting his antirejection drugs from somewhere; we figured he was buying them on the black market, so we started looking in that direction. Pretty quickly we developed three good possible locations for him. We knew the vehicle that he was driving, so we set up surveillance at all three places. I was watching one of them, and the DEA and the Dominican police were covering the other two. I was in my hotel about one A.M. when a DEA agent called and told me, "Get up, we got your guy." I met them at the local precinct. Moya was cuffed to a bench, and when I walked in, he looked up at me and shook his head and said something in Spanish that I was told meant, "I can't believe that you came all the way down here to arrest me." I went back to New York, and several weeks later he agreed to sign the extradition papers and flew back to the States. I went down to Florida and got him, and several times the next year I took him to medical checkups. We got to know each other a little, and he would laugh whenever he saw me walk into the room.

In 1996 Moya was sentenced to twenty-five years in prison, but he never finished serving that time, dying behind bars in 1999.

"A lot of it is just common sense and hard work," Mike Moran says about solving cases. "I tell people that I'm not necessarily smarter than anybody else, but I work harder. It's not glamorous; a lot of it is surveillance, locating people through databases and all the other sources of information we have, and most of it is just work. We don't catch them any differently than we did a hundred years ago; the difference is we have more tools and we don't have to tie up our horse."

And sometimes, as Vic Oboyski admits, finding a fugitive is simply a matter of experience meeting luck. One of Oboyski's simplest cases began when an administrative error enabled a triple murderer to walk out of a Washington, D.C., prison. The prisoner had been serving a life sentence without chance of parole. One morning a new guard called the roll of prisoners who had court appearances scheduled. When a prisoner whose name was called didn't respond, this killer grabbed hold of the opportunity and stepped forward. For whatever reasons nobody stopped him, nobody said a word. He went to court and worked the system to get his release. That afternoon he walked out of the courtroom into thin air.

Several months later two NYPD officers on patrol in Brooklyn were flagged down by a hysterical elderly woman who told them an incredible story. Her son had just stolen her stereo, she said. It was a sad story, but the cops didn't react until she added, "I don't know why he's out. He killed three people in Washington and he's supposed to be in jail." The Homicide Squad took the information and contacted D.C. officials and confirmed he had escaped. Because the District is considered a federal city, every warrant issued there is a federal case. Whether it's spitting on the sidewalk or shoplifting, it's a federal case. NYPD officers called the marshals and Vic Oboyski got the case.

We had learned over the years that one of the first things you do when you have a local guy is look up his arrest record. Local guys generally don't wander too far. This guy had been arrested several times within the same three- or four-block area in Flatbush. That area was all he knew. So I drove over there with a couple of NYPD detectives and we found out that he had sold the stereo and picked up a check for it. Metro Washington police had faxed an old photo to us so we knew what he looked like, and the person who bought the stereo from him told us he was wearing blue leather pants. Blue pants? It's hard to hide in blue pants.

So we started driving around Flatbush. Within a very short period of time we saw a tall guy wearing blue leather pants standing on a corner. The detective asked me, "What do you think?"

I shrugged. "How many guys are walking around Flatbush wearing blue leather pants?" We drove past him and stopped on the next block. I took out my 9 mm and walked up to him and said his name. He immediately turned and looked at me. That response was all I needed. "Put your hands up," I told him.

We got him in one morning. Sometimes it happens that way.

Each deputy has his or her own method of working a case, but most people start with the family. To survive, fugitives on the run have to have help, and the first place they're going to turn is to the people closest to them, family and friends. As bad as some of these guys are, there are still people who love them and believe in them. For that reason, deputies try to find out the birthdays of close relatives, especially mothers, because fugitives often contact their loved ones on meaningful days. Holidays like Mother's Day and Christmas are working days for many deputies, because a lot of fugitives want to be with their families on those days. The first thing Deputy Wendell Brock does when starting a case is run the criminal history of the person he is looking for.

> Most of them have a prior history. I'll pull the visitation log from the last place they were in jail, because when they're on the run, they've got to turn to that person who loved them enough or cared about them enough to visit or give them money while they were in jail.
>
> Then if they were ever on probation or parole, I'll get all that information. Those records may include distant relatives that might not show up on other reports.

"You know that eventually most fugitives are going to reach out to a family member," says New York deputy Craig Caine. He remembers looking for a woman who had been convicted of a narcotics violation and walked away from a work-release program.

It was a Friday and my partner, Juan Petersen, and I were just killing time driving around Queens. We knew this woman lived in the area so I suggested, "Let's call her mother and maybe go over there." I got her mother on the phone and she's telling me, "I don't know where she is. I can't stand her because I do all these things for her and she stole a hundred dollars out of my purse and if I see her again I'm gonna . . ." I interrupted to ask her where her daughter usually hung out. She started again, "How would I know where she is? She tells me nothing. Somewhere over by the projects. She's all over . . ."

As I'm listening to the mother Juan taps me with his radio and tells me, "Look what's coming down the block." We had a photograph of this woman taken while she was on crack; it wasn't an especially flattering likeness, but she had a distinctive mole on the side of her cheek. A woman with what looked like a mole on her cheek was walking in our direction. "I don't know," Juan continued. "Could that be her?"

"No way. Get outta here." But I continued looking at her; there definitely was a resemblance. She was wearing headphones and bebopping down the street. As she walked right past us, we got out of the car.

Juan called out to her, "Hey, girl, come over here." We told her to take off the headphones and asked her what her name was. Lisa, she told us; that wasn't our fugitive's name, but she did have that mole on her cheek. We couldn't tell. So just for fun I handed her my phone and said, "Here, your mother wants to talk to you."

I told the mother, "Talk to your daughter." The woman listened for a few seconds then said, "Mom?" It took her a few seconds to realize exactly what had happened. Meanwhile, Juan and I are high-fiving each other. Then she got angry, yelling into the phone, "Thanks a lot, Mom; 'cause of you these two cops just arrested me and they're high-fiving each other in the middle of the street."

Then we heard her mother starting in on her again.

Even some of the most hardened criminals in the world have a soft spot for their mothers. Deputy Harry Layne spent almost two years chasing a woman named Judy McNelis, who ran a $250-million-a-year drug smuggling operation and was regarded as violent and ruthless by investigators. Several members of her family were involved in the drug operation: her father had been convicted and sentenced to twenty years, her sister got ten years, her lawyer got ten years, and her partner in the drug operation and codefendant in the murder case, Jean Tumulty, got life. The "Black Widow," as McNelis had been nicknamed, had been arrested in 1983 and was getting ready to go on trial for the murder of a pilot for the organization when she escaped by sawing through the bars of her cell in the small Valdosta City, Georgia, jail with a hacksaw that had been smuggled into the prison. That's when the marshals were brought into the case. "It was very unusual to find a woman in this position. She had built a major drug organization mostly by herself," Layne says. "She had shrimp boats and three airplanes, and she was accused of being a ruthless enforcer. In addition to the drug charges, for which her father and sister received long prison terms, she was also charged with the murder of a pilot for the organization and at that time was believed to have been involved in several other homicides."

Judy McNelis was the first woman ever put on the Marshals Service 15 Most Wanted list. Deputies chased her all through Florida and Georgia and, admittedly, didn't make much progress. Every time they got close to her, she would disappear. The trail eventually led to an associate of hers who was believed to be running his own substantial marijuana operation in Sebring,

Florida. He was living in a house that was on posts in a lake, about thirty feet off the shoreline.

Layne and his partner went to Sebring to pump that person for information. As Layne remembers,

I was pretty new to Florida, so until this case I didn't know much about alligators. I had seen them on TV. But as we were crawling through the bushes to get close to this house my partner whispered pretty urgently, "Harry, get out of there, man; there's an alligator."

That gator was about thirty feet away. "I see him," I said. "But they run slow. I can outrun him."

"Dude, I don't know where you heard that, but gators run as fast as a horse. Get the hell out of there now." We left rapidly, very very rapidly.

This man, they discovered, was actually raising guard-alligators. He had several concrete pits stocked with alligators of different sizes. As they got bigger, he'd move them from one pit to a larger one so they wouldn't eat each other. Deputies eventually discovered that one of the pits literally had a false bottom, which was where he kept his stash. When he needed product, he would drain one of the pits and get the alligators out. But as long as they were there, he knew he didn't have to worry about anybody robbing him when he wasn't home. Eventually Layne and his partner interviewed him in his real house, which was on land.

He was a convicted felon who had done real time and he wasn't giving us anything at all. But while we were talking he got a phone call and excused himself to go into another room. When he opened the door, I saw a ton of guns in there. As a convicted felon he wasn't allowed to have any guns. Based on that, we got a search warrant and went back to confiscate those guns and search the rest of the house. He came home while we were there and we arrested him.

There was a big safe in a closet and I told him, "You need to open it for us." He couldn't, he said, he didn't have the combination. "That's okay," I said, "we'll just have to take the safe and open it."

He shook his head. "You can't. It's in concrete."

I smiled. "Wanna bet?" The tow truck showed up about an hour later; the driver pulled a cable and hook through the window and wrapped it around the safe. "I'll tear out the whole side of your house," I told him. "I don't care." His lawyer showed up just in time to prevent that from happening, but when the situation became clear to this guy, he decided to cooperate. He told us where McNelis was living with her two grown children and what name she was using. By the time we got to that address, she was in the wind. We never knew how she found out. But when we hit the place, a pit bull attacked me. I'd never had a case like this; alligators, pit bulls, and this was all before we found out that for the previous nine months she had been working as a topless dancer at the Office Lounge in St. Petersburg. She was known as Angel. She wore a blond wig, she'd had breast implants, and she easily passed for someone ten years younger than her actual age. "She would make you feel good," the owner of the place told me. Among the people who had come in regularly to see her were off-duty St. Petersburg police officers.

That was a very odd and completely unexpected career choice for McNelis. Nothing in her background indicated she would have suddenly decided to become a topless dancer. Fugitives usually try to keep a low profile and try to avoid being seen. There isn't a much higher profile job than an exotic dancer. Layne was amazed that a woman whose wanted poster was hanging up all over the place would stand up in front of hundreds of men dancing topless five nights a week, especially in a bar frequented by law enforcement. That certainly was one of the last places they would have looked for her, which is probably why she did it. As Layne says,

We were forced to spend three days at the Office Lounge just in case she showed up, but she never did.

Throughout all this time we were watching her mother, who lived in the Macon, Georgia, area. All of a sudden her mother started getting in her car and driving to pay phones to make calls. She rarely used the same phone twice. The fact that somebody has to leave their home to make a phone call would always attract our attention. We got the numbers she called from the phone company and traced one of them to the Ocean Way Motel in Fort Lauderdale. Local law enforcement raided the place and arrested McNelis's two grown children; they both lied to the officers, but the officers found enough information there to lead them to McNelis. They finally found her and made the arrest. She eventually pleaded guilty to federal drug conspiracy charges and tax evasion and was sentenced to twenty years, though she was acquitted of the murder charge.

Layne also brought charges against McNelis's twenty-year-old and eighteen-year-old children for harboring a fugitive. There were people who thought Layne was wrong to do that, but as he explained, it was important to make a statement: "When we tell people that if they assist a fugitive we will prosecute them, we've got to mean it. Once it becomes known that you don't screw around with the U.S. marshals, people respond to that threat. Her two children pleaded guilty and received suspended sentences."

Experience has proved over and over that fugitives will turn to their families—and no matter how heinous their crime, often the families will protect them. In 1990, Craig Caine had a deadly case that began when a Staten Island couple let their dog loose to run in a nearby landfill. The dog returned sometime later carrying a human bone in its mouth. The NYPD started excavating the site and discovered numerous body parts. Eventually this led them to a member of the Thomas ("Tommy Karate") Pitera drug organization named James Febbraio, or Jimmy February. Pitera's crew was known for killing its competition, then cutting up their bodies with a chain saw and leaving the parts in landfills. Eventually the DEA issued a warrant for Febbraio charging him with conspiracy to distribute and possess large amounts of marijuana, cocaine, and heroin. The DEA spent almost eight years looking for him, and eventually handed the case to deputy marshals Patty Quinn and Craig Caine.

The Electronic Surveillance Unit discovered that Febbraio's mother was living in Pensacola, Florida. Quinn and Caine took the lead to Deputy Scott Palumbo, working in the southern district of Florida. Febbraio hadn't been seen in almost a decade, so Palumbo asked a Miami Dade PD forensic artist to patch together an illustration of how he might have aged. "A lot of it was guesswork," Caine remembers.

> He asked me all these questions, does he drink, does he smoke, what does he eat? I told him, "If I knew all that, I would have caught him already."
>
> We also hit all the usual databases and found out that the mother absolutely was in touch with him, and that she was having her mail forwarded to an address in upstate New York. We thought he might be there. The local police department in that town discovered that the mail was going to Febbraio's sister, who also was in touch with him. We knew he was around, but we couldn't peg his location.

Scott Palumbo, meanwhile, had also been working on a DEA task force and as part of that assignment had developed a good informant. When Palumbo showed that informant the forensic sketch, he recognized it instantly and told him where Febbraio was staying in Brooklyn. It was in a building just off Eighty-Sixth Street, the location made famous by John Travolta in *Saturday Night Fever.* A task force composed of several deputies and members of the NYPD fugitive task force converged on the address. Before busting down the door, they debated putting on disco outfits, 1970s leisure suits, under their raid jackets when they made the bust, but decided they didn't have enough time.

Instead, Caine remembers,

We sat out there watching the house all night. About six A.M. we saw some activity, then some kids left the house and a woman was standing at the door. We decided it was time to hit the place. Febbraio's wife answered the door and told us he wasn't there. "I don't know who you're talking about," she said. A wife lying to protect her husband? That wasn't exactly unheard of. We went through the house in teams of two. Patty and I walked into Febbraio's bedroom; he was standing by his dresser putting his watch on. When he saw us, his face went ashen. I said, "You know why we're here. Jimmy February, right?"

Sometimes fugitives try to lie their way out of this situation. It never works, but they still try. He didn't, "Now that you call me that, I do." But he was stunned. After managing to stay free for a decade, he probably figured we'd forgotten about him. Patty put the cuffs on him.

Usually there is at least one family member who, if he or she doesn't know exactly where the fugitive is, at least knows how to get in touch with him. Caine remembers going to speak with the brother of a fugitive who had escaped from the minimum-security prison in Otisville, New York. There were no walls surrounding the place, so he had just walked off the grounds. When Caine asked the brother if he had seen or spoken to the fugitive, "He said to me, 'How come you're looking for my brother? He ain't here. He's being incinerated up at Otisville.' I didn't laugh when he said that, but then he added, 'He was arrested illegally, you know, so we're going to be suing the government for that radioactive back pay.' That's when I did laugh."

Deputy Thomas Smith uses a slightly different strategy. "If you want to find somebody, you find out who his or her lover is; if you can find out who the love interest is, male or female, you're going to find your guy or girl. It really is simple; find the girlfriend, you'll find the crook—but if you find the ex-girlfriend, she'll find him for you!"

Following the girlfriend is almost always as productive as following the money. Often, in fact, the girlfriend, the money, and the fugitive will be in the same place. The first fugitive Bobby Sanchez caught was appropriately known as Tony Gangster, a drug dealer suspected in multiple homicides. Sanchez recalls, "A local police department in Puerto Rico asked our assistance in finding him. His girlfriend supposedly lived with her mother. But we followed this woman one morning, and after she dropped off her child at school, she went to a house no one knew anything about. We set up surveillance in a neighbor's house across the street, and the second night he showed up and we arrested him."

In 1997, the DEA charged a man named Allen Jerome High with selling cocaine on school grounds and possession of a knife. Five years later, he disappeared from the federal prison camp in Atlanta and was in the wind for several months. Wendell Brock began looking for him by interviewing both the prison guards and inmates. "I didn't get a whole lot of information," he says.

But several months later I was hauling prisoners from the courts back to the camp and I asked one of them if he knew Jerome High. "You mean Big High?" he asked.

My fugitive was about 6'3", 300 pounds. "Yeah, that's probably him," I told him.

This prisoner was surprised. "You tellin' me you haven't found that guy yet? Then you need to talk to Miss Francis." It was a name I hadn't heard. "She works in the kitchen. They started f—ing the first day he got transferred to Atlanta."

This conversation took place almost a year and a half after High's escape. Eventually Brock uncovered the whole story. This was a minimum-security prison camp, so the restrictions were pretty lax. Apparently High had been paying one of the guards to let him walk out of the gate at the end of the day where a corrections officer named Denise Francis was waiting for him. They would go to a nearby motel and spend the night. The following morning she would take him back in time to make roll call. One day they were too late getting to the gate, so he missed roll call. She picked him up and they drove away. This was something even a veteran law enforcement officer like Brock had never seen.

He actually had been escaping and returning on a regular basis. When I confronted prison officials about it, they admitted they had suspected her of being involved with him but hadn't been able to prove it. She had been suspended but eventually got her job back. She was still working there.

They gave me all the information they had on her. According to these records, she was living with her parents, but very quickly I had determined that was no longer accurate. Finding out where she did live was a lot more difficult. She definitely did not want to be found. After a lot more investigation, I discovered she was stealing Social Security numbers and using them to help her rent apartments. She'd move in and not bother paying any rent, and after several months, she'd be evicted and repeat the same scheme. It took me almost six more months to finally track her down.

We set up surveillance and one night she came home from the prison in her uniform and walked into the apartment. About five minutes later she came out, followed by her teenage son, and then Jerome High, who was carrying the baby they'd had together. We let them get into her car—High was driving—and then swarmed all over it, using a vehicle to block their path. My team arrested him and I went over to arrest her. "You can't arrest me," she said. "I work for the prisons."

I told her, "Well, this isn't official; I'm not telling you officially you're fired, but I am telling you you're under arrest and you probably are not going to be working there anymore." Denise Francis served six months and a three-year suspension for aiding and abetting a fugitive.

Every deputy has learned from experience that a spurned—and often angry—ex-girlfriend or ex-wife is often a very good source of information. Wendell Brock verifies that strategy is an effective one, whether you're looking for a man or a woman.

I always look at their wife, their ex-wife, their girlfriend, the mother of their children, the one they just left to go to the next one, because I guarantee you that among those people there is going to be at least one person who is angry. Find the person who is mad at your fugitive and they are going to tell you everything they know. I was looking for a woman from south Georgia, for example, and I couldn't find a thing on her, although a couple of sources believed she was in Atlanta. A local Atlanta cable company regularly posted a police blotter with pictures and profiles of fugitives believed to be in that area. I put her information on this site, and out of the blue I got a call from a woman who told me her ex-husband was actually living with the fugitive. Then she gave me the exact address where I would find them.

The Midland County, Texas, Sheriff's Office had a case in which a man in the middle of a messy divorce had kidnapped his two children and fled. He was tracked down and arrested in Florida, the children were taken away from him, and he was released on bail. Only then did authorities discover that the entire time he was on the run he had been raping his twelve-year-old daughter. In 2002, warrants were issued for his arrest in both Florida and Texas, and the Midland County Sheriff's Office asked Texas deputy marshal Phillip Matthews for assistance.

We developed some information that our fugitive was bouncing around the transient motels in Albuquerque, New Mexico. We worked with the Marshals office there, and officers confirmed that people had seen the guy but no one could put their hands on him. He stayed to himself, didn't talk to other people, and kept a low profile. There are some cases that you take a little more personally, and this one continued to bug me. In November 2004, I went to Albuquerque for a Federal Fugitive Conference and took this case with me, figuring if we had a free day I'd go out and do some checking myself.

While Matthews was at this conference, his partner in Midland, Steve Clark, called and told him he had just received a message from the fugitive's ex-wife that he had applied for DIRECTV satellite service. There was some kind of records problem so they had contacted her. She provided an Albuquerque address that hadn't come up on any database. Matthews says,

Apparently the ex-wife was very happy to give us that information. We hit the street with several U.S. deputy marshals and local law enforcement. The address was an apartment in a strip of crappy one-story buildings. We didn't know which apartment he was in, and one of the deputy sheriffs wondered how we were going to figure that out. "It's pretty simple," I told him. "It's the one with the satellite dish hanging on the front door." The apartment manager confirmed that our fugitive lived in that apartment.

We surrounded it. I knocked on the door and a short guy with a Charlie Manson beard opened it.

He looked around and saw twelve guns pointing directly at him. "Man, don't shoot me," he said, raising his hands. "I'm not going to do anything stupid."

I'm not certain of my exact response, but it probably was a Clint Eastwood–like "No, you already did." I called the Midland County Sheriff's Office from the parking lot and told them that the case was closed.

Fugitives also leave a paper trail. It's incredibly difficult to move around the country without leaving tracks, and this was true even before the dawning of the digital age. Often fugitives live under an alias, which can make it more difficult to find them, but eventually almost everyone will have to make some transaction that's going to put them on the grid, whether it's taking cash out of an ATM, using a credit card to pay for a motel, or making a phone call. There are numerous databases available to law enforcement that collect an incredible amount of information, and in many instances fugitives are not even aware that their presence is being recorded. As directly as footprints left in soft ground, this information enables the modern deputy to track a fugitive across the country.

Obviously documents like credit cards and driver's licenses are the easiest things to track. For example, a member of Texas's Mexican Mafia had completed most of a previous sentence and was living in a halfway house prior to his release. When he got in an argument with a man in a wheelchair, his girlfriend brought him a gun and he killed that man, then the two of them took off. She wasn't difficult to track. James Benjamin discovered she was using her credit cards to buy gas and food stamps that she'd gotten through a federal program to buy supplies. By tracking those transactions, with some additional help from informants, Benjamin was able to electronically follow their paper trail stop-by-stop as they raced across Texas. When they finally stayed on a large ranch in south Texas for a couple of days, local authorities arrested both of them.

With the introduction of E-Z Pass technology, which registers every license plate as each car goes through a toll gate, it is possible to track and locate just about any vehicle's plate. To take one example, a Colorado burglar stole a car and made a clean getaway, disappearing for several months. Using the National Insurance Crime Bureau, a commercial database that records license plate numbers, deputies in the Marshals Service Technical Operations Group discovered the vehicle had been impounded by the Montgomery

County, Maryland, police department. Deputies then began digging down into the fugitive's file and were able to associate him with several people living in a community in Maryland. When local police officers went to that address, they found the fugitive staying there and made the arrest.

People on the run have to be able to communicate with people who might help them, and that means at some point they are going to use a phone. Although cell phones have necessitated the application of advanced technology, the basic concept of tracking a fugitive through whatever type of communications device he or she is using hasn't changed. And that proved to be a key element in protecting a Florida judge. As Mike Bunk admits, the relationship between the Marshals Service and the FBI has at times been strained, and he points out there is a lot of competition between the two organizations.

> There are a lot of great individuals working for the bureau. But we had a situation over in Tampa in which a mother and her son did not like the way a trial had turned out and had threatened the judge. It was believed they were capable of carrying out their threat. While deputies protected him, the bureau

was searching without success for the mother and son. After a couple of months, the judge decided he wanted his life back. He had gained a lot of respect for the people guarding him, so he insisted the Marshals Service get involved in the hunt.

I knew this was not going to be a good assignment. The following Monday morning my partner and I went over to the FBI's office. I remember specifically telling the agent, "Look, you don't want me here just as much as I don't want to be here. I know you all are doing what you can, so just throw me something. I don't want to step on your investigation." He threw me a bunch of year-old records of telephone calls made from the fugitives' last known address, calls that had been made before they were fugitives.

My partner and I went back to our office and began searching through them. This wasn't new for us; we'd done it many times before, and after a while you begin to develop an instinct for those things that just aren't quite right. Several numbers caught our attention and we began attaching addresses to them. There was one number they had called several times that was way out in the country, way out in the backwoods. It seemed like a perfect place to hide out. So my partner and I decided to take a ride up there the next morning. We took an exit off US 19 and drove about two miles deep into the middle of nowhere. We had cell phones with us, but there was no reception that deep in the woods. We were driving, driving, and suddenly we spotted a trailer off to our right, and standing in front of the trailer were the woman and her son. Normally my partner and I would have just gone over there and arrested them, but we figured this was an FBI case; we decided we'd better let them use their SWAT team.

When we got back to the main road I called my supervisor. "We got 'em," I said.

He didn't believe that at all. "Quit screwing around, I know damn well you don't have them."

"Okay, we'll just have to bring them in."

After a few seconds of silence, he asked, "You really have them?" It took some convincing before the FBI finally accepted the fact that we'd located these fugitives they'd spent several months looking for in one day. And when we did convince them, they told us not to do anything about it, which obviously was a decision we had already made.

Later that night Bunk and his partner went back into the woods—this time with the FBI SWAT team.

In fact, they rode up there in the SWAT team vehicle. When they arrived, FBI agents completely surrounded the trailer, then got on the PA and ordered the two fugitives to come out with their hands up. Bunk looked around at all of these people, every one of them heavily armed and wearing a protective vest, and then he started laughing. And he thought, *Wow, my partner and I could have had these people in custody twelve hours earlier.*

Among the first real advances in modern telephone technology was the pager, which allowed you to call someone and leave a phone number for the person to call back. The Marshals Service developed a wrinkle in that technology for a gun buyback program known as Gunsmoke. Although the technology wasn't very successful in that program, it eventually proved very valuable. Basically, this technology allowed Technical Operations to determine almost immediately where a phone call made to a pager was coming from. "That was the beginning of our Technical Operations Group," says Donald Ward. "It sounds pretty simplistic now, but back then it was a big deal. We didn't have any real budget for things like that. Our people built it mostly with things they bought at Radio Shack. But it was tremendously effective. We developed literally hundreds of investigative leads from this technology. People used pay phones then, and when they called a pager, we could pretty much locate that pay phone. Once we had the number of a pager, there were a lot of things we could do with it to track down the fugitive."

One of the many cases in which getting that pager number made all the difference began in late May 1994, three weeks before Nicole Brown Simpson and Ron Goldman were brutally murdered outside her Brentwood, California, home, when a convicted Mafioso named Joey Ippolito Jr. walked away from a prison camp in Pensacola, Florida. Ippolito was born to be a gangster; his father had worked for Meyer Lansky and the infamous Sam "the Plumber" DeCalvacante, and several other members of his family also were connected. Ippolito had been arrested on Long Island in 1988 for smuggling eight tons of marijuana. After completing a five-year sentence, he moved to California and opened an Italian restaurant, but his real business was a cocaine distribution network centered in Santa Monica and Brentwood. He had hired Al Cowlings, O.J. Simpson's close friend, to work as his chauffeur and bodyguard. The restaurant closed in 1991; a year later somebody put three bullets into the back of the head of one of Ippolito's cocaine distributors. Eventually the DEA arrested Ippolito and he was sentenced to ten years in prison on drug charges. When Ippolito disappeared in 1994, nobody paid too much attention—until Nicole Brown Simpson and Ron Goldman were murdered three weeks later. Suddenly law enforcement began connecting some very intriguing dots.

Harry Layne was running the North Florida Fugitive Task Force when he received a call from the office of California prosecutor Marsha Clark. "They suspected Ippolito Jr. might have had something to do with the murders and wanted to know if we had any idea where he was," Layne remembers.

When authorities arrested Al Cowlings after the televised pursuit of Simpson's white Bronco, they found a Pensacola phone number in his pocket and wondered who he had been calling. We discovered it was a phone at the Pensacola Naval Air Station Officer's Club—where Ippolito had been working in a work-release program. The fact that Ippolito had escaped three weeks before the murders made the LAPD suspect he might have had some involvement in arranging them, or that he had some foreknowledge that stimulated him to get out of custody before it happened. They requested that we make a major effort to find him.

The Marshals Service put Ippolito Jr. on its 15 Most Wanted list and began an intensive investigation.

It was a difficult case because he was a well-known mobster and people were afraid to cooperate. We really shook the bushes: we did a lot of interviews, we watched a lot of his old hangouts, and we put pressure on his known associates. We locked up some people and offered them an opportunity to help themselves, but for several months we didn't get much. Months passed, almost a year. Then we were told Ippolito was going to meet a friend of his who lived in Fort Lauderdale at the International Offshore Boating Championships in Key West. That made a lot of sense because Ippolito had raced cigarette boats and a friend of his was entered in the competition. Deputy John Cuff, an expert on the New York mob, met me there. A bunch of Jersey mobsters had come down for the event. We had been told Ippolito and a close friend were riding matching Harleys, one red, one blue. We found those bikes and spent the next few days watching them and following anyone who went near them. We actually developed one lead we were pretty confident would lead to him so we hit the hotel room; we found another coke dealer and made the arrest. But if Joey showed, we didn't see him.

Later we learned that our informant was terrified of Ippolito; she was convinced he would have her killed if he found out she was talking to us. We couldn't deny that was a possibility.

Eventually, out of the hundreds of phone numbers deputies were tracking, John Cuff was able to get Ippolito's personal pager number. Being able to associate someone with a phone number provides a huge advantage. As soon as the marshals got that number, Layne knew Ippolito's arrest was imminent.

We finally had a hook in him. We found out the pager was serviced by a store run by some Chinese people in lower Manhattan. We wanted them to turn the pager off and tell Ippolito he needed to come into the store and pay in cash to reactivate it. We thought this might work because only a few of his very closest associates had this number, and it would be a real hassle for him to change it. The Chinese knew he was a mob guy and didn't want to cooperate; they didn't want any trouble with anybody. But when we found out they were having their own problems with a Vietnamese gang that was extorting Asian store owners, we agreed to get the Vietnamese off their back in exchange for their help. We asked the ATF to put the squeeze on the Vietnamese, and whatever they did, it was effective. The store turned off Ippolito's pager and when he called to complain, they told him he had to come in to have it serviced.

Deputies surrounded the store and waited. For two days there was no sign of Ippolito. Marshals were positioned on rooftops, in vans parked on the street, and Layne and Cuff were in a stuffy room one flight above the store, watching a surveillance camera monitoring the front door.

We figured he might send someone else to take care of it so we had people in cars and on foot ready to follow that person back to wherever he was laid up. But suddenly Ippolito walked in the door all by himself. John and I ran down the stairs with our guns drawn; I screamed, "Police! We got you, Joey, get on the ground now!" He didn't hesitate; he got right down on the floor.

The front door was locked and had to be buzzed open, but when some of our people outside saw the bust going down, they immediately came running to help—and one of them slammed into the door and knocked himself over backward. The Chinese heard the crash and thought it was a gunshot, so they dived onto the ground behind the counter.

Although this arrest proved much too late to assist law enforcement in the Simpson case—and Ippolito claimed that he didn't know anything about it—the apprehension did have an unexpected benefit. Ippolito told deputies he'd been living in a rented house in the Hamptons; he knew he was being pursued and the stress had caused both him and his girlfriend to pick up a serious heroin addiction. Every time the two of them had gotten settled somewhere, law enforcement would pick up the trail and they would have to pack up and run; eventually the pressure got to be too much. When Ippolito was told his girlfriend was going to jail too, he reacted. "You can't do that," he said. "They won't take care of her when she comes down. She's in real danger."

"We explained to him that there were alternatives," Layne remembers.

We told him we could get her into a drug treatment center, but we had to have something in return. "You take care of her," he said, "I'll take care of you." We hoped that meant he wouldn't try to have us whacked, but in fact he meant he was willing to talk. We put him in with the U.S. Attorney's Organized Crime

Task Force and he did a complete 180 degrees from being a made guy to providing valuable information. He turned out to be an absolute gold mine. The information he provided enabled us to recover several bodies and solve as many as a hundred homicides. We were proud of the fact that we were able to find him and turn him, which was a little different from the way we usually operate. But without that pager number, we might still be looking for him.

Ippolito went back to prison, and when it became obvious that he was cooperating, the mob tried to kill his brother. As the brother was coming out of a restaurant they shot him, then ran over him, then got out of the car and shot him again. Somehow he lived. When Ippolito was released from prison, he was offered a place in the Marshals Service Witness Protection Program—but he wasn't interested.

"He did it all for a woman he loved," Layne says. "Eventually he died a normal death, for a mob guy, in 2006 and was described in his obituary as 'a self-employed restaurateur in the Florida area.'"

Tying a fugitive to a specific phone number is like putting an electronic tracer on him. When three convicted killers of police officers escaped from Puerto Rico's notorious state penitentiary, local officials requested the assistance of U.S. Deputy Marshal Bobby Sanchez. Río Piedras, or the White Bear as it was called, was an especially brutal prison; it was run by the inmates, who were reputed to kill other prisoners, cut up their bodies, and flush them down the toilet. The three escapees were known on the street as Papo Yuca, Landy, and Jerry. Papo Yuca was easy; he went right back to the place he knew best, his housing project, and was recaptured very quickly. The other two, the more violent two, remained on the loose. Sanchez told local law enforcement, "What we need to do is form a task force dedicated completely to this case. We're not going to catch them working part-time." The Group of the Hundred, as this task force was named, consisted of one hundred officers from several different law enforcement and military agencies and was commanded by an army colonel. At one of the early meetings, a local cop announced, "I think I have the cell phone of Landy." Landy had been in Rio Piedras for executing two police officers at point-blank range when they interrupted a robbery. Sanchez asked him, "Are you sure that's a good number for Landy?"

The officer was offended, insisting, "If I say I have it, I have it."

Sanchez nodded. "Good. I'm not questioning your investigative skills, but I have guys in the States I can reach out to who will come and track that cell phone and we'll catch him."

The next day Sanchez and several local officers met with the man who had provided that number. He was a drug dealer who ran a lot of drug points in Puerto Rico. Apparently Landy had been stealing from this dealer, telling his workers that he was picking up the money for this dealer. So the drug organization wanted him captured or killed as quickly as possible. They knew the cell-phone number was good because Landy had told one of the people he'd robbed, "Call me at this number if you have any questions or need to talk." Sanchez handed the dealer his phone and told him to call that number. He did, and a few seconds later he identified the voice of the person who'd answered it: "Yeah, that's him."

As Sanchez stood there one of the military officers told this dealer, "We want this guy caught or killed. We want him off the streets. Don't you have some guys who will kill him?"

Sanchez thought, *I guess that's the way things are done here.* Three deputies with the technical expertise flew down. They were able to track Landy's phone to a certain area—and the night before Sanchez's task force was planning to arrest him, local cops caught up with him. That was two down; that left Jerry. Sanchez recalls the capture started with a phone number:

Our technical people got Jerry's mother's phone number and used that to identify the numbers from which he was calling her. Then we began tracking him. We found the general area where he was when he made his first phone call every morning and his last phone call of the day, but we couldn't get his specific location. One morning when we pulled the phone records, we discovered that the last call he'd made the night before had been a local Pizza Hut. We went there and asked if they could give us the address to which a pizza had been delivered at that time. They did, which enabled us to identify the house in which Jerry was hiding out.

We were watching the house when a man walked in. He looked like our Jerry, but we weren't certain, and we didn't want to move until we were sure. We waited. It wasn't Jerry; it was a man that Jerry had formed a relationship with in prison. Our Jerry showed up a little bit later. When we were sure he was there, we hit the house and captured him.

The arrest quickly became a media circus. A helicopter carrying the police superintendent landed on the block, news people showed up, and the high officials began taking turns walking Jerry out of the house and putting him in the car. They repeated it several times: walk him out and put him in the car—then stop the cameras; take him back in the house, then another official would march him out and put him in the car. All Sanchez could do was watch with amazement as they got film for their résumés.

Even before the Internet and digital technology became key law enforcement tools, it was almost impossible not to leave some type of paper trail. In late 1997, Florida deputy Mike Moran got a call from a *Miami Herald* reporter asking him to confirm a rumor that law enforcement had apprehended Belgium's notorious Honeymoon Killers. Moran replied that he had no idea what she was talking about. He'd never heard about the case. But he checked the report anyway and discovered that no warrant had been issued for these European fugitives. "It sounded like a good case, though," he says.

One of our international people in D.C. checked with Belgian authorities and got the whole story. It was fascinating. Peter-Uwe Schmidt, a NATO officer, had been caught running a large stolen car ring. When Belgian law enforcement found out about it, his wife of only six months, from whom he was already separated, agreed to speak with them about what she knew. The day before she was scheduled to be questioned, she was drowned when the car that her estranged husband supposedly was driving suddenly skidded on a clear, dry road and went flying into a canal. Schmidt escaped without injury—in fact, it was noted that his clothes were completely dry when he reported the "terrible accident." He actually received a large settlement from his wife's life insurance policy. As a result of an investigation he was found guilty of "unvoluntary death," was sentenced to two months in prison, and paid a fine.

That's when the case really began to get fascinating, Moran discovered. In 1995, a woman named Aurore Martin, who had also worked at NATO headquarters, was on her honeymoon in Corsica where her new husband was killed when their car crashed into a ravine. She managed to jump free in time to save her life—and also collected a very large life insurance payment. The groom's parents didn't believe her story and hired private detectives to investigate. These investigators discovered that Marc Van Beers had been beaten to death by four men hired by Peter Schmidt and his body had been put in the car then crashed into the ravine. As the facts began coming out, Schmidt and Martin made their getaway. While few people in America knew anything at all about this case, it was a huge story throughout Europe. Belgian authorities had managed to track the couple to Florida and had requested assistance from the FBI. When the FBI failed to locate them, the Belgians asked the Marshals Service to join the hunt. Moran told them, "We can't get involved without the permission of the FBI. We don't want to step on their toes if they've got something going."

But when Moran checked with the FBI, he found out they had no leads. In fact, he was told that the FBI believed Schmidt and Martin already had left the United States.

So when I asked their approval to work on this case, they told me to go ahead but warned me that I'd be wasting my time. It wasn't a priority case for us, but we worked on it when we had a little time. And we eventually developed a source who told us precisely where Schmidt was living. When we grabbed him, he had a pistol in his waistband and about $100,000 in the money belt he was wearing. He told us if we let him go, we could keep the money; we laughed and told him that we were keeping the money but that he was going to jail. We seized everything—but Aurore Martin wasn't with him; in fact, he told us smugly, "You'll never find her." Unfortunately, that was very possible. When you're looking for two people and one of them is caught, you have a very brief window during which to catch the other one or that person will be gone.

As we were searching Schmidt's car, we found a receipt for some work that had been done by an auto body shop. When we checked it out, we learned that this body shop had a contact number for Martin that we traced to an apartment in Kendall, just outside Miami. We went from never finding her to arresting her in four hours. This case was on the front pages in Europe, and we went to Belgium to testify in their trial.

Any piece of paper that puts a fugitive in a specific place at a specific time is immensely valuable; it doesn't need to be an official document—anything that can be associated with that person can put a deputy on his or her trail. Deputy Craig Caine recounts a story of pursuing a career criminal who had violated his supervised release program, a type of probation, and disappeared.

He had been in the system for a long time so he was pretty good at covering his tracks. His release address was to his father's house in Queens, New York. Deputy Bobby Ledogar and I went to talk to his father, who played hardball with us. He didn't know where his son was, he told us. It was the usual, "he just took off and I haven't heard from him" story. Obviously we didn't believe him from the get-go. We kept going back to roust him, and there was nothing he could do about it because this was the release address on the warrant. Sometimes with people like that the more you bother them, the angrier they get, and we were hoping the father would get tired of his son putting him in this position and tell us where he was. But he didn't.

But one day while we were looking around the house we noticed a photo of the fugitive with some other people. We showed it to the father and pointed out how odd it was that he'd told us he wasn't in touch with his son but here's this recent photograph of him sitting on the table. "He sent it to me around Christmastime," he said. Naturally the envelope didn't have a return address, and even if it did he hadn't saved it. Who saves envelopes? Right, we agreed, that's too bad.

But what we didn't tell the father was that on the back of the photo we'd noticed the letters CVS followed by a number. We went right from the house to the local CVS drug store, and the manager there checked the store number and told us the photo had been developed in a CVS in Boca Raton, Florida. We handed that information to the Marshals Service office in that area and those deputies took over.

Employees of that store identified him as a regular customer. He had his prescriptions filled there, but there was no address on record for him. One of those employees happened to mention that he had seen the fugitive at a local bar, where he was working part-time as a bouncer. When a team of deputies went there to arrest him a couple of nights later, he spotted them and took off running. After a brief chase, he was arrested and eventually extradited back to New York.

One of the nation's more successful fugitives in recent history was Alphonse "Allie Boy" Persico, for a time the reputed head of New York's Colombo organized crime family. Allie Boy took off in 1980 to avoid going to prison after being convicted of extortion and was on the run for seven years, spending a lot of that time as one of the FBI's 10 Most Wanted. Vic Oboyski was one of a small team of deputies who decided to resurrect the case. The team began by tracking down and locking up one of Allie Boy's known associates in Florida, and then squeezing him. Oboyski says, "This guy told us that Allie Boy was somewhere in Connecticut, although he didn't know where. We got some other information that also put him there, but then we heard all kinds of stories, like he had been in a serious boating accident or he'd had a heart attack. None of it fit together." A task force was formed and set up headquarters in a hotel in Hartford. Many deputies believed that Persico was getting inside information about law enforcement efforts to locate him, which was one reason he had been able to avoid being captured for so long. So this whole operation had to remain secret.

Oboyski sat down with his team of six young deputy marshals and told them not to trust anybody who wasn't sitting in the room at that moment. He said, "Throughout this entire investigation, as long as it lasts, we're going to talk like the wise guys. No one will ever, for any reason, mention our target by name. I don't want to hear anybody say the words 'Allie Boy' or 'Persico.' He's going to be 'our guy' or 'that guy.' Nothing else. The people we interview are going to be 'the other guy.'" Oboyski continued, "Talk like you're being taped and you can't divulge nothing." He knew that if Persico found out marshals were in the state looking for him, they could forget about finding him.

I was afraid if we even whispered the name Persico, he'd be up and gone.

We didn't want anybody knowing we were there. We rented cars with Connecticut plates on them and set up our command post in a Sheraton. We did everything possible not only to look for our guy, but to hide the fact that we were there looking for him. We even had a plaster bust made of what he might look like after surviving a heart attack and probably growing a mustache, and we carried photographs of that bust with us.

The task force knew that "our guy" had to be living under an alias, and most likely had used that name to obtain the basic public documents necessary to live a normal life. Nobody can go through life without identification, even if it isn't real. Oboyski's team assumed Persico had gotten a driver's license, which is the basic form of ID. They decided to go through the state Department of Motor Vehicle files looking for people with birth dates around the same time as his, who had a name beginning with a vowel, probably an "A" because they were told "our guy" had his name, "Al," tattooed on his hand. Deputies found about seven hundred names that fit those parameters, then narrowed the search further by using additional known information, like his height. They kept knocking down the probabilities and eventually cut the list to 128 names.

One name, Anthony Parry, had the exact same birth date as Persico, and another was off by a month and a day. The task force focused on those two names, doing an exhaustive search for all documents in those names.

They started getting some hits. As Oboyski remembers,

At some point on a DMV form one of them had identified the high school he had attended and the year he graduated. We checked with the high school and they had no record of anyone by that name ever being a student there. Then we checked birth certificates and other records; neither of those two names had established any credit record prior to the date our guy had taken off, so we knew these were made-up identities.

We lived in Hartford for almost three months, working on nothing but this case. At the end of every day, we would sit down together and have a complete debriefing, and then the following morning we would go through our plans for the day. We lived in a total attack mode. We did a lot of work on these names and finally narrowed it down and narrowed it down until we knew we had his alias—although we still didn't know where he was. But once we had the name, it was just a matter of time. We just kept following the document trail until we got a good address for our guy. It turned out he was living in West Hartford, no more than three miles from the place we'd set up our command post.

After all the work we'd done, the arrest was not very dramatic. When we busted in, he was standing over the stove stirring a pot of marinara sauce. Just like in the movies. We told him, "Alphonse Persico, you're under arrest."

He looked at us, "What do you want me to do?"

I told him, "Put down that spoon!" As we were taking him back he wondered how we'd found him, guessing somebody had "dropped a dime" on him. I told him no, "We found you just doing regular police work." Then I added, "But I got to tell you, I'm glad to be getting out of the state of Connecticut because you can't find good Italian food anywhere."

"I got a good idea," he suggested. "Let's go back to my place. I got some great sauce and pasta for you."

4

Details They'll Tell

In 1875, [freed slave] Bass Reeves began his career as a deputy U.S. Marshal under the guidance of Federal Judge Isaac "Hangin' Judge" Parker of the Western District of Arkansas. Reeves was responsible for chasing and apprehending criminals. To do his job, Reeves employed a number of clever tricks and techniques. . . . As a 6'2" man, Reeves learned from the Native Americans how to make himself appear smaller on his strong white and grey horse. At times he would surprise outlaws by adopting their clothing and mannerisms. Just as the Lone Ranger gave out silver bullets, so too did Reeves give out silver dollars as calling cards. Reeves was also often accompanied by one particular Native American, whose name is unfortunately unknown to historians at this time. According to contemporary reports, Reeves apprehended more than 3,000 outlaws and killed 14 during his time as a marshal.

—*National Museum of Crime and Punishment*

While almost every investigation at one point requires that deputies get out on the street, bang on endless doors, and ask innumerable questions, the technological capabilities of the Marshals Service have kept pace with the growth of the digital world. Deputy Jimmy Bankston, who has been working in the Technical Operations Group since 1997, says unequivocally, "We are the best agency in the world in technical surveillance. The absolute best. There is no dispute about that. If one of our people wants to intercept a communications device, or find out where it is, that person will come to us and if it is possible, we will find it."

For most of a century, telecommunications consisted of phones anchored to a spot and connected to the rest of the world by wire. When deputies hit the street, they always carried a roll of dimes with them in case they needed to use a pay phone. That's history. People now communicate by voice and vision and through the Internet on a variety of devices. And every one of those devices can be used to gather information about a fugitive. Computers, for example, have become a vitally important tracking tool—for a talented technician, a fugitive's computer can be a digital gold mine. In February 2001, for example, Clayton Lee Waagner, who was about to be sentenced to anywhere between fifteen years and life for interstate transportation of a stolen vehicle and possession of a firearm, escaped from prison by breaking through a flimsy wall. Using sophisticated electronic surveillance tools, the Marshals Service was able to track Waagner as he bounced around the country, robbing banks, stealing cars, and threatening to kill abortion providers, but marshals were always just a little behind him. They could pinpoint where he had been, but not where he was going next. Eventually he was placed on the Marshals Service's 15 Most Wanted list and, not long after that, the FBI's 10 Most Wanted. Waagner hadn't killed anyone yet, but his movements were becoming more erratic and his threats more violent.

On September 7, 2001, on a highway outside Memphis, Waagner crashed his Crown Victoria into the back of a truck and ran away. In the car Memphis police found a pipe bomb, a rifle and a shotgun, fifty-four rounds of ammunition, handcuffs, rope, a blue police car light, and a laptop computer. By carefully examining that computer, technicians determined that Waagner had a very specific browsing pattern: when he went online, he would immediately visit the same three far-right websites, usually in the same order. Much like a phone number, that unique browsing pattern could be traced. Technicians worked with his Internet provider to set up an alert when someone using this specific pattern showed up online. Then they waited.

A couple of weeks later Waagner went online. The Technical Operations Group was able to locate the computer, but deputies missed him by less than a half hour. Then he disappeared again. He continued moving around the Midwest, leaving a trail as law enforcement's frustration grew. Finally, in early December, Waagner showed up online once again, this time from a rented computer in a Kinko's located in the Cincinnati suburb of Springdale, Ohio. He was still surfing on that computer when local enforcement got there and arrested him. He immediately surrendered, although he was carrying a loaded semiautomatic pistol. Arresting officers also found $9,000 in cash and ID cards in twenty different names. With his extensive rap sheet it is unlikely he will ever get out of prison.

In addition to using state-of-the-investigative-art tools and an array of public and private databases, deputies also utilize the new online media to provide intelligence, a great advantage being that much of that information is publicly available. A lot of people just don't realize that. The Criminal Intelligence Branch, which was created in 2005, essentially searches numerous computer databases and other sources to create a profile of the fugitive. As the assistant chief of the Fugitive Targeting Unit, Kevin McSorley, explains it, "While deputies are doing the cat-and-mouse game in the street, we have the luxury of doing the cat-and-mouse game sitting behind a computer. If there is a trace of information about a fugitive out there in cyberworld, our job is to find it."

Debra Jenkins, who served in the U.S. Marshals Service from 1972 until her retirement in 2011, established the criminal intelligence program for the agency. According to Debra, "The criminal intelligence program focused on information collection and analysis to develop investigative leads and to generate strategic intelligence, which is used to make sound law enforcement decisions."

The Criminal Intelligence Branch initiated automated, high-speed, and regular WIN data comparison routines against the records of other agencies and entities, which helped to discover where fugitives might be active or have a corresponding record. The resulting investigative leads were quickly handed over to investigators to make arrests. Debra recalls the first time the analysts started to send these leads to the investigators:

> I guess [the investigators] were surprised that a lead could come out of nowhere. They did not realize that a group of analysts hundreds or thousands of miles from them were working with information they—the investigators—put into WIN and using it to look for new addresses or other information that might lead them to a fugitive. At first, the information we provided to the investigators was met with curiosity, and sometimes they seemed bothered. After receiving six solid addresses for separate open fugitive cases, one such investigator complained, "What am I supposed to do with this?" But once they began to follow up on our information and it either furthered their investigation or led to an arrest, they began to look forward to receiving more.

For example, after a Florida mother lost custody of her son, she took the child and ran. While Florida authorities believed she had stayed in that state, the CIB was able to determine that this woman had applied for certain federal benefits, which were being sent to an address in New York State. Generally the most difficult part of tracing fugitives through electronic surveillance is finding the name or names they are using. Investigators had a phone number for this woman, and by tracing that number on social media, they discovered she had used it as her contact number in an ad she had placed on Craigslist looking for a job as a nanny. That ad also included her e-mail address. She used her cybername on that e-mail, and a search for that alias revealed she had registered with a dating website in New York. All this information confirmed she was living at a certain address, and deputies arrested her there the next day. A deputy sitting in front of a computer had successful tracked, identified, and located her.

It isn't only the fugitive who may unwittingly provide vital clues. When a man violated his sentence by walking away from a halfway house and not returning, the CIB watched his family members on Facebook and noticed they were talking about him in their posts. One relative wrote that he believed the fugitive was at his sister's house. His sister's address was listed on Google and deputies found the fugitive hiding there only hours after the search was initiated.

Although the digital universe has been the source of significant leads in numerous cases, that information is not infallible. In one unusual case, evidence from a variety of Internet sources indicated an individual wanted for a murder in Texas was hiding in Washington, D.C. It didn't make a lot of sense; the fugitive had no known contacts in that part of the country, but that same address kept popping up. Among other things, the fugitive was receiving Social Security benefit checks at that address. When deputies knocked on the door, an older woman answered it and invited them in. After asking her some questions, it was apparent that the killer wasn't there and, in fact, probably had never been there. But as the deputies got up to leave, one of them noticed a stack of checks and credit cards on a table, most of them made out to different names. The answer quickly became obvious: the woman was running an identity theft operation—and she had unknowingly stolen the ID of a wanted murderer. The U.S. Secret Service was called in to investigate her use of stolen checks and credit cards.

There is no single best way to find a fugitive. Everything counts. For example, deputies began tracking the leaders of the very violent Los Tres de la Sierra drug organization after they were spotted on TV sitting in the stands at the Sydney, Australia, Olympics in 2000. And while many cases have been solved by picking up the document trail or tapping into the digital world, without exception every case is going to require a human connection at some point. While it is very difficult, a fugitive can move through the world without using a phone or a credit card, but it is impossible not to be seen or have some connection to other people, whether it is the person the fugitive loves most in the world or a clerk in a hot-sheet motel. People talk; sometimes people talk a lot. For a veteran investigator, even people who don't want to snitch can unknowingly provide good leads by not talking.

Deputy Marshal Tony Burke learned that even in the digital world few things are more accurate than human intelligence. The legendary computer hacker Kevin Mitnick apparently had a sometimes partner named Justin Petersen or, as Petersen referred to himself online, "Agent Steal." Petersen had established his own reputation as a computer geek; instantly recognizable because he had lost a leg in a motorcycle accident, the one-legged man with undeniable charisma had become a regular at some of the trendiest clubs on L.A.'s Sunset Strip. But what eventually made him infamous was the way he paid for his lifestyle. Working with several other hackers, Petersen ingeniously broke into PacBell's system and compromised the call-in lines of local radio stations. When these stations held on-air contests, Petersen's group were the only people able to get through, eventually winning $50,000 in cash, two Porsches, and several trips. When Petersen found out he was being pursued by the FBI, he fled to Texas and supported himself by using counterfeit credit cards issued to stolen identities. After being arrested, he pleaded guilty. He was looking at a sentence of up to forty years and a fine of $1.5 million; but rather than going to prison, he agreed to work undercover for the FBI, helping them pursue other hackers, among them his former partner, Kevin Mitnick.

Petersen burned the FBI. While working for them he had continued committing financial crimes. When his deception was discovered, he took off again. The FBI was both embarrassed and furious, and after failing to find him, they brought the Marshals Service into the chase. Deputy Tony Burke, who was assigned to the case, explains,

> I didn't know much about computers, but I did know if I was going to catch this guy, it wasn't going to be online. It was going to be the traditional way. I did his background and found out he was very into S&M. Apparently women found him practically irresistible, but he treated them really badly. Just about every woman he'd dated hated his guts. I hit all the S&M clubs in Hollywood, especially some of

the underground clubs, and it's fair to say that I got to meet a lot of interesting and unusual people.

One of those places I remember very well was a bar called the Zoo. I don't know if it even had a license, but it was wild. Usually, when I was working a case, I tried to dress to fit in; so in this case I put on an old AC/DC T-shirt, clipped a fake earring in my ear, and tried to blend in, but I looked like I belonged about as much as an Amish person. The Zoo had no real walls, just a chain-link fence that went all the way up to the ceiling. And people with all kinds of piercings on their face with spiked hair were clinging onto that fence like geckos. It's so hard to describe. I went to the bar and there was a guy holding another guy on a dog leash, and the guy on the leash had a birdcage covering his head. The guy holding the leash was taking peanuts from the bar, opening the cage, and feeding them to his lover. They had all kinds of weird rooms, people slapping each other with whips; it was incredible. I had never seen anything like this before. And I had to ask people a lot of questions.

There weren't a lot of computers in the place.

But eventually I managed to collect a lot of info on Petersen. I found out where he hung out, who he had been hanging out with, and who might still have some contact with him. I was told he had hooked up with a woman and was staying at her apartment in West L.A. It was on the sixth floor of a ten-story building. Normally when we hit a place, we always cover the back entrance, but I figured, the guy's six stories up, he's got one leg, where's he going to go? My team decided to go up to the sixth floor, knock on the door, and kind of bust in.

He saw us coming through a locked screen door. I could see him too; he had his artificial leg in his hand, and he was hopping pretty fast toward the back of the apartment. By the time we got the door open, he had thrown his leg out the window and dived out headfirst right after it. He dived out the window! I couldn't believe it. I'd seen plenty of guys go out the back, but never from the sixth floor.

When we got to the window we saw that about six feet away there was a big birch tree. He'd jumped out and grabbed onto a branch and slipped down it like he was going down a fire pole. I saw him on the ground, putting on his leg. He looked up at the window—and flipped me off. Then he took off running. I was with some young deputies and they wanted to call the LAPD to get a chopper up. I stopped them. "Dude, you know what? That was badass. You got to respect that. That was f—ing awesome! He deserves to run a couple of days for that." Then I asked them, "What would you like to say to your wives tonight, hey, I caught a computer hacker or we went into this one-legged guy's sixth-floor apartment and he went out the window? We got a great story to tell now."

But Petersen was now aware the marshals were on his trail. He wrote about his narrow escape in his online blog: *"Those fat assed Marshals couldn't catch a one-legged guy!"* In a later blog he claimed he had made it safely to France and couldn't be extradited. Earlier in the case Burke had turned another hacker into an informant who tried to hack into Petersen's blog to find out his location and failed. Burke suspected Petersen had a contact inside Earthlink who was helping him, but there was nothing he could do.

With his investigation going nowhere, Burke started retracing his steps, once again hitting all of Petersen's favorite places. And he found out that he actually hadn't gone to France; he hadn't gone anywhere. He was still around L.A.

About a week after his escape, I got the information I needed in the same way we'd been getting it forever: somebody told it to me. I'd gotten to know the bartender at a restaurant called the Rainbow Room. Apparently a guy had come into the place and started whining to the bartender that some one-legged motherf—er had stolen his girlfriend. The bartender asked him, "You talking about Justin Petersen?" Then he gave him my name and phone number and told me I was looking for him. That guy called me and told me exactly where Petersen was. I knew I had him, so that night I went on his blog. I was sitting there watching him typing away, bragging, and I just couldn't resist. I sent him my own message. The movie *Tombstone* had just come out, in which the U.S. marshals Wyatt Earp and his brothers shot down Ike and Billy Clanton and their gang at the O.K. Corral, so I wrote to Petersen, *Hey, Justin, remember the movie Tombstone, you f—k. We're coming and hell's coming with us.* I signed it Marshal Anthony W. Burke.

This time I didn't take any chances. I took about eight guys with me and we showed up at that address about 5:30 in the morning. We bashed down the door as we announced ourselves. He was in the bedroom, lying there with his leg off, typing on his laptop. "Lemme see your hands!" I ordered him. "Don't even think of going for the window again." I told him to walk toward me; he said,

"I can't get to the door, I don't have a leg."

I told him, "F—k you, you jumped from six stories, you can make it to the door." He actually crawled on his hands and knees, and we cuffed him. After we had him under control, I asked him if he had gotten my message the night before. At first he didn't know what I was talking about. I said, "I told you we were coming for you and hell is coming with us." I showed him my ID—then he figured it out. He couldn't believe it: "How did you track me? That's impossible!"

He was absolutely convinced that we had managed to track him through his computer; he was so deeply involved in that world that he couldn't even imagine we were capable of finding him using traditional techniques. He served three and a half years in prison, and after he got out, we actually ran into each other at a federal courthouse one afternoon. He stopped me and we started a casually friendly relationship; he'd call me about once a year until authorities found him dead in his apartment in 2010.

There is no better lead than an informer telling a deputy exactly where a fugitive is hiding. In August 2005, George Hyatte pleaded guilty to a robbery charge in Roane County Courthouse in Kingston, Tennessee;

Hyatte was a repeat offender so he was facing a long sentence. As two Department of Corrections officers were taking him from the courthouse to the transport van, his wife, Jennifer Forsyth Hyatte, pulled up in a borrowed Ford Explorer and held the two guards at gunpoint. Jennifer Hyatte was a nurse who had met and fallen in love with her husband while working inside the penitentiary, so she knew both guards. As George Hyatte ran toward her car with the officers in pursuit, he screamed at her, "Shoot them!" She opened fire, killing one officer and wounding the second man. The officers returned fire, hitting her in the upper thigh. Ultimately George and Jennifer Hyatte got onto Route 95 and raced north. The borrowed Explorer was found abandoned several hours later, but the Hyattes had disappeared.

A day later, deputies working in Covington, Kentucky, found the Hyattes' own vehicle parked outside a motel. They had stayed there but were long gone. John Bolen, who had just formed the Southern Ohio Fugitive Apprehension Strike Team in Columbus, Ohio, says,

> I remember telling my team, get ready, they're coming north. It was a big story in the Cincinnati region. When a taxicab driver named Mike Wagers

saw it on the news, he realized that he had picked up these two people in Erlanger, Kentucky, and driven them all the way to an America's Best Value Inn in Columbus. He called local law enforcement and said, "I'm sure it's them, although her hair had been cut and dyed. They said they were going to an Amway convention." That's when I got the call telling me that an informer had told us that he had dropped them off at a motel.

A team of marshals and the Columbus PD SWAT team surrounded the motel. Bolen sent a female deputy into the lobby and she was able to determine that the Hyattes were in a room at the rear of the second floor.

We got up the stairs and outside that door without being detected. When we were in place, I had that deputy call the room. From outside, we could hear the phone ringing and somebody pick it up. I couldn't hear the conversation, but we had decided that if someone answered, the female deputy would tell them that the room was surrounded and there was no way to escape, there was nowhere to run, nowhere to hide.

At that moment we had every reason to believe they were still armed. They had already killed one officer, so there was a real threat that this was going to end in a shoot-out. The deputy asked Jennifer if George was still with her and she said he was. From my position on the balcony I was in visual contact with my deputy on the phone in the lobby; she gave me a thumbs-up, meaning both of them were there. The deputy told Jennifer not to hang up the phone, but to set it down, walk to the door, and follow our instructions. Incredibly, she did. Within a minute or so she opened the door.

She had been wounded much worse than anyone knew and was bleeding badly. I told her to raise her hands and walk backward toward the sound of my voice. With her hands still in the air, I told her to turn around several times and pull up her shirt so we could see her waistband. Then we had her walk out the door and grabbed her. "Is George still in there?" I asked. She nodded her head, and started crying, saying, "Please don't hurt him."
"Does he have a gun?"

"No, we broke it apart and threw it in a dumpster in Cincinnati."

We took her into custody and hustled her away from the scene. But George was still inside that room, and no matter what she said, I would've bet he was armed. He wouldn't come out. I suspected he had climbed up into the motel ceiling and was trying to crawl across on the supports and drop down into an adjoining room; I've had several fugitives try to escape that way. But when we finally burst into the room, we found him hiding in the bathroom. He saw four or five long guns pointed at him and decided pretty quick he didn't want any part of that. We gave him the same orders we had given Jennifer, hands up, turn around. Both of them eventually pleaded guilty to first-degree murder, to avoid receiving the death penalty, and will spend the rest of their lives in prison.

In most cases, though, marshals don't have an informant come forward that quickly to provide that level of information. Instead, as Deputy Jim Schield explains, "When you work a fugitive case, you're usually going to be talking to many different people; some of them are going to tell you the truth, a lot of them are going to lie to you. The key is how it all fits together. It's like doing a big puzzle. The best fugitive investigator in the world is somebody who can sit down and talk."

Generally people don't want to get involved, so they need to be convinced that cooperating is in their own best interest. There are a lot of different ways of accomplishing this. Certainly among the most effective is reminding them that lives are in danger, maybe the fugitives', maybe some innocent people's, maybe even their own. For example, Harry Layne was once looking for a carnival worker who had shot a fellow carnie. Layne had information that this fugitive was hiding out in Gibsonton, Florida, or Gib town as it is known, a small town famed for being the winter home of circus sideshow and carnival attractions. As Layne discovered, carnies and circus people have their own strict code of silence, much like the traditional *omerta* of organized crime. Or, as Layne puts it,

They wouldn't tell you if your hair was on fire.

But eventually someone led us to Lobster Boy, a man who was born with a birth defect that resulted in a sort of web holding all his fingers together, except his thumb. His hands really did look like lobster claws. Lobster Boy's girlfriend was a midget and when we went in to speak to them, she hopped up on a chair and her feet stuck straight out; her legs didn't even reach the end of the seat. After doing this job for a while, you begin to believe that you've seen just about everything there is to see, but this was different; this was very different. At first they didn't want to talk to me, but I after I explained to them that this was a dangerous guy—

he had shot at one carnie and eventually he was going to kill somebody, maybe even them—they began cooperating. They told me where he was, giving me the address of a small house in town. We decided to hit that place before dawn the next morning.

It turned out to be a very foggy Florida morning, so foggy you could barely see your hand in front of your face. The house was a very small, cheesy little place, and a little travel trailer was parked about thirty yards away from it. As we were creeping up on the house, we suddenly heard a tremendous roar. My first thought was, *That sounds like lions and tigers.* My second thought was, *That is lions and tigers.* The hair on my head and my whole body stood up. Then I remembered we were in Gib town. I thought, *Jeez, I hope they're chained up.* It was weird, especially because we couldn't see anything. As we got closer a light went on in the trailer. We intended to hit the house first because Lobster Boy had told us they were there. But when a light went on in the trailer, I figured the roaring must have woken up whoever was in there, which meant we had to secure that person first.

We hit the trailer. We made our entry and found our bad guy actually was living there. We hooked him up, then asked him where they were keeping the lions and tigers. "They're in the house," he said. In the house? They were living in the house. The lions and tigers were living in the house; the people were living in the trailer. These people would feed them by tossing food through a window. If we had gone into the house in the dark, we would have had a very serious problem. Every deputy has had to deal with dogs, including pit bulls, at some point in their career—but lions and tigers? Our informer hadn't told us about that.

People also will give you information when it's to their advantage to see the fugitive caught; it's not at all unusual, for example, for members of a drug organization to provide information about competitors. Generally, by the time a case gets to the Marshals Service a fugitive has already made a lot of enemies, and identifying them and finding them often makes a big difference. Women especially will tell law enforcement pretty much everything they know if they suspect a man is lying to them or cheating on them. Geri Doody made a point of empathizing with wives and girlfriends, saying she understood how really hard it was to deal with a guy like that—before casually mentioning that she had seen their man with another woman.

Every deputy knows that anger can be a great motivational tool. One very cold winter day, for example, Deputy Robert Leschorn was looking for an escapee in Brooklyn and started at his last known address, his father's house. Leschorn and his partner knocked on the door, and the elderly man who answered was crying. His son had come home looking for money, he told them, and when he refused to give it to him, he had kicked in his TV set, and that TV set was about all he had. Leschorn showed him the fugitive's photograph; that was his son, he said, then told them, "He's down on Fulton Street. He's looking to rob somebody."

"Our perp was a street crook," Leschorn remembers.

This was the kind of guy who gets up in the morning looking to commit a crime so he can get what he needs to survive that day. They're people who prey on other people and make a hard life even more difficult, especially in a neighborhood like this one where people don't have a lot of things. When you take a guy like this off the street, you've made a real difference in people's lives. We went down to the Fulton Street area looking for him. At that time, it was a very rough neighborhood. There were shootings and holdups in that area every day. But we didn't see him. At that time I carried two six-shot snub-nosed .38s in holsters that had been sewn into the pockets of my jacket. I know that sounds a little strange, but my theory was that when I'm in a bad neighborhood, I'm not going to have time to get my gun out so if someone starts shooting at me, I'll fire back right through my coat. I felt it gave me a slight advantage, but in certain situations that slight advantage could make a big difference. Like this turned out to be.

It was freezing cold, but we were standing outside showing a picture of the fugitive to people and asking if they had seen him when suddenly somebody stuck something in my back and demanded, "Gimme all your money. I'm not playing around." It definitely felt like a gun. I put my hands in my pockets and turned around—and it's my perp. The guy I'm after. And he's holding a metal pipe in his hand. "I'm not playing with you," he said again.

I took one step backward and pulled both my guns out of my pockets and pointed them at him. "You're under arrest," I said. "I could've shot you already. How dumb can you be?" Actually, I already knew the answer to that question: my partner and I were the only two white guys in the middle of a very tough block and it hadn't occurred to him that maybe we were cops? We took him in, and the judge later gave him a long sentence. After we made the arrest, my partner and I went back to the father's apartment and told him his son was in jail. We felt so bad for him that we gave him some money toward a new TV.

For some people, informing is a business; they know information is valuable and expect to be paid for providing it. A lot of people who live in this world are pretty far down on the economic ladder, or they're using drugs, so a few dollars will make a big difference in their lives. They are willing to do whatever is necessary to feed their personal beast. Deputies understand that and in many cases are willing to negotiate a reasonable payment. Deputy Chris Dudley had an informer who helped him with several major drug trafficking cases, and expected to be paid. "His first request was always one million dollars and we would negotiate down from there," Dudley said. "We'd usually end up paying him about a thousand. He carried around a silver briefcase. He helped out on a couple of good cases, but like many informants a lot of the information he tried to sell us wasn't very reliable. The Internet was just becoming widely available, and it became obvious that much of the information he was trying to sell us came from online fugitive posters. That's actually the problem with most informers, you have to sift through the material they give you to figure out what is real."

"They all want something," Bobby Sanchez maintains.

I had a Miami case, this guy was on the FBI's local Top 10 list. One of my informants told me he could give him to me, but he wanted a lot of money. We settled on $10,000. The FBI told me they would make that deal if we could grab the fugitive. My informant told me he was going to meet him in an apartment. The plan was that as soon as he left that meeting he would call and tell me exactly which apartment it was, "but you have to hit it and grab him right away because if you miss him he's going to know it was me who called you and I'm dead." That's the way it went down. We were waiting outside, ready to go. As soon as he gave us the apartment we hit the place and grabbed our guy. He was doing it for money.

They all want something. Getting handcuffs on fugitives who flee to Mexico has always been a long and often difficult process. Two decades ago, one deputy had informants inside Mexico who needed things that couldn't be bought there. Obviously this doesn't work the same way today, but this deputy would let his contacts there know exactly who he wanted and they would let him know what they needed in return. Within a reasonable period of time he would receive a phone call informing him that his fugitive could be found handcuffed to a chair in a local McDonald's.

Sometimes what people really want is help for the fugitive. When the Marshals Service set up its Puerto Rico Fugitive Task Force in an office previously occupied by the FBI, they decided to go after the FBI's most wanted fugitives. The first person on the list was known as Purletia, Little Pearl, whose real name was Juan Zuniga. He was associated with a drug organization and had broken into the New Rochelle, New York, home of a man who owed $500,000 to that organization, held the man and his wife at gunpoint, and taken their one-year-old child. Ten days later the child was discovered alive in a San Juan apartment; three people were arrested, but Zuniga escaped. Deputies got word that Purletia's girlfriend was flying to New York, and they were waiting for her when she got off the airplane. To their surprise she seemed genuinely happy to see them. "He wants to turn himself in," she said. "Right now he's in hiding, and he's afraid that if the local cops catch him on the street, they'll kill him. He won't turn himself in to the FBI because he doesn't trust them."

And he did not want to be locked up in a Puerto Rican jail because he was afraid the other prisoners would kill him for kidnapping a baby. He was faced with an odd choice: his only way to be certain he would survive was to surrender to U.S. marshals. Purletia's girlfriend told them she would contact them to make the arrangements the next day. They didn't know whether or not to believe her, but they had little choice; there was no reason to hold her.

In fact, as promised she called the following morning. She would arrange his surrender, she said, but in exchange, he wanted their word that he would not be held in a local jail and would be flown back to New York that same day. Deputies couldn't guarantee it would be the same day—legally he had to appear before a judge—but they did agree that he would be held in a Marshals Service's cellblock where he would be protected and as soon as he appeared before a judge he would be flown back to the United States. Given those assurances, Zuniga's girlfriend made the necessary arrangements for the meeting—and he actually was pleased to surrender to U.S. marshals. Mike Earp crossed the first name off the list the FBI had left behind.

Charlie Carneglia was a stone-cold killer, a made member of John Gotti's crew in the Gambino crime family. Carneglia eventually became infamous for disposing of victim's bodies in a barrel of acid. After a warrant was issued for his arrest, he went into the air. Deputies hit all his usual haunts, but there was no trace of him. As Mike Pizzi remembers,

We decided to shake things up by interfering with the family business. We started hitting their chop shops, the places they tore up stolen cars for parts, and generally making it obvious we weren't going anywhere until we had Carneglia. Just before Easter, Charlie's brother John paid me a visit. This was about the last person I expected to help us. John was a pretty heavy guy himself; at that time he had a pending drug case with Gene Gotti for which he eventually got fifty years. Turned out he was offering more than information. He came in and he asked, "You think we could have an Easter dinner with the family without having to worry that you guys are going to come busting in?" I asked him what was on his mind. "If we could just have a little family dinner with my brother, I'll bring him in Monday."

That's all he asked for, one Easter dinner. I spoke to our supervisor, who told me nobody had any plans to go after Carneglia on Easter Sunday and let me make the deal. Monday morning, John walked Charlie in the door.

Daniel Stoltz got one of the strangest requests of his career while hunting for a Puerto Rican prison escapee believed to be in Florida.

I had an informant in Miami and it was clear he had some information about the person we were chasing, but he wouldn't talk to me. He wasn't interested in money, but finally he told me what he really wanted: a goat and two chickens. Okay, a goat and two chickens. I didn't ask what he intended to do with them. I knew a place in Orlando that raised goats, so I drove up there in my small Camaro and bought a goat and two chickens. I put them in the backseat of my car and drove them all the way back to Miami. There were times I wondered about the wisdom of this decision. That goat made a terrible mess in my car. And I also wondered how I was going to put a goat and two chickens on my small expense account. But when I showed up with the animals, my informant gave me the escapee's cell-phone number. I gave it to our international desk, and we were able to get up on his phone and we found out exactly when and how he was coming into Miami from the Dominican Republic. We missed him at the airport coming in but caught him walking on a beach in Miami a little while later.

Often informers are looking to make a deal to improve their own legal situation or to help a family member or friend solve a problem. In return for information, they want the deputy to tell a prosecutor that they were helpful or to tell a cop that they provided good information. Sometimes they want to help a specific person get a reduced sentence or, if in prison, some form of better treatment. "Informants are a mixed bag," explains Jerry Lowery.

Ideally you'd want to work with a member of the church choir who had been an Eagle Scout, but we don't run into too many of them. A lot of the people we use are down in the gutter where they can produce the information we need. We had a murderer in Miami whose street name was Boobie and he was running a crew of about nine guys known as the Boobie Boys. The Boobie Boys were responsible for as many as twenty murders. I had an informant who was a true pain in the ass. He would show up at my office drunk; he would promise to set something up, and it would be delayed five or six times. He was always getting into trouble, but he could produce just about anything I asked him to produce. He set up a buy with Boobie and we successfully took him down with two kilos of dope, some other drugs, buyers, and weapons.

But about three weeks after that, my informant got arrested again. His defense attorney called me and wanted me to confirm that he worked for me. He certainly did, I said. Did he do good? I said he did good. He asked me to testify on his behalf and I said I would, but before I did that I'd better make sure he knew the other side of the story. I told him all the negative things, then asked, "You can swear me in and put me on the stand and ask me any question, but then the prosecution gets to ask me questions that I have to answer. Do you really want that?" He laughed. "Forget it," he said.

Most informers working for the FBI or the DEA are eventually going to be asked to wear a wire or make undercover buys or risk exposure by testifying in court. The Marshals Service is a lot easier to work with: when marshals catch a fugitive based on the information he or she provides, they will tell the prosecutor or the judge that the informant helped them—while protecting his or her identity. Whenever Joseph Lobue made an arrest, even on a minor probation violation, he would take part in the booking and at some point in the process, tell the suspect, "You want to help yourself maybe? You know I can help you out, but I need something. You know anything about any homicides, any drug information? You know where there's a stash house?"

And whenever I got information I would share it with the proper agency. At one point I had a guy out of Brooklyn looking for a little help with his problem and he told me about a local Chinese takeout place that was selling guns. It was an interesting situation: I'll have a quart of wonton, Uncle Tao's chicken, and a .38 Special to go, please. I contacted people I had worked with in the ATF and we sent in an undercover, who came out with fried rice and an automatic in a little Styrofoam box. We made three gun buys and ended up arresting the people who worked there and closing down the place.

Convincing people who don't want to help law enforcement to give up information is an art that can be mastered with practice. Each situation is different and requires its own approach. A veteran deputy will use all the various strategies until he or she hits on the right one. Often it's simply persistence, going back to see the same person again and again until that person gets so sick of being bothered he or she will talk just to be left alone. When a young Memphis, Tennessee, girl finally told her mother that two men living in their home, forty-five-year-old Winfred Scott and his twenty-two-year-old son Akeem Scott, had been raping her for several years, her mother reported them to law enforcement. Both men fled before they could be arrested. The Tennessee Bureau of Investigation put both men on its 10 Most Wanted list and requested assistance from the Marshals Service. The Marshals Service has focused on sex crimes, especially those involving minor children, for a long time; the Sex Offender Investigations Branch (SOIB), which was created in 2006 following the passage of the Adam Walsh Child Protection and Safety Act, made the Marshals Service the primary federal agency offering assistance to state and local departments tracking and pursuing people like the Scotts.

For almost two years there was no sign of either Scott, but in 2008 the case was assigned to Deputy Stephanie Creasy. She remembers,

Winfred and Akeem Scott had told everyone they were going to California to become rappers, but we found no evidence that they actually had moved there. As I was going over all the reports, one name kept popping up and when I asked about it, nobody knew who she was. From talking to people I found out that this was Winfred Scott's biological daughter. We were able to determine that she hadn't been in contact with him for a long time, but she'd recently found him on the Internet and reached out to him. She was living in California—it turned out that he had been out there and she had helped him establish a window cleaning business. But apparently he'd felt some heat coming down and by the time we got there he had left the state.

While doing background research about the daughter, Creasy was able to connect her to an apartment in Kansas City. She gave that information to the Kansas City Career Criminal Task Force and they found Winfred Scott living there under the name Travis Best.

Creasy continues,

We had the father, but we still couldn't find Akeem. What made it even more difficult is that there were no fingerprints on record for him; he'd never been arrested or detained for any reason. I was convinced other members of the family knew more than they were telling me, so I just kept going back to see them over and over and over. I interviewed the same people endless times, and every time I called them out on their lies. They just didn't want to tell me anything. You try to put people in an uncomfortable position so they'll talk to you just to get rid of you. I would go see them at work, and they definitely did not want to be bothered in the workplace; they didn't want their coworkers knowing there was an issue with them. I would interrupt them at a relative's house or a friend's house; I just wouldn't go away. And I kept warning them that until we find him I was going to continue coming back. Finally an informant who initially would not talk to me at all got so sick and tired of being bothered that this person gave me a few bits of new information. This person told me Akeem's girlfriend's first name and, most importantly, the fact that his older brother had been born with a serious birth deformity: at birth the doctor had pulled him out and messed up his arm. Akeem's brother had a bad arm, a fact no one had ever mentioned to me. I don't think this informer realized how important this might be. I think they told me this just to get rid of me.

Creasy suspected Akeem might be using his brother's ID. In checking she found out that someone using the brother's name had had some minor issues with law enforcement, parking tickets and things like that.

I put out the information that Akeem could be living under his brother's name, and that any officer who came in contact with him should look for that deformity; if that person had two perfectly formed and usable arms, it was Akeem. That's exactly what happened. Two weeks after Winfred Scott was arrested, deputies found Akeem at the apartment he was living in with his girlfriend. As he had done before, he claimed to be his brother and produced his brother's ID as well as a photograph. This time he didn't get away with it. When deputies arrested him, he started fighting and had to be Tased, and even then continued fighting. Eventually he was subdued and extradited to Tennessee, where he was sentenced to ten years in prison. His father was sentenced to eight years. But what made that arrest possible was the information we got from an informant.

Getting a person to talk often comes down to the carrot or the stick, the carrot being the knowledge that there are good reasons to cooperate. Family members

especially want to protect a son or brother, but sometimes they have to be convinced he is going to be
arrested eventually and it would be best for everyone if
it was the Marshals Service deputies who caught him.
Deputy Donald Ward always tried to give people a good
reason to work with him. "When we were in New York
looking for someone wanted on a federal drug charge,
for example, I would explain to those people who really
cared about the fugitive, 'If we find him we can get
him into a program, we can get him somewhere where
he can get some help, but if the NYPD arrests him he's
going to Rikers Island and they don't have any programs there. By helping me you're helping him.'"

Geri Doody would tell them, "Look, if they put a
wanted poster up in the post office, it's going to say
armed and dangerous, and you're better off having
your son in jail than having him shot or killed." Doody
never hesitated to tell a fugitive's relatives, especially
when drugs were involved, that her own son had once
been a heroin addict—even though she actually doesn't
have any children.

Invariably, according to James Benjamin, parents
would say, "If he gets in touch with me . . ."

And I would stop them and tell them, "It isn't if,
it's when. Then you have to decide if you're going

to call me or not. We want to get him off the street for his own safety as well as the public's safety. Believe me, this warrant's not going away; he's going to stay a fugitive until we catch him. If he's asleep in a hotel somewhere, tell me now, because we don't want him getting stopped by some uniformed police officer who doesn't know he's a federal fugitive and it ends up in a gunfight."

I remember speaking with the grandmother of a major drug smuggler who was living on the west side of San Antonio. His mother was dead and the grandmother was his closest relative. She lied to me and told me she hadn't heard from him. I told her we had two eyewitnesses who had seen him at her house the day before. I reminded her that we were going to catch her grandson, it was just a question of how tough it was going to be for him. She called us the next day and told us he was there and we made the arrest.

When the carrot doesn't work, marshals will bring down the stick. Deputies will tell people, especially family members, that if they are withholding information they will be arrested for harboring a fugitive, and in some cases after the fugitive has been apprehended they will do just that. There is a federal statute that makes aiding or abetting a federal fugitive a crime. In many situations it's an effective tool—but only if it is enforced. "If you don't arrest them," Don Ward said, "you've lost all credibility forever. The word gets around and people pay no attention to you."

Sometimes it is absolutely necessary to put pressure on people to force them to talk. The very first case assigned to brand-new deputy Rick Gainey involved a Dominican wanted by the ATF for running guns and drugs. The fugitive had been on the run for more than seven years when the case was reopened. Gainey and his partner started from the very beginning, going back to reinterview most of the same people who had refused to cooperate years earlier. But there had been some changes in their lives: seven years earlier the people who had signed the fugitive's bond had no property, so they had nothing to lose by not talking. Since then their building had become a condo and they'd bought the apartment they were living in. The value of their apartment had appreciated tremendously, so suddenly they had considerable equity to protect. The government could put a lien against their property and potentially foreclose if these people didn't cooperate. Given that choice, they changed their minds. Although they didn't know where the fugitive was living, they gave Gainey the names of two people who were in touch with him. "We looked at both of those people; when we interviewed them, we knew they were lying to us," Gainey says. "But we also knew that as soon as we walked out they were going to contact the fugitive to warn him that we were after him. We tracked them and discovered they had contacted someone in Providence, Rhode Island. That phone number came back to a pager. That pager led us to a restaurant and eventually we were able to connect him to that place and finally make the arrest." But without forcing the people who had signed his bond to cooperate, the fugitive may never have been found.

In another case, a man named Jonathan Sampson George, who had been charged by the federal government under the Armed Career Criminal Act, which basically added twenty years to life to the sentences of felons who commit crimes using a firearm, walked out of a county courthouse in Chula Vista, California. He had been left alone in a small glassed enclosure, broke through a door, and made his way through the judge's chambers to the street. He was gone. Jim Schield was working with a county marshal named Adam Truitt and, as he describes it,

We were like magic together. We arrested a lot of people. We had tremendous chemistry and even before we walked into an interview we knew exactly how it was going to go depending on which one of us opened his mouth first. A few days after Jonathan George escaped, Adam got some information that he had been hiding out in a pet shop in southeast San Diego. I wasn't working that day and Adam went over there to speak to the owner—it turned out George was still there. He surprised George, who managed to make his getaway by stopping a car, ripping open the door, and throwing the driver into the street. Everything immediately got ratcheted up a few notches.

Adam and I sat down with the pet shop owner and I explained to him that Adam was the local guy and I was the federal guy and that we were about to become his worst f—ing nightmare. The owner claimed he hadn't known George was an escaped felon. George's father used to bring his dog to the shop, he said, and George had asked if he could sleep in the back one night. Since then he had stayed there on and off. We came down hard on the owner and he was scared to death. I told him, "Look, you're done. It's too late. The only way you can change this is if he comes back and you call me." A few nights later we got that call. I jumped in my car and Adam jumped in his car and we raced there at a hundred miles an hour.

We believed George was armed. We were told that when he hijacked that car he had a gun. I was carrying a sawed-off short-barreled shotgun. When we got there, we set up a perimeter. A deputy named Ralph Garafala and I were out in front, two other guys were in the back. We were waiting for additional support to arrive when George spotted us. We couldn't wait. As we busted open the front door George kicked open the office door; I was sure he was coming right to me. I leveled that shotgun and got ready for him, but instead of coming out the front he ran through the store and out the back door—right into the hands of our people waiting for him. He was big guy and he slammed into a fence, which stunned him a little bit. The guys in the back were rolling around in the dog shit trying to control him. Finally we managed to get cuffs on him. We put him under arrest and that was it. At least we thought that was it.

Three months later as George was being transferred to a court hearing by a lone female sheriff's deputy, he managed to get out of his transport chains and kicked open the side of the van. When the deputy tried to stop him, he overpowered her and beat her with her own gun. Then he took off running toward downtown San Diego. During that escape he carjacked another car—but this time the owner resisted. George didn't hesitate; he shot and killed him. Schield says,

For the next week this was the only case we worked, twenty-four hours a day. We retraced all the steps we'd originally taken, talking to the same people over and over. This time, because it was a cold-blooded murder case, there was a lot of media attention. A fugitive has to have resources to stay on the run so we knew he was either going to commit more crimes or convince somebody to help him. We went to see his mother, his sister, his sister's friends, his girlfriend, his old girlfriends—we kept the pressure on. For a time we thought he might have gone south into Mexico; instead he went north, north to an old drug connection who tipped us off he was going that way. We hit every place he might go and made sure everybody knew that if they helped him in any way they were going to jail, because this was now a death penalty case.

I was never much of a believer in surveillance. There are guys who will sit on a house for hours and days. I never thought that was a good use of my time; I like to go out and ruffle feathers to make things move along. I would just as soon go knock on the door and talk to people and tell them we're looking at them. Once they knew we had associated them with the fugitive I could cross that off my list; that was one less place for that fugitive to go. If I had five places I could associate with a fugitive, I might hit four of them and then have a neighbor watch the fifth one for me.

During the investigation, task force personnel interviewed several men who had been friendly with George in prison. One of them was a gang member living up in Irvine. Schield's team took a state parole officer with them when they hit the guy's house. "We really rattled his cage," Schield explains.

I took him into the garage with me and explained exactly what was going to happen to him if I found out he had any information he wasn't giving us. I did not paint a nice picture of his future. I told him flatly, "I know you've had contact with him." Truthfully I didn't know that for sure, but we had closed down so many other people and places that I just felt sure he did. But I said it in a way that didn't leave any doubt that I knew it. He had to believe I had some information I wasn't telling him.

He thought about it for a minute or two, then gave us an address in Compton.

I told my supervisor, "We got him." We sent an army up to Compton. I threw my informer into the back of my car and told him, "You're not making a phone call—and if he's not there you're going back to jail." We had six people there when we hit the house. George went running out the back into the arms of our people waiting there for him. He was on his stomach, his hands cuffed behind him, and I went up to him and told him, "Hey, Jonathan, we caught you again."

We tracked him almost entirely through informants; most of them had a lot more to lose by helping him than helping us.

In terms of playing hardball with informants, there are legal actions that can be taken and others that are strictly prohibited. For example, when police officers across the nation were searching for serial killer Kenneth Allen McDuff, Dan Stoltz felt certain McDuff's parents knew where he was but were refusing to cooperate, so he told the helicopter pilots to shine their searchlight on the house every single time they flew over it. He wanted to remind them that law enforcement was still looking for their son and wasn't going to stop until he was captured or killed. Stoltz's hope was that they would become so irritated by the light they would tell authorities what they knew. It didn't work, exactly: "While his mother never gave us any information, when I interviewed her she complained that the federal government was sending radiation into her house through those searchlights. I thought she was very serious when she said it."

U.S. deputy marshals strictly follow American law, but those laws don't apply in other parts of the world. Sometimes law enforcement officers in those countries make up the rules as they go along, interpreting them very casually. When the Marshals Service was looking for a killer who had escaped to a Caribbean island, for example, deputies learned he was hiding somewhere in a certain region. A high-ranking island police official told marshals, "Just give me the information. I will catch the guy." A week later he handed over the fugitive. When asked how he did it, he explained, "We found out this guy had a sister. We grabbed the sister's husband off the street, put a bag over his head, and the guy peed himself. He believed we were going to kill him and so he told us everything he knew." Apparently the sister visited her brother in a building every weekend. It was a three-story building with four apartments on each floor. The husband knew the address of the building, but did not know exactly which apartment the fugitive was in. Local police brought buckets of water into the building and sloshed water under the front door of each apartment. When the people inside the apartments saw the water flowing in, they opened the door to find out where it was coming from—until finally the right door opened and the fugitive was standing there. He was immediately arrested.

Some informants provide information because they're desperate for attention. Knowing how much power they have makes them feel important, and they enjoy it. The problem with many of that type of informants is that they lie often and too easily. In fact, almost all informants lie much of the time. They lie for a lot of reasons beyond not wanting to help law enforcement; sometimes they are afraid to tell the truth because they've been threatened, occasionally they want to screw with law enforcement, and sometimes it is just because they want that feeling of power. The reason why they lie isn't important; a lie is a lie. Mike Bunk admits he is a terrible interviewer:

Most of the time I don't count on people to help me, especially family members. One time we were looking for two brothers who had escaped from prison in Florida. We went to speak with the family, and I pulled the head of this family aside to speak with him. He was a polite southern gentleman. I told him right away that whatever he said to me I was going to think he was lying, that it didn't matter what he said, I wasn't going to believe him, but he was still willing to talk. We actually talked for more than an hour and finally I asked him if he would take a lie detector test. All of a sudden he got very defensive and said, "You think I'm lying?" and just started going off on me.

"Yeah," I said. "I do." Then I reminded him that right at the beginning I told him I was going to think that everything he said was a lie, "and I've kept my word!"

He started laughing and admitted, "You got me on that," and agreed to take the lie detector test, which he passed.

Most deputies just assume at least a portion of everything an informant tells them will not be totally accurate. The question usually is how much of it is a lie. Bobby Sanchez was looking for a killer in the Dominican Republic and went with local law enforcement to the man's mother-in-law's house, where his wife supposedly was staying. The mother was there with a woman who introduced herself as the fugitive's sister-in-law. She told Sanchez, "Yeah, that's my sister's husband, but he's not here. My sister knows where he is but she won't tell me. Leave me your card and if I find out anything, I will call you." Over the next few weeks, Sanchez and the sister developed a good working relationship; she would call him regularly with updates: "He's in Europe, but he's supposed to come back next month."

When Sanchez asked to meet his informant's sister, she told him that wasn't a good idea. "You can't do that. She doesn't know I am talking to you. If she finds out, she's going to go crazy and stop telling me things." It was obvious this woman did not like her sister; she was constantly complaining about her to him; once she was furious because her sister had borrowed her car and wrecked it, another time she had stolen money from her purse. She painted a picture of a very troubled and difficult person.

This continued for several months until Sanchez got a call from the mother, who told him, "I want to tell you this is not my business, but you need to be careful." When Sanchez asked why, she continued, "That is [the fugitive's] wife you're talking to and I don't think he appreciates that you are asking her all these questions all the time." The fugitive's wife? Sanchez had been completely fooled. Just about every word out of his informer's mouth had been a lie, and he had wasted a lot of time working with her.

When a case goes national, deputies will receive literally hundreds of tips, almost all of them turning out to be worthless. In one case, seven prisoners killed a police officer after escaping from a Texas penitentiary, and the hunt for them became major news. "We got calls from everywhere," Jimmy Bankston remembers. "The volume of calls was amazing. Our problem was trying to determine which leads were worth following up on. Sometimes you can tell just by asking a few questions. For example, a woman called to tell us she'd been with one of the escapees, 'I danced with him in Niagara Falls and at the end of the night he proposed to me. He said he was going to take me on his jet across the world.' We figured we could discount that tip pretty quickly. But we have to listen to every call and then try to figure out how to use our manpower."

At times it is very easy to determine that someone is lying. Deputy Bill Sorukas always carried both a photograph of the fugitive he was pursuing and a second photograph of a person who had absolutely nothing to do with the case.

If I got up on the doorstep and there was something about the house that made me wonder if I could trust this person not to alert the fugitive, I'd show the second picture and ask if they had seen him. One time a woman opened the door and I told her that I needed to talk to her about a fugitive I was looking for, then I showed her my credentials. She looked at my credentials and nodded, then said, "I've seen that guy." Thank you very much.

Even when deputies suspect people are lying, or telling less than the entire truth, they will continue to ask a lot of questions. They do that because people often give away a lot more information than they intend to, even when they're lying. When they do reveal potentially important information, most deputies won't react; instead they'll act as if they didn't hear it and continue asking questions.

One of the basic tenets of conducting an interview is to never let the subject know what you already know. If you do, they'll sometimes feed it right back or make sure they stay away from that subject. Asking the same questions to several different people can begin to tell a bigger story: When was the last time you saw him? What did he look like? Did he dye his hair? Did he tell you where he had been or where he was going? Was he alone or with someone? Information gets confirmed, places the fugitive has frequented get mentioned, past events get brought out, names of associates get dropped, the fact a person travels by bus rather than train is revealed—every fact counts and eventually it all begins to add up. "If you're persistent," Stephanie Creasy says, "you're going to get something out of them. It's often a piece of information that person has no idea is valuable to you; they don't think it means anything, and they just want to get rid of you, but it turns out to be the turning point in the investigation."

The goal of any interviewer is to make subjects comfortable; that requires making them feel important, showing them that they are needed and that you have great respect for them. Once people get really comfortable they relax and sometimes lose control of what information comes out of their mouths. Deputies in Atlanta had a street informer who sold information for cash. One night they were driving through an especially rough area of the city when this informer suddenly jumped into the back of the car and crouched down behind the seat where he couldn't be seen. He stayed there talking about what was going down on the street, trying to find something he could sell to the deputies. So when they asked him about a certain fugitive, he got very excited. "I know him," he told them. "I know exactly where he is." When they asked if he was sure the fugitive was still at that address, he told them, "Damn right I know it. Because I just sold him a pound of weed." And as he heard those words coming out of his mouth, he realized exactly what he had just done. "Ah man," he said, "you got me." And, in fact, they did have to charge him.

Alcohol and drugs often make people so comfortable that they really can't control what they are saying. Although obviously deputies can't provide either one to potential informants, when they find someone who has been drinking or doing drugs, they can ask any and many questions. John Bolen and his partner, Roger Daniel, had been chasing a man through eastern Kentucky for several months. Bolen remembers,

> We knew that he frequented this one bar but we could never pin him down there. The bartender was a good source of ours and he would call us when the guy came in, but this place was about forty minutes from our office, and by the time we could get there, he'd be long gone. No one knew where he lived or who he was staying with. It was just one of those unlucky deals; those nights we would go sit on this bar he wouldn't show up and when we weren't there, he'd stop in for a quick

drink. Our bad luck was consistent. But one night we got a call from the bartender telling us our guy had come in early, and if he stayed as late as he usually did, we might get lucky. Roger and I both raced to get there.

When we got there he wasn't in the bar; the bartender didn't know where he'd gone but pointed out that his truck was still in the parking lot. More importantly, the man he'd come in with was still there drinking. As this second man came out of the bathroom we double-teamed him. We could smell the alcohol on his breath from several feet away. He was three sheets to the wind, just out of it. But he was game; he tried very hard not to give us any information while at the same time he was telling us everything we wanted to know—although he had no idea he was doing it. He was the perfect informant. At the same time he told us he hadn't seen his friend, he also told us he was with a woman he'd been sitting with at the bar; at the same time he insisted he didn't know where they had gone, he was telling us they were out in the parking lot in her car. That's where we found them, having sex in the car in the parking lot. We knocked on the window, then ordered him to pull up his pants and step outside of the car.

Actually, finding a wanted person while they're naked or having sex isn't that unusual, and it's not necessarily a bad thing. As most deputies have learned from experience, naked people are less likely to run. And it's pretty simple to determine they aren't armed.

Many people are naturally intimidated when speaking with law enforcement officers, which will lead them to provide good information. In 1969, Harry Hantman had been found not guilty by reason of insanity for the rape and murder of an eleven-year-old girl and had been committed to a Washington, D.C., mental hospital for the criminally insane. Five years later a staffer took him out of the facility to Christmas mass and he escaped. For almost two decades he had successfully evaded capture, but when the Marshals Service initiated an intensive effort to track down violent sex offenders still on the loose, the case was assigned to Bill Bonk and Geoffrey Shank. The two deputies dug through all the records but found nothing. Very few fugitives are able to stay out of the system for two decades, but somehow Hantman had managed to do it. During their investigation, Bonk and Shank learned that Hantman's brother, Bill Hantman, had killed their mother only a few years earlier and had then committed suicide. Looking at photographs of the crime scene, both deputies were struck by the fact that there was no blood anywhere in the room. That was very strange, like Arthur Conan Doyle's dog that didn't bark, and it stood out. It was obvious that someone had cleaned up the crime scene. But there was no reference to anything like that in the records.

A Montgomery County, Maryland, detective told the deputies that when Bill Hantman had killed himself, he'd had a close friend named Nick, and the detective provided Nick's contact information. Shank drove up to Bethesda, Maryland, with a Marshals Service contract employee, parked outside Nick's workplace, then called him; "Hey, Nick," Shank said, identifying himself as a deputy marshal, "I need to talk to you." Nick replied that he couldn't talk at that time, he was at work. "I know, I'm sitting outside. You need to come out and talk to me right now, or I'm going to come in and grab you in front of everybody."

As they waited for Nick to come out, the contract employee wondered, "What are you going to ask him?"

Shank shook his head. "I have no clue, man, we're just going to play it by ear."

Nick sat down in the front seat. Shank introduced himself and said somberly, "I think you know why we're here, right?"

With that Nick turned ashen white and said, "You're here for the tape, right?"

"That's it," Shank told him, although he had absolutely no idea what tape Nick was referring to. "I knew you had it. We can do this the easy way or the hard way, it's up to you. I'm coming back here tomorrow morning, and I expect you to get your thoughts straight. You bring me that tape and tell me everything you know and we're good; otherwise I'm going to have to put you in jail."

Nick was terrified; Shank was mystified. He didn't know if Nick was talking about an audiotape, a VCR tape, or even if it was related to the search for Harry Hantman. All he knew was that Nick was too frightened to be less than totally honest. The next morning Nick produced a cassette tape from an answering machine. As Shank recalls,

When we listened to the tape, we heard Nick's voice, which we assumed was the reason he took it. He definitely did not want to be associated with the murder-suicide. We played the tape over and over, and one of the messages was left by a person we would later positively identify as Harry Hantman, who was calling in with a coded message for his family. The message didn't seem to make any sense, even after we had it transcribed. We actually asked the CIA to try to decipher it, and they worked on it without success for two weeks. Bill Bonk's wife worked at another government agency and we drove up there to give it to their cryptologists. We handed it to one of their people and sat down to have a cup of coffee. Practically before we'd finished he came back, tossed an English-to-French dictionary on the table, and said, "I cracked it."

Yeah, right, we thought, *the CIA couldn't do it in two weeks, he did it in less than a half hour?* But, in fact, he had broken the code. Hantman was giving instructions to his family, telling them how to send him money, where to meet him, and what he was doing. It was the first piece of new evidence uncovered since 1974. It provided evidence that Hantman had been in Fairfax, Virginia, within the last few months.

After that, as Shank remembers, the investigation moved rapidly.

We sent fingerprint cards and wanted posters to every state, asking them to check them against their databases—and we got a hit. We discovered that several years earlier Hantman had been picked up by the Secret Service for counterfeiting under the name of Thomas Andrew Dorian. Incredibly, when they submitted his fingerprints to the FBI, they had been misidentified. That happens once in about a hundred million searches, but it happened in this case. The Secret Service had had him and they'd let him go. But once we had his alias, the pieces began fitting together. He had been living in the Pacific Northwest for two decades as Tom Dorian, an identity he'd taken from a George Washington University student who had died in 1973; even more amazing, under that name he actually had served eighteen months in a Multnomah County jail for burglary, kidnapping, and assault and was currently wanted in Oregon on four felony charges for the kidnapping, rape, and sodomy of an Oregon State University coed.

Once the Marshals Service had Hantman's alias it became much easier to track him. Like so many other fugitives, Hantman may have been relying on the fact that local law enforcement didn't have the authority, or the manpower, to pursue him out of state. Three weeks after he had been properly identified, deputies arrested him outside a Lewiston, Idaho, motel. He was returned to prison—and eventually he killed himself. No one knows for certain how many crimes he committed during the twenty-year period after escaping from St. Elizabeth's, but there is strong speculation he may have been involved in several other unsolved murders.

Deputies never know what they're going to learn when they start asking questions, and no matter how many years a deputy has been doing the job, no matter how many questions he or she has asked of how many hundreds and thousands of people, there still are going to be surprises. During a sweep of old and cold cases, Bill Noble went to speak with a man about a relative who had escaped from prison almost two decades earlier and hadn't been seen since. It was a case that had come from another federal agency. Noble wasn't expecting much of anything when he sat down with the man and started talking to him. So he was surprised when the man suddenly broke down and started sobbing. That definitely was not the reaction he had been expecting.

I sat there and let him cry, then explained to him that sometimes it's really tough to do the right thing, but in the end it works out best for everyone. And then this man told me, "I've been waiting for over twenty years for someone to ask me what you just asked me." He proceeded to tell me the name this relative had been living under and what city he was living in. I went back to the office and did a computer search and found his exact address. Then I called the Marshals Service office in that city and told the supervisor that I really didn't trust my informant not to have second thoughts about what he'd done and call up to warn the fugitive. "I need deputies to respond right away," I said. They did, and they found him at the address I gave them and arrested him.

A final lesson every deputy has learned is that no matter how long you spend interviewing someone there is always one more question that should be asked. Jerry Lowery was hunting a fugitive in Puerto Rico and interviewed his female associate, who was serving time in a California state prison. "We interviewed her three or four times," he remembers.

It had been a long and very tedious process because we were using an interpreter, so every question and every answer had to be translated. And then it had to be asked again because we were never sure the translation was completely accurate. Finally, near the end of the final interview I said something to the interpreter, and before he could answer, she turned to me and responded in clear English. It was stunning. For more than a month we had been totally convinced she didn't speak a word of English. I just looked at her and asked, "Why the hell didn't you tell us you spoke English?"

And she answered as if it were the most obvious thing, "Nobody asked."

5

May the Task Force Be Watching You

It was decided that the marshals would use covered wagons, a common sight in those days which would not arouse suspicion. On the night of September 8, 1893, two wagonloads of officers stopped outside of Ingalls [Oklahoma]. However, a small boy playing nearby had not only seen them arrive but had overheard them making plans. He scooted back to town inflated with importance because he knew, as he told the gang who were playing poker in the hotel, "that the marshals are coming." . . .

Marshal Shadley, a fine officer, was in the lead, running and firing. From the window on the second floor, Arkansas Tom fired three rapid shots. Shadley spun around and fell, to die later.

—*Zoe Tilghman, describing the 1893 Battle of Ingalls; from* The Lawmen, *by James D. Horan*

When the Marshals Service was established by the Judiciary Act of 1789, its duties were described only in the most general terms as the enforcement arm of the court system. The real power in law enforcement at that time was held by local sheriffs. Essentially marshals were to perform similar duties—but on a very limited federal basis. There is no explanation in history why the founders chose the name "marshals" instead of a more accurate term like "federal sheriffs."

The actual duties of the Marshals Service have evolved and been expanded throughout American history to basically fulfill whatever need exists. While marshals are best known for tracking down fugitives, people who are already known to the legal system, because of their legendary prowess as manhunters marshals often have gotten involved in the hot pursuit of suspects on the run. On a Friday night in August 2007, for example, in Marble Falls, Texas, bartender Michael Jay Allred was shot and killed. The killer then apparently drove to Jonestown, where he killed a woman, her boyfriend, and two teenaged girls. Then he started running.

The Travis County Deputy Sheriff's Office very quickly identified the killer as a man named Paul Devoe. The woman was his ex-girlfriend. They learned that Devoe was from Long Island and believed he might be heading in that direction. They also discovered he had stolen a station wagon and a cell phone belonging to one of his victims. The sheriff's office contacted the Marshals Service Violent Felons Task Force and asked for assistance in apprehending their "prime suspect."

USMS Tech Ops discovered that Devoe was using the stolen phone as he made his getaway. They traced his calls as he moved up the East Coast. The last phone call that could be traced was made from Pennsylvania to Devoe's sister on Long Island. She told deputies that he had called and confessed to his mother that he had killed five people. His mother already had a restraining order in place against him, and in response to that call his sister and mother immediately left the house to stay someplace safe until he was caught. Deputies traced another call he'd made to a friend and former coworker living in Shirley, New York. They set up surveillance on that house but didn't spot the stolen station wagon. Eventually they knocked on the front door, and the owner of the house answered. He had no idea what was going on, he said, and told deputies Devoe was asleep in his back room. As they were talking, Devoe came out of the bedroom holding a gun. "Don't hurt me," he pleaded. "I'm not going to hurt anybody." He put the gun to his head and threatened to commit suicide, but deputies talked him out of it. He was arrested without any additional problems.

The station wagon wasn't there. The car he had been driving belonged to an eighty-one-year-old woman from Greencastle, Pennsylvania. When local law enforcement went to her house, they found Devoe's station wagon in the driveway and the body of his sixth victim in the house. In 2009, a Texas jury voted to give him the death penalty.

In the Old West, after a crime was committed, the marshal would put together a posse, make each person raise his right hand, and deputize them; then they would all climb up on horseback and take off after the outlaws. Often this posse would stay on the trail for long days and even weeks until they could track down the outlaws and dispense justice. That broad concept of forming a posse to go after the bad guys is the foundation of the Marshals Service's fugitive task force program. It works essentially the same way today as it did more than two hundred years ago. The task force, the modern-day posse, is composed of members of numerous law enforcement departments and agencies from the local, the state, and the federal government who, as mentioned earlier, are generally referred to as force multipliers. A local police department may have one murder case in six months, and will not have the resources, the state-of-the-art equipment, the funding, the access to databases, or the manpower to work that case. In addition, their jurisdiction is confined to their borders. By participating in the task force they can present that case and suddenly have an extraordinary crime-fighting team working it. It makes life on the run very difficult for fugitives. In return for providing even one officer to the task force, that small department gets hundreds of law enforcement officers from numerous departments, plus a Technical Operations team and a SWAT team, as well as the ability to pursue a local fugitive anywhere he or she goes in the country.

All the members of the task force are deputized, but in addition, according to Deputy Tony Schilling, "We give them state-of-the-art training in fugitive operations, in everything from building entries to vehicle takedowns. We train them with one objective in mind: we're all going home tonight. By the time we're done, they have become manhunters."

There really is nothing else in law enforcement like a Marshals Service task force. As deputies, task force members have federal arrest authority, meaning they can chase fugitives anywhere in the country, and each of them brings with him or her into the task force unique knowledge—and information sharing is paramount. Very often the result is exactly the same as it was on the

American frontier. And just as it was a hundred years ago, sometimes a deputy simply has to drop whatever case he is working on and join the posse. For example, one Saturday morning Deputy Marshal Thomas Smith was at his home in Bulverde, Texas, a town just north of San Antonio at the start of the Texas hill country, when he got a call from Texas Ranger Lance Coleman, who had worked with the task force on many cases. "I need help, Tom," he said. Three women had been shot; one of them was dead, a fourteen-year-old was fighting for her life, and the shooter was on the run. The Rangers had identified the killer and gotten the warrants. But that had taken them some time, which gave the killer several hours' head start.

Smith was the supervisor of the regional task force, "I started sending text messages to our guys telling them to stand by, because we probably were going to be rolling in a bit. When I got the call to go, I sent up the balloon. We met at a rallying point, briefed everybody about who were looking for, handed out photographs of the suspect, and went to work."

The shooter had vanished. Deputies began looking into his past and his current history, trying to find out who was important to him in his life. His jail records were pulled to see who was on his visitors' list, who had put money on his books. He didn't have a lot of friends, they discovered, but he had kept in contact with some people he'd met in prison. Officers were assigned to watch all of these people. If he called any of them, or showed up on their doorstep, law enforcement would know within minutes.

"We cast a wide net," Smith explains.

We found out he was not a man of means, so likely he couldn't go far. We put a trace on his vehicle. A task force headquarters had been set up over in Gonzales County and we were caravanning over there, driving eastbound through a rural area on Interstate 10, when one of our people spotted his car on the other side of the road, parked right off a ramp. We turned around and tactically approached the car. We were pretty certain he wouldn't be in the car, but nonetheless you take these precautions. We didn't know if his car had broken down or run out of gas, or if he had just abandoned it, but he wasn't there. The only thing nearby was a little service station and a little store with some outbuildings behind it. There also was a trailer that somebody was living in. None of the people in the gas station or store recalled seeing him. We thought he might be hiding in one of those buildings so got permission to search them. Everybody was on edge and we went through them slowly and carefully, but he was not in any of them. Now where?

I asked my team, what's next, throw some ideas out there. There was a school of thought that he had hitchhiked out of the area and was long gone. That was possible, I thought, but we also needed to do some due diligence and try to eliminate the possibility that he'd hit the brush. If it was me I wouldn't have hitchhiked, not right there by my vehicle. On both sides of the road there was thick brush, trees, bushes, swamps. I would have gone in there and walked for so many miles and then maybe come out and hitchhiked where whoever picked me up wouldn't necessarily associate me with that car.

The deep woods were a perfect hiding place. Smith contacted John Moriarty, then the inspector general of the Texas Department of Criminal Justice, which means he ran the entire state penal system, and asked him to get some horses and dogs out there to track him. Just like in the movies, prison authorities have long relied on dogs to pick up the scent of escaped prisoners.

As darkness fell, Deputy Bobby Hoglan, who was at the fugitive's sister's house, called Smith and told him, "Tom, he just called here. He's wanting his sister to come pick him on up." Then he gave Smith the phone number that the call had been made from. Smith traced the call.

The number came back to a landline at the Acme Company Clay Quarry, a rock quarry just a few miles from where we were setting up. I sent one of my people over there to do a quiet drive-by, but the building the call had come from was back a ways; you couldn't see it from the access road. About all I got from him was that the entire area was very dark and he didn't see any lights. I called the county sheriff and filled him in. He knew the owner of the quarry. I asked him if he could get us a key to the big front gate, 'cause if we ripped it down going in, the suspect definitely would hear us coming. The owner ended up bringing the key down to us. We asked Texas state authorities to provide some air support, so they sent us a helicopter equipped with thermal imaging cameras and high-intensity lighting. This boy had already shot three people, killing one of them, so we knew he wouldn't hesitate to shoot any of us; we were stacking the deck in our favor. Finally, when everybody was on the site, I held a briefing and made our decisions.

We had convinced his sister that the best way for her to ensure that her brother came out of this alive was for us to be able to catch him by surprise. She just didn't want her brother hurt. He had told her to call him when she was leaving her house, drive down the quarry road, and flash her lights; then he would come out from hiding and jump in her car. Of course that was never going to happen. We never had any intention of letting him get in her car. I put two guys in the backseat and told them to lie down so he couldn't see them. While the night covered some of our movements it also made it impossible for us to see him. We wanted to time the pickup so the helicopter could track his thermal image and tell us where he was. We had the dogs ready too; the state penal authorities had dogs that would circle and bark if the man they were tracking stood still, but if he tried to run, they would pounce.

Smith put cars in front and behind the target vehicle. The fugitive's sister would never be out of direct sight. At the scheduled time, she went to the quarry and flashed her lights; he came running out—but for whatever reason she drove away. Later she explained that she hadn't seen him. Observers in the helicopter could see the killer's thermal footprint and reported his movements to officers on the ground. After the failed pickup, he had gone back into the building, but then he'd come out carrying something in his hand. Smith explains,

> We believed it was a gun; I had asked the owner of the building specifically if there was a cordless phone in there and he said firmly, "No sir."
>
> He called his sister again. The deputy in the car with her relayed her side of the conversation to us. Meanwhile, the helicopter had only ten minutes of fuel left. I did not want a large group of armed men out there in the dark, so we had to make a move. I told everybody, "Listen up. This guy's bought and paid for already. He already shot three people, you guys do not hesitate. If he makes any move whatsoever, you do what you need to do. Because we are all going home tonight."
>
> The dogs were going to go in first. I was going in right behind them on horseback with Lance Coleman and several correctional officers. The posse was behind us, everybody armed to the teeth; most of us had AR-15s or some type of semi-automatic weapon. The prison guys had long guns. There were a lot of fired-up people on the ground, a lot of testosterone going through the air. We all took a big deep breath as we got ready to go. Then we moved in.

The spotters in the helicopter kept us informed exactly where he was. As soon as the dogs went in, the chopper pilot hit the spotlight and lit up the entire area. There he was, standing outside, caught in the bright light. We got on the speaker and ordered him to drop his gun. Turned out it wasn't a gun. It was a cordless phone. The only reason he survived that night was because he didn't lift up his hand.

Every member of a task force has the legal power to cross state and local borders without limits to their authority. Deputy marshals can make an arrest in any jurisdiction in America, and they can extend that unique right to anyone working with them. In December 2004, for example, a robber described as a young white male with vivid blue eyes held up a jewelry store in Westbury, New York, escaping with an estimated $100,000 in merchandise. Two weeks later, the owner of a Glen Cove, New York, jewelry store was shot in the chest four times at practically point-blank range as the killer escaped with more than $100,000 in jewelry. In January 2005, a Nanuet, New York, jewelry store was held up and the robber escaped with rings valued at $80,000. But what was an active armed robbery investigation instantly became a massive manhunt on February 2 when the robber walked into a Fairfield, Connecticut, jewelry store and, after a brief conversation about engagement rings, took a semiautomatic pistol out of a shopping bag and calmly killed the husband and wife owners of the store.

Twenty-three-year-old Christopher DiMeo, a drug addict, was identified as the primary suspect. Among the numerous law enforcement departments working the case was the New York/New Jersey Regional Fugitive Task Force. Vinny Senzamici, an officer with the State Division of Parole, who had raised his right hand and been deputized in 2002, was assigned to that team. "It was a good fit," Senzamici says.

> Joining the task force gave me the federal arrest authority that I did not have as a member of the Parole Department. We had a lot of parolees who fled the state and we were able to go outside the borders, put boots on the ground, and track them down. And when my other law enforcement partners in the task force were looking for parolees for other crimes, in addition to our physical presence, we were able to contribute a lot of information from our database.
>
> Like everybody else I was following this case

through the media. Those cold-blooded killings in Connecticut really shocked everybody. But what surprised me was that the Nassau County PD published the suspect's name. I'd worked with those homicide detectives, and it was rare for them to do that. That was pretty strong evidence that they really were desperate to catch this guy. So while I was sitting at my desk I thought I'd run his name through our system to see if he was on parole and sure enough, he popped up.

DiMeo had a long parole history. He'd previously been arrested three times. After serving two years in prison, he had been released on parole. The previous October he had stolen money from his grandparents' bank account as well as other items of value and skipped out on his parole. His whole record was right there.

Senzamici started digging deeper.

I pulled up the names, phone numbers, and addresses of everybody that he had contacted while he was in jail, everybody who contacted him, anybody that sent him packages—every bit of information we had. I started checking the phone numbers and we found that they were still viable; the people he had been in contact with still lived

at those addresses. I contacted Nassau County
and told them what I had, and they asked me to
come down to assist them. Everything had to be
done immediately. Nobody slept. When a guy is on
the run, he needs money and the more desperate he
gets, the more dangerous it is for everybody. This
guy already showed that killing meant nothing to
him, so there was every reason to believe he
wouldn't hesitate to kill again. This really was a
race until he killed somebody else.

Senzamici packed up all his research and gave it to
the Nassau County Police Department. That included
the addresses of DiMeo's mother, an old girlfriend
he was still in contact with, all the people in his life.
Nassau sent people to sit on those residences while the
Marshals Service's Technical Operations Group got
subpoenas for those phone numbers to see if he tried to
make contact.

"Once the Technical Operations crew gets onto
something, they're like pit bulls," Senzamici says.
"They don't let go. I began interviewing DiMeo's
former parole officers to see if they might have some
additional information that could help us. Everything
I got I relayed to Nassau County. Once we got the
subpoenas we were able to find out what phones he

was hitting. Nassau PD started interviewing people; eventually his old girlfriend gave up his new girlfriend's cell-phone number, which was the phone he was using while he was on the run. We were able to trace that phone to the Ascot Motel, a run-down place in Atlantic City."

Deputies and state and local police officers surrounded the motel. All the nearby streets were barricaded, sharpshooters were posted on rooftops, and all the other rooms in the motel were quietly emptied. DiMeo's girlfriend was with him, and when she went to the front desk to pay for another night's stay there, officers grabbed her. Then they began negotiating his surrender with him. Eventually he stepped out of the room with his arms up in the air and was arrested—for violating his New York State parole. In 2011, he received consecutive life sentences without possibility of parole in New York and Connecticut for the three murders.

Surprisingly, while the Marshals Service has so often played an important role in tracking down wanted felons, very few people are aware of it. The reality is the Marshals Service only occasionally receives public credit for its contributions. There are a variety of reasons for this. Many of the cases worked by deputies are brought to them by local law enforcement agencies and those departments get the credit in their local media for resolving it. As a federal agency working mostly local cases, the Marshals Service is never the home team. And deputies often enter a case after a tremendous amount of work has already been done by another agency. Maybe more important, as everyone who goes to the movies or watches TV knows, the competition between different law enforcement agencies can be detrimental. At times it actually discourages the sharing of information. The task force concept adopted by the Marshals Service both requires and emphasizes the complete cooperation of numerous forces, and sharing the credit for success encourages that type of relationship.

In numerous instances when a case is reported in the media, the fact that the Marshals Service was involved isn't even mentioned. The hunt for the D.C. Sniper is one of those cases. Without question this was one of the most dramatic manhunts in recent American history. Beginning in September 2002, ten people were murdered and three additional victims survived what appeared to be entirely random shootings in the Washington Beltway area. The shots came without warning, for no known reason, in different places at different times of the day and week; the victims included men, women, and even children. The entire region was terrorized. No one felt safe. Normal life was suspended; events were canceled and people stayed home at night. Almost every law enforcement agency in the region concentrated all their resources on this case. Although the Montgomery County Police Department was the lead investigative force, in addition to the Marshals Service numerous other local police and sheriff's departments, the DEA, ATF, Secret Service, and even the FBI were actively involved in a desperate race to stop the killings. Each agency had an "incident commander." Mike Earp was put in charge of the Marshals Service participation in the operation. He brought together about fifty investigators who were assigned to various regional task forces and a dozen Technical Operations Group inspectors.

"They were drawing on every possible resource that was available out there," remembers Bill Sorukas. "They told us, we're looking for anything here, just give us some direction to go. We talked about a hundred different options of how to use our technology to attack this thing, including some of the techniques we had used at Ground Zero. After the World Trade Center buildings had collapsed, there were numerous reports that cell-phone calls were coming from the pile; we investigated every single one of them in the hope that it was true. Unfortunately, we never found one in the debris field."

Because these crimes were committed in different jurisdictions, several different command posts with different people in charge had been set up, which created some confusion. Earp assigned his personnel to work with the various command posts. Mike Moran, for instance, was assigned to the Montgomery County Police Department command post. Geoff Shank was assigned to the Washington, D.C., Metropolitan Police Department. Lenny DePaul was sent to the Richmond and Prince William County command posts.

Task force members spent hundreds of hours patrolling and surveilling points of interest throughout the area, checking out everything from gas stations to strip malls. The Technical Operations Group developed some very innovative concepts, and although they didn't lead to a specific person, they did allow law enforcement to eliminate several people who had surfaced as potential suspects. These techniques saved considerable time and investigative effort.

Fortunately for investigators, the killer continued to make phone calls and leave notes at crime scenes. In one of those calls the killer boasted about a previous murder he had committed "in Montgomery." Authorities mistakenly believed he was referring to an unsolved killing in Montgomery County, Maryland—until a priest called the hotline and informed them that he had gotten a call from an unknown person telling him that this first killing actually had taken place in Montgomery, Alabama. When the task force investigated they discovered that a woman had been killed, and a second woman had been seriously injured during a liquor store robbery—in Montgomery, Alabama. A partial print had been found at that crime scene. Alabama law enforcement had run that print through its system and hadn't come up with a hit. The Montgomery PD ran that same print through NCIC and this time, bingo! They finally had a name. As Sorukas explains,

> Now they went ahead and processed it and managed to find a thumbprint on a page torn out of a firearms catalog. None of the people up in Maryland attached any significance to it. Mike Moran contacted the Technical Ops group and told them that print had been positively matched to the immigration record of a seventeen-year-old Jamaican named Lee Boyd Malvo and suggested if that information was of interest we should go ahead and do a full workup. Why nobody else was curious about it I never found out. But we got to work on it immediately.

Meanwhile a supposed witness to one of the Beltway shootings claimed he had seen a white van racing from the scene of a shooting, so investigators began tracking and searching every white van in the region. At the same time profilers had suggested the killer was probably a lone, white, middle-aged divorced, unemployed, disgruntled person, maybe former military—which definitely eliminated Lee Boyd Malvo. Sorukas says,

We started gathering all the information we could on Malvo and kept coming across a man by the name of John Muhammad. Every time Malvo had a problem with law enforcement, it was John Muhammad who bailed him out, not his mother. In some of the reports Muhammad had claimed to be his father. So now we started on the Muhammad end of it. He had legally changed his name from John Allen Williams to John Allen Muhammad. He had been in the military, so we got all his military records: he had served in the Gulf War and had been discharged as a sergeant in 1994. In the military he had qualified as an expert marksman. It just felt like this was worth pursuing, and we began briefing the people in Montgomery, but they just weren't getting it.

All the pieces were starting to come together. At one of our daily briefings we were told that

Muhammad's ex-wife was living in the area, which gave him a reason to be here. I saw that he had a California driver's license and a Washington State license, and Malvo didn't have any of that stuff. I got copies of everything I could get my hands on. I called the FBI Task Force in Montgomery and asked my contact to run Muhammad's name through their Rapid Start Database, where they were collecting all the information. We discovered that someone who claimed to have been in the military with Muhammad had called and identified him as the sniper. In one of the letters left at a crime scene, the shooter had demanded $10 million and threatened to shoot children in that area if it was not paid. He gave a credit card number in that letter. I found out that credit card had been stolen in Arizona and there had been only one attempt to use it—at a gas station in Washington State. Now I had a link between a credit card used in Muhammad and Malvo's home state and the killers. It was pretty flimsy, but it was real. In another letter there was a reference that Vinny Senzamici, a parole officer permanently assigned to the New York Violent Felons Task Force, recognized as coming from a well-known Jamaican song, so we had that ethnic connection.

The Sniper Task Force began to believe the deputies were onto something when the Marshals Service's entire canine corps, which then consisted of a single dog named Beacon, found an expended cartridge at the Benjamin Tasker Middle School in Bowie, Maryland, after a thirteen-year-old boy was shot and seriously wounded. It had a partial print on it, which they were able to match to the print left at the Montgomery, Alabama, liquor store murder scene. According to Sorukas,

Meanwhile, at about three A.M. I sent a request to the Criminal Justice Information Services Division in Clarksburg, West Virginia, asking them to conduct an offline search for John Muhammad. Then I followed up with a phone call. I just had a hunch. Basically, if an officer checks a name through the national wanted persons system, even if there is no record of that person, there will be a record that the search was made and the name of the person requesting it. I wanted to find out if anybody had been interested in Muhammad, if anybody had run his driver's license, for example. I was sleeping on the sofa in my office a few hours later when the fax machine started ringing; it started pumping out thirty or forty pages of information on John Allen

Williams and John Allen Muhammad. And in all that data, there was one hit in the Beltway area.

Earp's team learned that the task force had finally begun focusing on Muhammad when they heard a news report that police officers had cordoned off the backyard of a home in which Muhammad had lived in Washington State. Apparently when Muhammad lived there he would fire weapons into a tree stump and investigators were trying to dig out bullets to see if they could match the rifling on them to any of the shootings. Sorukas was surprised when he heard the news:

Why did they let that news out? Now Muhammad knew we were onto him. That one hit I'd gotten on Muhammad had come from Baltimore. It was the right name with the right birth date. There wasn't much information, just that a Baltimore police officer had submitted a routine check on Muhammad's driver's license. I got hold of Brian Shepherd, who works in our Baltimore office, and told him I needed him to find out the circumstances of this inquiry. I gave him all the data, including the time and the date the request had been made. I asked him to find out who the officer was, why he had made the inquiry, and where he encountered the guy.

When Sorukas got back to the office at Technical Operations, someone said to him, "Good job finding Muhammad."

I asked him, "What are you talking about?" And he told me they'd found the information about that stop; they'd found the Baltimore police officer. He had encountered Muhammad sleeping in a car in the parking lot of a 7-Eleven, roused him, and asked him what he was doing there. Then he'd made an inquiry to Criminal Justice Information Services to find out if this guy was wanted for anything. When he was advised there were no outstanding warrants on the name or the license plate, he had given Muhammad a warning then let him go. The officer knew it was the same John Muhammad because he'd used his Washington State driver's license for identification. He was the only person in the car at that time. Malvo could have been anywhere; he could have been inside the 7-Eleven, walking the streets, or asleep in the trunk. The officer had taken good notes; he'd written down the license plate number and the make and model of the car, a dark Blue 1990 Chevy Caprice. That was huge; we now knew for certain they were in the area, and we had a description of the car they were driving.

So I sent out a nationwide BOLO, alerting officers to be on the lookout for a blue 1990 Chevy Caprice being driven by . . . I knew from my past experience that as soon as this went out to patrol units, the media was going to pick up on it. In fact, within thirty minutes I saw the license plate number on the news with a report that police were looking for this car. Very shortly after that report was broadcast, a supermarket refrigeration specialist coming home from work just after one A.M. spotted the dark blue Caprice in the back of the lot at a rest stop just off Interstate 70 near Myersville, Maryland. It took him several attempts to get through to 911, but once he did responding police used their patrol cars and borrowed trucks to block all exits to the rest stop and then quietly arrested Muhammad and Malvo.

John Muhammad was executed in 2009; Lee Boyd Malvo will spend the rest of his life in prison. And as in many other cases, the contributions of the Marshals Service to the identification and arrest of the killers went largely unnoticed.

During the D.C. Sniper investigation, several phone calls had been made to law enforcement from various pay phones. The Technical Operations Group traced all the calls made before and after those calls in the hope that the killer had used the same phone to call someone else. The task force also started watching those phones. One night a crew of deputies set up shop in the back of a van in a Virginia parking lot to watch a public phone that the killers had been known to use; at two A.M. an unmarked van pulled up, and several men dressed in black and carrying rifles jumped out and began dismantling the phone. The deputies called Craig Caine at one of the command posts to figure out what was going on. Caine called Lenny DePaul at the Command Center in Richmond, who found out that, without telling any other agency, the FBI had decided to grab the phone and examine every quarter in it for fingerprints. It was a dangerous situation that almost resulted in the kind of friendly-fire confrontation that can end with serious injuries.

Sitting in the back of a van watching pay phones in the middle of the night actually isn't that unusual. Like every other law enforcement officer, deputies spend a lot of time just watching, watching some more, and waiting, waiting sometimes for a long period of time. Doing nothing can be very difficult, but surveillance has proved to be a vitally important investigative tool. And for a group of people who like action, it requires mastering the art of patience. While standing in a courtroom for hours can be tedious, sitting in a hot van for days can be considerably more trying, and dangerous. According to Craig Caine,

> It definitely ain't like the movies. When you're sitting there for twelve hours in the heat or the cold it gets boring, it gets frustrating, and sometimes the air-conditioning or the heater doesn't work so well. You have to fight to stay awake. The worst is when you have to go to the bathroom. I am an expert in the skill of how to pee in a car. It's either that or break off the surveillance, which we don't want to do, so this is one of the important skills that we learn early.
>
> If we know we're going to be on a location for an extended period of time, we'll prepare ourselves. I usually keep my favorite cookies in the car or a big bag of peanuts or almonds. It's very rare that we have only one car sitting there; usually we cover the whole block from end to end so we can cover for each other if we get desperate.

"You get to know your partner really well," says Joseph Lobue.

Really, really well. You do anything to stay awake, and you talk about anything and everything. But there are times you doze off and when that happens, you're relying on your partner to nudge you if anything changes. There were times we would go as long as thirty-six hours without sleeping. You drink coffee, but then you have to go to the bathroom; but if you don't drink it, you can't stay awake. You go through waves when you're completely exhausted and then suddenly you're alert. Mostly you depend on your tenacity; you're not going to let that guy you're looking for get over on you. But even worse than being in the front seat of a car is being in the back of a closed surveillance van in the middle of the summer.

Part of the excitement of a deputy's job is that every day is different. When deputies come in to work in the morning there is absolutely no way of predicting or anticipating what will happen that day. That's just as true for surveillance; no one knows when or where they might end up. Jerry Lowery ended up sitting in a van across the street from a funeral home for a week, and as he remembers, "There was nothing going on to maintain some level of excitement, so it was really hard to stay awake. The most exciting thing was watching them bringing in the bodies for burial in the middle of the night."

Deputy Joseph Abdullah ended up sitting on top of an Arizona hill for several days without even knowing what he was looking for. In the 1990s Mexican drug cartels had dug numerous tunnels under the border between the two countries; they would park a large tractor-trailer directly over the entrance on the American side and load the truck with product being smuggled in from Mexico without being detected. It was one-stop shopping for moving almost any type of drugs. When the FBI raided an unloading operation one night, the man who appeared to be running the operation jumped into his car and raced off. After a high speed chase, the car crashed and the unknown suspect took off into the night. The only thing agents found in the wreckage of his car were a crumpled black-and-white photograph and a list of street names. But that information led nowhere. The FBI couldn't identify the suspect and certainly couldn't catch him. After almost two years, they handed the case over to the Marshals Service.

All Abdullah had to go on was that crumpled photograph and that list of streets. Slowly he began developing some leads, just threads that seemed to go nowhere, in hopes he might be able to tie them together.

We made several arrests of low-level workers in the organization, just moving up the ladder. Among the people we were interested in was a female who might have had a connection to this guy. We couldn't know for sure, but she was definitely someone we wanted to look at. We followed her to a ranch in the Sabino Canyon, which is in the Santa Catalina Mountains north of Tucson, Arizona. I took a crew of guys with me and we sat on top of a hilltop in the boiling sun, looking down at the ranch. We were just burning alive up there. We didn't know what we were looking for, or waiting for, or even if there was a connection, but it felt right. So we just sat there for several days watching through binoculars to see if anything happened.

The heat was brutal. Because we didn't know what we were waiting for, we didn't know how long we would be there. But suddenly, without any warning, a car pulled up to the house early in the morning. A man came out of the house, accompanied by several bodyguards, and quickly slid into the backseat of the car. It took off fast. He was obviously somebody pretty important in the organization. I called it out to the chase cars we had in position and they started to follow, but I called it off. I knew that if he noticed them, he would do whatever he had to do to escape—he would have driven over anybody and everybody—and we'd have to start all over again. And once he found out we were on him, it would be that much more difficult to find him again. We did have air support standing by, but the plane was refueling when this happened and we couldn't get it up in time to follow him. We had to watch him go and then spent the next few hours baking in the sun once again. It was torture.

I thought, *Tomorrow is Cinco de Mayo, and it would be great to celebrate by arresting him.* But we didn't have to wait. About six hours later he came back, once again moving very quickly from the car right into the house. But a little while later, I remember, he came out of the house and just stood there, looking totally relaxed. *Wow,* I thought at that moment, *this guy doesn't have the slightest idea we're on him. So now's the perfect time to take him.* I decided, we're gonna take him right now. I got on the radio and we very quickly assembled a team of about sixty people from the task force, deputies and state and local police. When we had the whole place surrounded, all the roads blocked off, I drove up to the front of the house and politely rang the doorbell. When the woman answered, we moved in and began clearing the front of the house. Soon as we did he took off out the back, where our people were waiting for him.

His name was Filiberto Castro Rascon and it was believed he had moved as much as fifty tons of marijuana through Arizona into Michigan. The ranch house looked like a set from *Scarface;* everything was lavish and overdone, from the large-screen TVs to the $60,000 in cabinetry—inside his closet. Rascon turned out to be a much bigger player in the cartel than anyone had imagined, and the fact that the marshals had just reached in and plucked him off the grid apparently created a lot of problems for the organization. No one knew how he had been identified, and there was some speculation that someone within the cartel had become an informant. In fact, a DEA agent told Abdullah that after Rascon's arrest the heads of four of these narcotics organizations met—and somebody interrupted their meeting and killed them all. Abdullah later learned that the whole case had started when Rascon had showed up unexpectedly to spot-check a transaction, just to make sure nobody was stealing from him, and got caught up in the FBI raid. "In that case," as Abdullah says, "all those hours sitting in the sun paid off for us."

Although today law enforcement officers tend to rely on the new and futuristic tools of technology that allow investigators to burrow deeply and unseen into a suspect's life, there still is no substitute for locking eyes on a person or a place. As most deputies have learned through experience, surveillance can often be days of tedium interrupted by seconds of violence. After an inmate escaped from prison, for example, Mike Bunk and several other deputies set up way down the block from the house in which his wife and child were living, figuring he might show up there. That was just one of several locations that were being watched. They sat there for three days, three long days, carefully watching nothing happening. They were killing time, and the more time that passed, the less likely it seemed that the fugitive would show up there. It was far more likely that he had taken off, trying to get as far away as quickly as possible. "In the meantime," Bunk recalls, "we got some information that he might be running with another fugitive from South Florida. And sure enough, on the fourth morning the two of them, plus another guy, came out of the house and jumped into a big SUV. We called for backup and began following them. They did not know we were on them." Bunk continues,

They pulled into the parking lot of a Walmart. The two other fugitives got out of the car and got into a second car. By that time additional deputies had arrived, and we decided to take them down right there. Three days of nothing had led to this moment. We drew our weapons. My partner went for the second car, I went for the prison escapee; when he saw me coming, he didn't hesitate—he stepped on the accelerator. As he raced by me, my arm got tangled up in the side mirror, and the car started dragging me. He didn't even slow down. I started slamming the hell out of the window with my gun, trying to smash it, trying to keep my feet from dragging on the pavement. My partner opened fire, putting several shots into the car. Just about the time I managed to break free I heard another gunshot and thought my gun had discharged. The fugitive was a few feet away from me, but I didn't see him get hit. The car kept going for about another fifty yards then rolled slowly to a stop. My first thought was, goddamnit, now I've got to fill out all that paperwork for an accidental discharge. But the fugitive wasn't moving. I got up and ran to the car and pulled him out. As I did I saw the glass on the ground from the back window and thought, good, it wasn't me that had an accidental discharge. I started administering first aid, but it was too late. He was dead. My partner did the right thing, and he may have saved my life.

But that's how quickly a surveillance situation can escalate.

Lenny DePaul and Craig Caine learned the same lesson on the streets of Brooklyn. A car in motion is a deadly weapon. The New York office had gotten a tip from an informer that a kid out of Buffalo wanted for rape was going to be delivering drug money to a building on Eastern Parkway in Brooklyn. The informant described the car and gave deputies the address, but he didn't know the exact apartment number. The deputies knew that whatever apartment he was going to, eventually he had to come back to his car. So about one o'clock in the morning, a team of four unmarked cars and a surveillance van started driving around the neighborhood searching for the fugitive's vehicle. DePaul recalls,

There is a narrow street there called Lincoln Place. It's so narrow that cars have to park on the sidewalk so traffic can get through. For a while we couldn't find his car. Then a deputy needed to relieve himself so he went behind a dumpster, and low and behold, he spotted the car. He got right back in his car and told the rest of us, "I got it. I found the car." We set up a perimeter using our vehicles to block it in. I was parked on the other side of the street, about three car lengths in front of him. Lincoln Place is so narrow our van couldn't get through, so they backed up and stayed off the block. Then we waited.

Like every deputy, DePaul had spent what seemed like years just watching and waiting for something to happen. Surveillance never gets any better or worse, it just is. There is no way to make the time go faster. And if it turns out to be a waste of time, it's usually a waste of a lot of time. During the day, at least, life is going on all around you so there are things to watch that help keep you alert; at night there's nothing. But in this situation, the deputies didn't have to wait very long. Two hours after they had settled in, a man got into the target vehicle. As DePaul remembers,

We hadn't even seen him coming. He came out of a side entrance to the building, which opened onto an alley. We didn't know about it. But in an instant we went from relaxed to on the very tip of the edge. We all took our guns out and got ready to make the arrest.

Our people jumped out of the surveillance van and raced toward the car. He spotted them, locked the doors, and turned on the engine, then we saw him reaching down between his legs to grab something. He put the car in reverse and slammed into one of our cars, then shifted into drive and took off. I blocked the street with my car and got out. No way he's getting by me, I figured. He figured differently. He hit the accelerator. I could hear the wheels squealing. I was racing diagonally toward him; to avoid my car he aimed right at me. There was no place for me to go. No question he was aiming right for me. As I dived out of the way he clipped me. I went rolling over his car just as Craig Caine and Billy Knaust opened up on him. They put fourteen rounds into that car. One round blew the trunk lid off, another one ripped a big gouge out of the roof. That car looked like Swiss cheese. As I came rolling off the back, another deputy began firing and blew out the rear windshield.

I hit the ground hard. I was sure I was hit. While I was lying there I looked at him trying to get away; the kid had opened his door and was using it like a shield—he was hunched over behind it, looking under the door while he drove. His head was practically scraping on the sidewalk as he tried to make his getaway.

Deputies spend their entire careers training for moments like this, going through every scenario imaginable, but when it happens, you just react and hope that training kicks in. There isn't time to think or plan; it's all response and it's over in seconds. The kid swerved across the road and slammed into a van. Jeez, I figured, no way he's surviving that one. He's got to be dead. I pulled myself up and yelled to my partner, "Am I hit?"

"Nah," he said. "It's just glass." I brushed it off and started walking toward the car. Smoke was coming up out of the engine. I took a deep breath, bracing myself to see the guy's body. I got about five feet away—and suddenly the kid sat up.

I leaped into the air. That was the one thing I hadn't expected.

The car was riddled with bullet holes. There were three holes in the headrest, holes in the horn, holes in the dashboard. The suspect had a small Afro and one round had literally parted his Afro. Another round had just skimmed his forehead, so he was bleeding, but it was a superficial wound. A couple of the guys hand-cuffed him and put him down on the ground. Within minutes it seemed like the entire cavalry showed up. An NYPD borough captain arrived at the scene and asked DePaul, "Who are you guys?"

"U.S. marshals," DePaul said. He told him what the guy was wanted for.

The captain looked over the whole scene and asked, "Who are you guys again?" When DePaul repeated the answer, the captain just walked away, shaking his head.

A lot of younger investigators, people who have grown up in the digital age playing video games, people who never used a dial telephone or touched a type-writer, rely greatly on technology. They have to be taught that sometimes the older methods—eyes on the fugitive, feet on the ground—are still vital. As Bill Sorukas explains,

> I've always preached to them that you still have to do your homework, you still have to be a good interviewer, and you still have to be willing to do surveillance. Surveillance requires making a real effort; you don't want to do it from nine A.M. to three P.M. if you think the guy's working. But you do want to be out there at three A.M. to see what time that person is going or coming from work and what kind of car he's driving. When I was watching

a house, I also would find out as much as I could about the neighbors on either side, and maybe I'd even go talk to them.

In the fall of 1996, Sorukas was looking for a legendary bad guy named Craig Forrest Jones, a methamphetamine producer for the Sons of Silence Motorcycle Club. Jones had been convicted of distributing meth in Denver in 1982 and sentenced to ten years but had jumped bail and disappeared. When Sorukas's former partner became the warrant supervisor in the Marshals Service's Denver office, he learned that Jones could be in the San Diego area and asked Sorukas to take a look.

He gave me some background about him: law enforcement had been close to getting him several times, but he'd always managed to escape. Once when he was trapped in a house, he had broken free by crashing his car through the garage door; another time during a chase he'd gotten away by driving the wrong direction on a freeway and firing shots at people on the side of the road so his pursuer would have to stop to make sure everybody was okay. He was definitely a resourceful and dangerous guy.

Sorukas was given a package of material that had been found in a car seized during a police stop in Arizona. Among the contents were several store receipts and as he began pinpointing them, he saw there was a concentration in the La Jolla area. That caught his curiosity:

I thought, that's a nice area for a methamphetamine fugitive to be living in.

I started doing my homework on Jones's family and found out he had a daughter living right around there, on the other side of Interstate 5. Maybe a half mile away. We also got information that he had rented a post office box under the name Maynard Harding Dorf Jr. so we set up surveillance on it. I sat in a van for a whole week, from five in the morning till eight at night, with San Diego PD and other task force members, watching people go in and out of that post office. We checked out every license plate. We never saw him, but we were able to get Dorf's fingerprint from the DMV and confirm through our sources that Dorf actually was our guy, Craig Forrest Jones.

We found out he was living in a town house condominium complex, a long single-story building consisting of six adjoining units. They were worth about $2 million each. The person living in the town house adjoining his was an investigator with the Naval Criminal Investigative Service who was on assignment in Hawaii at that time. When I finally got in touch with him, I told him exactly what was going on; I thought I could trust him because he was a cop too. He identified a photograph of Jones, although he didn't know his name, and told me he didn't see him very often. He wasn't around a lot, he said, and he'd often be gone for as long as a month. They never talked, but he knew he had a white Mustang in the garage that might be up on blocks, that among his few visitors was an elderly woman, and that he would often ride a bicycle around the area. Then he told me one additional fact; a crawlspace stretched the entire length of the building, going through the garages. That meant a person could move from one condo to any of the others undetected, then drop down and go out through any of the six garages. The residents hadn't bothered to block them off, he said; they kind of trusted each other. Then he in detail described the layout of his unit, which we assumed was similar to Jones's.

Sorukas set up surveillance on the block, but for several days there was no activity in the town house. Finally he spoke with another neighbor, a woman who told him she would see Jones on occasion, but that he was rarely out in the yard. Sorukas gave her his phone number and to his surprise she called a few days later, on a Thursday night. Jones was home, she said; she had seen him out on the porch smoking a cigarette. As Sorukas remembers,

It was early in the evening and I figured I'd go over there and just take a look. I was just going to sit down the road and watch the place for a little while to see what was going on. But as I parked the car and started to get settled, here comes a guy on a bicycle, and he rides right past me out onto the main street and down the road. I recognized him immediately. I followed him and watched from across the street as he stopped and made a call on a pay phone. That's strange, I thought, I know he's got two phones in his place, why is he doing that? I decided not to wait to find out.

Sorukas got on his radio and requested assistance. Although at that time of night everybody was on their way home, they turned around. The team assembled in La Jolla, and Sorukas laid out the whole situation.

We knew that he had busted out through a garage door in the past and that we had to cover the entire six–town house building because he had access to the crawlspace. It took about twenty-five people to secure the entire perimeter. I reminded the whole task force that Jones was a clever guy who would do anything to avoid being caught. I was driving a big Oldsmobile touring car that we had seized from one of our 15 Most Wanted a couple of years earlier, and I drove it up his driveway and parked it flush against his garage door. He wasn't going to smash his way out again. He wasn't going through that car.

We didn't have to wait very long. His wife opened the front door and walked out. She was visiting from Colorado, she said, and then she told us he wasn't coming out. "He told me that he loves me and our girls," she said. "But he isn't coming out." And, she told us, he had a lot of guns in there. And gas cans. And he had vowed that he wasn't going to be taken alive.

The deputies evacuated the other town houses, and SWAT team members took up positions in the residences on either side of Jones's house. Then they waited. A deputy made contact with him and tried to negotiate his surrender. He wasn't interested. Eventually the team began pouring tear gas, flash-bang charges, and sting-ball grenades that sprayed rubber pellets into the house, trying to force him to surrender. They used every tool they had to get him out of there alive. They blasted a hole through a cement wall with a gas gun then poured tear gas into the house. Nothing worked. He had been preparing for this for years; he even had gas masks in there.

In the middle of the night a fire started on an upper floor; either Jones set it or one of the marshals' canisters ignited something. The SWAT team eventually was able to get firefighters close enough to put it out. A couple of times during the night Jones fired warning shots, trying to make the deputies believe he had killed himself. There was no change throughout the whole morning. The entire neighborhood was shut down.

Sorukas had been on the scene for almost twenty hours and was exhausted and frustrated. He remembers,

> I didn't see this having a good ending. I was just sitting on the curb, trying to figure out if I could have done anything differently. A San Diego PD sergeant asked me, "Everything okay?"
>
> "Sure," I told him. "It's been a long day." He asked me what I was thinking about and I told him the truth: "I don't know whether I should wear my blue suit or my black suit when I have to go before

Congress and explain what happened here." In my mind I saw this $12 million building exploding.

On Friday evening the SWAT team blew open the front door with a water charge and sent a dog in; Jones shot at the dog and the dog came out. A deputy continued negotiating with him, but he wasn't getting anywhere. Finally it was time to take him. The SWAT team began closing down his space, moving people into his garage. Eventually four members of the team appeared at the front door. As they did he pointed his weapon at them—they had no choice: they opened fire with submachine guns, a gas canister launcher, and disabling beanbag cartridges. He was hit several times and died at the scene.

A search of the condo revealed he was carrying three loaded weapons and had six more loaded guns stashed around the house. They also discovered a methamphetamine lab in the condo. A subsequent police inquiry ruled that the officers had been justified in killing Jones.

As Sorukas explains,

It took us four or five days to clear the crime scene. The HAZMAT team was in there, the DEA, the San Diego PD—a lot of people had a stake in this.

Finally they told me I could take my car, which had remained up against the garage door. The SWAT team had been using it as a shield when they were putting tear gas into the house. I started driving home, thinking about all the reports I was going to have to write and file. And as I was driving south on I-5, tear gas started spreading throughout my car. It had been in the engine and as the car heated up, it got blown right in my face. I pulled over and put my gas mask on and continued driving home. I was exhausted. And I drove right past a California highway patrolman, who saw a guy driving wearing a gas mask and figured something had to be very wrong. He pulled me over and approached my car cautiously. I explained I had been part of the incident in La Jolla. He stuck his head in the car, took a deep breath, and started coughing. I had to wear that gas mask all the way home.

While cell phones and the Internet have eliminated much of the need to watch phone booths and mailboxes, deputies still find themselves staking out parked cars and trucks, waiting for a suspect who lives in some unknown place nearby to show up. In the late 1980s, Don Ward remembers, the DEA had done a tremendous job taking down a Dominican drug operation known as the Black Sunday Gang. They had arrested most of the leaders, but there were a few stragglers they couldn't catch.

So we started putting together the group's family tree using presentencing reports and information from numerous sources. Most of these people had their phones under the names of their wife or girlfriend, and once we figured that out we were able to get an address for them. The problem was in some of these neighborhoods we could identify the building they were living in, but not which apartment. There were a lot of people living in those buildings who weren't interested in being found, so there was no directory. We knew the top guy still out on the street was driving a gold Oldsmobile, a real tricked-out muscle car. We cruised the neighborhood until we found it on the street—it was a gold Oldsmobile, it was hard to miss it—and then we sat on it. But first we did let the air out of a tire so he couldn't go anywhere, which was a pretty standard thing to do back then. Then we waited. We waited a long time.

They knew he would show up eventually. Finally he came out of the building; when he spotted the flat tire he got out his spare and started changing it. The Black Sunday Gang was known to be especially violent. So when the suspect was down on one knee, four deputies rushed him with guns drawn, screaming, "Lie down! Get on the ground! Now!" They quickly established control and got his hands cuffed behind his back. Then he was arrested.

Then, as Ward remembers,

We hit his apartment. There was another member of the organization there. He ran into a bedroom and when I walked in, he had his hand in a drawer. This was one of those times I admit to being scared because I couldn't see his hand. I drew down on him and told him, "Don't do it. Get your hand out of there slowly." He did exactly what I told him to do; and when I searched the drawer, I found a 9 millimeter and $60,000 in cash. As we searched the apartment, we found several cans of tennis balls on the top shelf in the closet. Tennis balls? I thought, *Something's wrong with this picture. These people do not play tennis.* So I took one of those cans down. It was unusually heavy; there was a lot of weight on the bottom. I opened it up; it was vacuum sealed but I saw that there were only two tennis balls in there. And then we found the false bottom.

The entire lower third of the can was filled with cocaine. We called the DEA. They came in and took over.

Actually, it isn't at all unusual to discover evidence of additional crimes while doing surveillance. Jimmy Bankston once arrested a high-profile fugitive and began searching him. The local news was filming the arrest. While Bankston was frisking him an envelope filled with crack cocaine fell onto the sidewalk. "That's not mine," the suspect said.

A reporter said, "I saw it fall out of your pocket."

The suspect didn't even hesitate: "But these aren't my pants. See how baggy they are."

Fugitives hide in those places where they fit in best, environments in which they won't draw too much attention. So criminals like to be in neighborhoods where people know enough not to speak with law enforcement, where the residents are careful never to see anything unusual going on, where everybody seems to have a relative in the system and knows how that world works. In 1989, Eddy Severino had been running one of the largest heroin rings in Philadelphia history, but when law enforcement arrested thirty-seven people and took down his multimillion-dollar empire, he somehow managed to make a clean getaway. For more than a decade there was no trace of him. Authorities believed he had fled to the Dominican and accepted the reality that he probably would never be apprehended, but in 2001, an informant suddenly and surprisingly provided the address of the apartment building in the Bronx in which he was living. "When we went there, it was not what we expected to find," Joe Lobue says.

This was a very nice, middle-class apartment building. We set up a major surveillance operation; in addition to deputies in vehicles, we had several undercovers in the area disguised as the kind of people you would expect to see on the street, Con Ed, FedEx, all the usual people. But while we were sitting on it, watching to see if Severino actually lived there, we saw a series of livery cabs pull up in front of the place. They stopped and sat there for a while, then somebody went up to the cab and handed a bag to the passenger and then the cab took off. Nobody ever got out. It was obvious what was going on, so we called some of the fine people we knew in the DEA and got them down there. From a simple surveillance, this had grown into a major operation involving deputies, agents from the DEA and ATF, and several NYPD personnel.

Eventually we were able to pinpoint the apartment; we had the phones, so we finally decided to go in. We took down the door and busted into a full-blown heroin packaging operation. While we were breaking down the door we could hear the toilet bowl flushing as they tried to dispose of the drugs; in fact the toilet bowl actually got plugged up with bags of heroin. It was like a movie set; people were sitting at long tables with white powder on their hands. We arrested eight people and confiscated eight pounds of heroin, a pound of crack cocaine, several guns, and $125,000 in cash. But the one person we didn't get? The one person we were looking to arrest. I knew he was somewhere in the building because we had his phone number and when we called it, we could hear it ringing, but he wasn't in that apartment.

We found out that the super was his watchman. He carried an alarm around with him and pressed it when he suspected police were in the building. We shut down the entire building, nobody was allowed in or out, then we began searching it door-to-door. When we knocked on one door, our fugitive opened it; and he claimed to have no knowledge of any drug operation. Drugs? Absolutely not. Unfortunately for him, several other people we arrested testified that he was the head of this little heroin organization. We got him on the old case, and we got him on the new case. We even got the super.

Although surveillance often can be conducted from a distance or from a fixed position, at times it becomes necessary for a deputy to go undercover to get closer to the action. Harry Layne remembers being on an early FIST operation in Detroit in which they were trying to get close to a drug dealer in the projects. This guy's crew controlled the building and it was just about impossible to get anywhere near him without being spotted. So, as Layne recalls,

About four o'clock in the morning one of our people crawled into the dumpster next to the building. That was more than being undercover, that was being under garbage. But that's how badly he wanted this guy. It was smelly and foul, and first thing in the morning people started dumping fresh garbage in there, but he stayed in there with his radio completely undetected, waiting to see if this guy came out of the building. We parked way down the street and waited for his call. Finally, around lunchtime our target came outside and we got the call to move in. We drove up, chased him, and caught him. The only problem we had after that was how that deputy was going to get back to headquarters. That smell was awful. He definitely wasn't riding with any of us. Eventually he made it back; we knew that because we could smell him coming.

In August 1989, sixteen-year-old African American Yusef Hawkins was attacked by a gang of as many as thirty teenagers in Bensonhurst, Brooklyn. Hawkins and three friends had gone to that predominantly Italian neighborhood to look at a used Pontiac that was for sale. Nineteen-year-old Joey Fama shot Hawkins twice in the chest and he died at the scene. Several members of the gang were immediately arrested, but Fama disappeared. With the entire city on edge, law enforcement searched desperately for him. When a member of Fama's family died, the Marshals Service got word that he might risk showing up at the funeral. The problem was how to get close enough without being spotted. Just before dawn, a task force including deputies Lenny DePaul and Scott Palumbo moved quietly into the cemetery where the burial was to take place. DePaul and

Palumbo were dressed in camouflage gear, their pockets filled with food and water. They climbed up into a very large tree overlooking the plot. "Even though it was still officially summer," DePaul remembers,

> it was cold. We were basically disguised as a tree as we got up there and tried to make ourselves comfortable. I found a branch way up high that was just like a natural chair, two vertical branches crossed by a horizontal branch, and settled in. We knew we were going to be there for a while. About nine o'clock in the morning the workers decided to take a break, and they sat down against this tree and lit cigarettes. The smoke just drifted up, and Scott and I couldn't move. Finally a cemetery security guard who knew we were there asked them to move.
>
> We sat in that tree for seven hours, right through the entire funeral. But Joey Fama never showed. Then we had to wait until the entire funeral procession cleared the area before we were able to climb down. By that time our muscles were just frozen into position.

That's the thing about conducting a surveillance operation, you just never know. Fama eventually surrendered to upstate New York authorities.

At least DePaul had a comfortable seat. Deputy David O'Flaherty was looking for a dashing con man named Juan Battalia-Ponte, who had successfully convinced at least a dozen gullible women at various times that he was an FBI agent, a CIA agent, an Immigration and Naturalization agent, a DEA agent, a foreign diplomat, or a commander in the Argentine navy. He was wanted on a minor charge, a passport violation, but authorities were developing another far more serious case against him. Later he would be accused of trying to extort money from Argentines living in America, claiming he had connections to people in their country's repressive government detaining their relatives and for the right amount of money could secure their release. In fact, he actually may have had some connection to the CIA. In New York, he would dress up in an Argentine navy commander's uniform and take ten people to dinner in an expensive restaurant. At the end of the meal he would direct the restaurant to send the bill to the Argentinean embassy. He had two known wives and possibly a third, and he was taking money from a variety of women. O'Flaherty says,

He was so brazen that he convinced one of his women to rent a limo for him so he could pick up another one of his women. He actually had both women in the limo at the same time, but had convinced them that they were not allowed to talk to each other about him because he was a CIA agent.

One wife finally gave us enough information to track him to another apartment he had in New Jersey. It was a real dump. When these women were paying, everything he did was first class—when he was in the city, he would stay at the St. Regis, for example—but when he had to pay for it himself, he was a lot less extravagant. He lived in a cheap, shabby apartment. We staked out this apartment, but for various reasons we couldn't get close to it. So I had one of my guys literally climb a telephone pole and spend hours up there watching the apartment. I don't know how many hours he was up there. Finally Battalia-Ponte showed up. We were close by, watching another place in that same area. As Battalia-Ponte came out of a store I was able to grab him. He kept denying his identity, telling me I had the wrong guy, and he actually produced CIA credentials with his photograph on them that looked better than mine.

He was a real nut, but clever. When we searched his house, we found several uniforms, some weapons, and even a fake bomb in his closet.

Even with all the advances in technology, no one has yet discovered a way to make time move faster, and waiting and watching remain a central part of every deputy's job. Maybe the most difficult decision is accepting the fact that the suspect isn't going to show and ending the surveillance. In the back of every deputy's mind is the belief that if he or she waits just a little bit longer, watches for another day, another hour, the suspect is going to appear. Harry Layne spent more than two years pursuing a drug dealer named Elton Winchester, who had been indicted by the DEA but successfully evaded arrest. As Layne recalls, "This started out as a relatively simple drug case, but the more we looked, the more we discovered about him. By investigating his associates and putting the squeeze on people who were involved with him, we were led to believe that Winchester had been involved in a Salinas, California, murder and done a lot more drug dealing than we'd known about."

Elton Winchester was a flashy guy—he drove fancy cars and wore a lot of jewelry—but he was actually pretty good at staying on the run. He liked to be known as a bad guy, and when he found out that Layne was tracking him, he made it personal between the two of them:

He actually would taunt me. I'd never had that happen before on this level. He would send me

Christmas cards telling me, "I know you talked to —, well go f—k yourself because they won't help you." He sent me an Easter card on which he'd written, "You can't even find the Easter Bunny!" Once he sent me a Dick Tracy detective kit, which included little handcuffs, a magnifying glass and fingerprint ink, and the note, "You're never going to find me but I thought I'd give you a chance."

It's fair to say that annoyed me, although at the same time it was pretty funny. But what really made me angry was a card he sent me, and inside was a Polaroid of him with his pants down mooning me with the message, "Harry, if you're really missing me bad enough, kiss this!" This job rarely gets personal, but this had become personal. I really wanted to get this guy, and he had made it pretty clear that he had no intention of being taken alive. We put the squeeze on anybody who had ever passed him on the street. We spoke with every associate he had ever had, and we were closing all his potential sources of cash and information.

Finally, we were able to charge the wife of a close friend of his who lived in Elberton, Georgia, with a serious drug crime, and this friend then agreed to cooperate to help his wife. We were cutting off Winchester's money, cutting off his friends, but we left this one guy open on purpose. We believed that Winchester eventually would have to contact him. We installed cameras and microphones in his house then set up shop in another house we'd rented several blocks away. I moved up there from Florida and settled in. We sat there for days just staring at those monitors, the days became weeks; after a month, they gave me permission to keep the surveillance going for another thirty days. I just didn't want to give up; I knew this was the best chance we had to catch this guy. But it was very expensive and very boring. After another month, I tried to get the surveillance renewed again—I just knew he had to come there—but they told me, nope, wrap it up. Two more weeks then, I pleaded, just give me two more weeks. Nope, wrap it up. The guy ain't coming.

That's what happens sometimes with surveillance, you just have to pack your bags and walk away. I closed down the operation and drove to Tampa to see my family—and that night Elton showed up at that house. This couple was terrified he would find out they were cooperating with us. We hadn't removed the cameras yet and they thought he would see one of them. Apparently they walked around the house saying loudly, "Oh, Elton

Winchester, it's good to see you" and "What kind of gun is that in your waistband?," hoping we would hear them and bring the cavalry. But we weren't coming because we weren't there. We'd ended the surveillance one day too soon. Eventually Winchester told the couple what he wanted them to do to help him. They agreed to everything he said and got an accurate description of his vehicle. It was a pretty unique car, a 1972 Dodge Coronet.

As soon as I heard about it, I got in my car and raced back to Georgia. I was going a hundred miles an hour. We put a surveillance aircraft piloted by Jerry Lowery up in the air. Jerry actually spotted the car parked near a boat ramp, next to a lake. I got a good team together; it consisted of deputies, Georgia state troopers, deputy sheriffs, local police, Game and Fish Department employees, maybe even a few Boy Scouts. If you wore a badge, you were part of this posse.

Jerry kept watch from the air. He never lost sight of Winchester's car and kept telling us its location. We set up a roadblock just over the crest of a hill so by the time he came over the top and spotted us, it would be too late to do anything about it. When he came over that hill, we put a lot of guns on him. He was carrying a .32 but he didn't go for it; he pussied out at the last second. Instead he threw up his hands and said, "I don't have a gun."

We took him to jail, to the Marshals Service lockup in Macon, Georgia. We were all real happy that the chase was over, and we were celebrating when one of the guys said to me, "Harry, you got to do it."

"Do what?" I asked.

"You got to moon him."

"I can't do that," I said. "It's unprofessional."

They insisted, "Dude, you got to do it." And I thought, you know what, they're right. I do have to do it. So I went back to cellblock, dropped trou in front of him and told him, "Hey, Elton, kiss this!"

He said, "That ain't right." The next day we transported him all the way back to Tampa. Along the way he told me that friends of his in different parts of the country had mailed the cards to me, that was his way of sending me on a wild goose chase. It turned out he was a very funny guy who happened to be on the wrong side of the law. But he definitely was the kind of person you'd enjoy having a beer with—as long as he didn't kill you.

6

Arresting Developments

I _____ do solemnly swear that I will faithfully execute all lawful precepts directed to the marshal of the Territory of Arizona under the authority of the United States, and true returns make, and in all things well and truly, and without malice or partiality perform the duties of the office of Deputy United States Marshal of the Territory of Arizona during my continuance in said office, and take only my lawful fees; and that I will support and defend the Constitution of the United States against all enemies, foreign and domestic; and I will bear true faith and allegiance to the same; that I take this obligation freely, without any mental reservation or purpose of evasions; and that I will well and faithfully discharge the duties

of the office upon which I am to enter: So help
me God.

—*Deputy U.S. Marshals Oath of Office,*
August 21, 1900

All the tracking and trailing, all the watching and
waiting, all the paperwork and the interviews, all
the tips and the clues, almost always enable a deputy to
finally say those three big words: *You're under arrest.*
Every step deputies take during an investigation is done
to move just a little bit closer to that moment when
they can slip the cuffs on fugitives, give them their
Miranda rights, and put them into the system. Many
deputies will make literally thousands of arrests in their
careers—and every one of them brings with it a feeling
of satisfaction, completion—on occasion, there's also
some physical pain involved—but there is always tremendous professional pride: We got you!

When a man named Marshal Fitzgerald was
arrested for the murders of two women, he was sent
to St. Elizabeth's Hospital for the Criminally Insane in
Washington, D.C., for a psychiatric evaluation. Because
one of the women was the mother of a popular radio
DJ, the case got a lot of publicity. As Fitzgerald was
being transported by van from one wing of the hospital
to another, he suddenly pulled out a syringe and held it

against the driver's neck. It was filled with blood taken from an AIDS patient, he told the driver, warning him that if he didn't stop the van and get out, he would stab him in the neck. Fitzgerald smashed the van through the perimeter fence and drove away. A desperate killer carrying a vial of potentially deadly blood was on the loose in Washington. The manhunt began.

This was a high-priority, drop-everything case. Deputies began working around the clock, trying to catch Fitzgerald before he could get settled. Nobody went home. "We all slept in the office and basically just nodded off when we could," Harry Layne remembers. "We worked all our informants, we were on the streets, we began reaching out to every name we could associate with him. On the third day we got to the right guy. An old acquaintance of Fitzgerald's admitted to deputies that Fitzgerald had contacted him and told us that he had agreed to meet him in Baltimore to give him enough cash to get out of the area. The meet was supposed to take place in a few hours."

Baltimore is less than an hour from Washington. Layne's team alerted the Baltimore authorities and raced down there. "We had people from several state and local departments going down with us," Layne explains.

It was a rotten day; it was pouring and the traffic was terrible, and we had to get there before our informant was scheduled to meet Fitzgerald. Our lights were flashing and our sirens were blaring and we were driving on the highway apron when I got a call from our assistant chief who wanted me to brief him and the marshal on the status of the case. "I can't come back," I said. "We're on our way to Baltimore. We're going to bring this guy back."

Just like in a bad movie he snapped at me, "I don't care what you're doing, you get back here right now."

"I can't hear you," I yelled. "There's something wrong with this radio. Hello? Hello? Can you hear me?" He repeated his demand that I turn around and get back to Washington. "What's that? You're breaking up." I never heard another word he said. I always valued putting a bad guy in jail above the chain of command.

Layne's team made it to Baltimore a few minutes early. By the time they got there, the informant was scared to death. "He's got a gun," he told the deputies. "He told me he'll kill me if he finds out I gave him up."

"Okay," Layne told him, "we'll put a vest on you."

"No, what if he sees it?"

"Okay," Layne agreed, "we'll take the ballistic panels out of the carrier and put them under your shirt."

When that was done, the informant put on his jacket and examined himself critically in a mirror. Then he panicked. "You can see it; he'll see it and he'll kill me." The deputies took it off and then he got even more anxious. "Put it back on, put it back on."

Layne was slowly losing his temper. "This was the most difficult informer I'd ever had to deal with. We went through this two or three more times, take it off, put it on, until I told him, 'Look, if you don't decide this once and for all I'm going to kill you myself.' No vest, he decided. That's the way he went to the meeting."

The meet was going to take place in Baltimore's Inner Harbor, a sort of outdoor mall with stores and tourist attractions. It's a big, crowded plaza. Layne arranged his team in a loose perimeter in case Fitzgerald started running. The plaza was crowded with tourists, among them many school classes visiting the exhibits, so there was no way they could risk any gunplay in that environment. They changed the plan: when Fitzgerald was spotted, they would follow him out of the area until it was safe to arrest him.

Layne explains what happened next:

I stayed several feet away from our informant, but close enough so he could see me at all times. Then we started walking through the plaza. Suddenly the informant seemed to lose all his color. His eyes just got real wide, and he looked like he was going to faint. I turned to see what he was looking at and Fitzgerald was walking right toward us. Fitzgerald noticed the same thing I did, and then he looked at me, and when our eyes met, he knew what was going down. This situation was about to turn very nasty. I didn't hesitate; I ran right up to him and clotheslined him, hit him right in the neck with my forearm. I hit him so hard I thought I decapitated him. He went down like a sack of rocks. We jumped on him and pinned his arms, and I screamed in his face, "You try to stick anybody with that needle and you're a dead man."

We got the handcuffs on him and searched him; we didn't find a gun, but we did find the needle full of blood. Meanwhile, our informant was just standing there. Part of the plan was that we were going to arrest him to protect him; we didn't want Fitzgerald to know he had given him up. So I jumped up and yelled at him, "Get on the ground, you're under arrest too." In my entire career, I'd never arrested anyone so happy to be arrested. He laid right down and we handcuffed him too.

I took a deep breath. It was done, I thought. But this was just about to become even more like a movie: in the course of making the arrest, my gun had been exposed and some people eating in a restaurant right there saw it; they called Baltimore PD and reported that some poor man was being robbed on the plaza and needed help. The police officers came rolling up on us in a golf cart with sirens blaring and lights flashing. A waitress from the restaurant pointed at me and said, "That's him! That's the robber! He has a silver gun!" The police put their guns on us. They didn't know who to believe. I knew we were okay. I had a lot of guys in the crowd, and I knew they were going to come rushing in to help us. They were coming. I was waiting. They were coming. They were somewhere, coming, sometime.

They didn't show up. I was thinking, *Where the f—k are my guys?* It was just me and my partner. My people weren't anywhere at all. We explained to the cops who we were and what was going on; we produced our badges and finally got everything straightened out. The Baltimore cops took control of Fitzgerald and the informant. I went to look for my people.

Layne walked around the entire area, wondering what could have happened to his team. And then, as he walked past a Hooters restaurant and looked up at the outside deck, the mystery was solved. Several officers had gone inside to use the deck as a vantage point. It gave them a view of the whole area. But then they started talking to the Hooters girls and missed the whole takedown. In retrospect, that part of the operation went less well than initially planned.

Even considering the thousands of arrests a deputy will make in his or her career, few of them will ever forget their first one. Even in the most basic cases— a failure to answer a summons, for example—being able to take away an individual's freedom serves to emphasize the enormous power that badge gives to deputies. Initially deputies assist experienced people on the job, but eventually they get to go out on their own. Deputy Tony Schilling was working in North Carolina when he was handed his first case, a cold warrant for an individual wanted on drug and gun charges.

The warrant was at least a couple of years old, but I worked it like it was the most important case in the world. I sent the leads I had to different parts of the country and eventually we developed information that he might be living in a little hilltop town right across the North Carolina border in Virginia. I ended up hiking up the backside of a mountain with a local officer to get a view on a trailer. It was a perfect hideout. Two trailers were sitting in the open on the top of the mountain. They had a view of everything around them, and anyone coming toward them. We stayed hidden in the woods, watching the trailers through binoculars, trying to determine who was there and what they were doing. We sat on that place for several hours until we saw some activity. Then I radioed our backup team to drive up the mountain while we cut through the woods to get close enough to cover the back. When the suspect saw the cars coming up the road, he started to slide out the back, but when he spotted us, he closed the door and went back inside. He knew he wasn't going anywhere. His girlfriend opened the door for us. He had a gun but made no attempt to do anything with it. I arrested him. I was a young kid and I was excited. I was pumped. That first arrest got me hooked, and I knew right away this was definitely the area I wanted to concentrate in.

A decade later, the now very experienced Schilling found himself walking up another, far more dangerous mountain. This one was in Jamaica in 2002. Jamaica was an important destination for fugitives, who could disappear into its small towns and villages until the heat in the United States cooled down and they might return. Although the Marshals Service now has a permanent office on that island, at that time deputies would go down there for a few months and close out as many cases as possible to demonstrate the value of having a full-time presence. "We were highly motivated," Schilling says. "When the TV show *America's Most Wanted* ran a segment about a guy who'd shot and disabled a police officer, we got a tip that he was hiding out in the central part of the island. There are large parts of Jamaica that are like a tropical rain forest; once you get outside the cities and tourist destinations like Kingston or Montego Bay, you're in another world. It's the jungle. That's where we were told this guy was staying."

Schilling and his partner hooked up with the Jamaica Fugitive Apprehension Team and some local law enforcement, then went to try to find him. Until they had evidence he was there, they couldn't get a warrant. As the newly formed task force drove up into the mountains, Schilling was warned not to get out of the vehicle, even to use a restroom, because people would know he was an outsider. The word would get to the fugitive pretty quickly that there were strangers in the area. So the team did its surveillance from the cars and eventually spotted someone they were pretty sure was the fugitive. That enabled them to get a warrant; very early one morning they went back.

This time, as Schilling recalls, they intended to arrest the fugitive.

We parked about a mile from this little village and began hiking up the road. It was a very uncomfortable feeling. I was in a place where I was pretty sure no American law enforcement officer had ever stepped before, walking up the road alongside people I didn't know who were carrying rifles, into a situation we knew almost nothing about. I knew I was a long way from home. At times like that I really did wonder how I got into that situation. The whole thing was surreal; I didn't have any control. It was a scary, scary experience. I'd arrested hundreds of people, but I'd never been in a situation like this one. All I could do was stay on edge and be ready to move if I had to. We hiked into this little village and surrounded the house. When he stepped outside and saw our faces, he knew he was

done. He just dropped his head, and we moved in
and I put him under arrest.

From the ninety-four independent districts operating
across a young nation, the Marshals Service has been
transformed into a semicentralized organization with
tentacles that currently extend far beyond our national
borders. The Marshals Service currently maintains
permanent offices in countries including Mexico,
Jamaica, and the Dominican Republic.

When deputies begin working on a case, they never
know where in the world it will lead them. The pursuit
of a fugitive may take them to a drug shooting gallery
in an inner-city project or to the top of a Caribbean
mountain, or the trail may wind through a city or
through a rural area—the possibilities are as extensive
as the reach of the American legal system. When the
United States invaded Panama in December 1989, for
example, there was a dispute between the FBI and DEA
over who would actually arrest Panamanian dictator
Manuel Noriega. General Noriega had been indicted
for drug trafficking and money laundering. Attorney
General Dick Thornburgh ultimately decided that the
apprehension authority for Noriega actually rested with
the Marshals Service and sent a team of deputies led by
Tony Perez into that country. He recaps the arrest.

We landed on the second day of the invasion. Fires were still burning, and there was some shooting going on. Noriega had requested sanctuary in the Vatican's Panamanian embassy and refused to surrender. We tried psychological warfare to get him to come out: we blasted rock music through loudspeakers around the clock. After ten days, he finally surrendered. I stood face-to-face with him— he did not look happy—and said curtly, "I'm Tony Perez, U.S. Marshals, and you're under arrest." He nodded his head; he understood. We brought him back and he was sentenced to forty years in prison, although that sentence was later reduced.

There is no way of predicting how a fugitive is going to react when confronted by deputies. The general rule is always be prepared for the worst possible reaction. Actually, there are some people who are resigned or even happy to be caught. Life on the run is tough: in most instances there are few nights when a fugitive can sleep peacefully, money is always a problem, there is no way of knowing who can be trusted, and the simplest things in life like using an ATM or cashing a check or getting a driver's license become major issues. "When you're on the run, you're always looking over your shoulder," points out Deputy John Bolen.

You're always wondering what's around the next corner. Fugitives live with continued anxiety and stress. I opened a two-decades-old parole violation case in 2003. Going through some notes from a Lexington, Kentucky, police officer who had made the original underlying arrest, I saw the fugitive had a cousin who no one had ever talked to. I spent some time with that cousin, who had led a normal law-abiding life, and ultimately he gave me the information that allowed me to find the fugitive. When I made the arrest, the fugitive told me he was relieved, that he'd been waiting for this day for twenty years, and that he was even considering turning himself in. I didn't believe that, but I have seen many people so tired of running and living life as a fugitive that they welcome being arrested.

There have been numerous cases in which a fugitive who supposedly has the ability to "live off the land" successfully escaped into the woods and managed to survive there—for a period of time. But the woods are a hostile environment: even with the proper equipment, there are things there that live to bite and sting or poison you. So when people who believed they could survive in the woods are caught, they often admit they are glad it's over. The same thing is true for people trying to survive in the urban jungles, who move from flophouse to flophouse or who sleep in drug dens and survive on the few dollars they can beg or find or, when necessary, steal.

Some people just aren't equipped to be fugitives. Famed computer hacker Bill Landreth, whose IQ was supposedly 163, was convicted of breaking into several high-security top-secret government computers and given three years' probation. One day he simply disappeared. His probation officer got a warrant and deputies began searching for him. Eventually he was traced to Puerto Vallarta, but by the time deputies got there he was gone. Almost a year after he disappeared, he was finally caught in McMinnville, Oregon, when a woman called police after finding a barefoot and disheveled man drinking water from her backyard hose. Life on the run had reduced this genius to a vagrant who risked his freedom for a drink of water.

Others can survive for an extended period of time, but when cut off from all help, they eventually get desperate. Consider Eric Rudolph, who killed two people and injured at least 150 more with a series of bombings, including the Atlanta Olympics and several abortion clinics. He spent five years on the FBI's Most Wanted list as both the bureau and the Marshals Service searched unsuccessfully for him. He lived during that time in the Appalachian wilderness—only to be arrested when a young policeman found him picking through the dumpster behind a Save-a-Lot store in Murphy, North Carolina.

Some arrests really are that easy; the fugitive surrenders or simply gives up without any resistance. Wendell Brock, for example, had to arrest a husband for domestic violence—his crime was he'd hit his wife with his walker. Brock's biggest problem in this arrest was getting the suspect to the curb and into the special handicapped transport van.

Whenever possible, deputies like to make a show of overwhelming force; they know that when a fugitive accepts the reality that he has no chance of escaping or resisting, he will surrender. Rick Gainey received information that a fugitive who had jumped bail on a major counterfeiting case was flying into Atlanta from Chicago.

This was a guy who counterfeited checks. He would have people steal checks out of mailboxes and use the information on them to create his own dummy accounts. He was at it for a long time before he got caught. And when he finally did get caught, he skipped. We got about eight deputies and went to the airport. We waited for him in the terminal just beyond the jetway. As the arriving passengers began walking out of the jetway, each of us held up a little sign, as if we were limo drivers waiting to pick up a passenger. And on each sign we'd written the name of a person whose identity he had stolen. He came off the plane and looked around, and it took a few seconds before it clicked in. He didn't exactly smile, but he realized he had no place to go and surrendered.

Unfortunately, many arrests aren't that simple. A lot of the fugitives pursued by the Marshals Service are career criminals; they've been in prison and know that if they go back in, they will be there for a long time. So they're willing to do whatever is necessary to get away. Almost without exception every deputy has had to fight someone to get the cuffs on them. Being injured is just part of the job. "They're cornered, they fight," Dave O'Flaherty says flatly. "I tell young deputies that if they think for one minute that holding up their badge and identifying themselves as a deputy U.S. marshal is going to scare anybody, they better find a new profession. It's more likely they're going to tell you to take that badge and shove it up your ass. Or offer to do it for you. When you're making an arrest, you have to be ready for absolutely anything."

O'Flaherty had a warrant for a man wanted on a nothing case, a parole violation. No big deal. But he figured there might be a problem when he learned that the guy's street name was Monster.

Turned out there was a reason for this. Without exaggerating, he was 6'6" and weighed 350 pounds. He was a big, big guy who lived in a building in Brooklyn. We finally tracked down the place, but we didn't know which apartment he was in. We knocked on the door of an apartment we thought might be a neighbor. The man who opened the door was the largest person I have ever seen in my life. He was bigger than the Monster. As soon as we told him who we were looking for, he slammed the door and talked to us through the closed door. "I don't want to say anything, leave me alone, please." The biggest guy in the world was scared of the man we were trying to arrest. If that guy was scared of the Monster, imagine how we felt.

We finally found out which apartment he was in. I dressed up my smallest guy, an extraordinary deputy named Mike Hollander, as a telephone company employee. Mike dressed the part; he put on the hard hat, and he was carrying the tool belt, phones hanging from clips—he looked like the real deal. He knocked on the door and when the Monster opened it up, Mikey found himself looking directly into the man's belly button. "Phone repair," he said.

"I ain't got no problems with my phone," the Monster said, slamming the door.

Now we knew he was in there. We came up with a plan: Mikey would knock on the door again, and when the Monster opened it, we would all charge in and tackle him. Mikey knocked again—the Monster opened the door and began, "I thought I f—in' told you to . . ." and we hit him. We charged into the room and brought him down. We wrestled him into submission, then tried to put the cuffs on him. He was so big that his arms didn't come far enough behind him for the cuffs to hold both wrists. We had to click together two sets of handcuffs to restrain him.

"Every deputy has had his or her share of knock-down drag-out brawls," according to Craig Caine.

It goes with the territory. You never know what to expect, never. We had a guy who put out the word on the street that if the cops came, he was going to shoot it out; he wasn't going to be taken alive. But when we busted into the guy's house, he put his hands behind his back and pleaded, "Please don't hurt me." It's the ones you don't expect a fight from who get crazy. A lot of times it's family members who get it started; the fugitive is passive in the beginning but when we separate him from his family and put the handcuffs on, here comes a wife or a mother screaming at us and swinging a broomstick at our heads. When we protect ourselves, the perp gets involved to help his people, and suddenly we're in the middle of a brawl.

Because of injuries suffered on the job, Harry Layne has had one serious back operation, two knee surgeries, and two shoulder surgeries—which he estimates is roughly typical for any deputy who has been serving warrants for an appreciable period of time.

We have to go hands-on a lot of times or let the guy get away. We're not in the business of letting people get away. One time my partner and I were looking for a drug dealer, and he had a girl he was working as a prostitute. When we pinched her, she told us he was out scoring some heroin and they were going to meet later at her apartment and shoot up. We went back to her apartment and waited there for him. It was a second-floor apartment with stairs outside leading directly to the ground. While we were waiting she told us, "He's got a secret knock. I've got to knock back or he won't come in, he'll take off. And sometimes he carries a gun, too." Okay, knock-knock, go ahead.

The drug dealer showed up at the apartment about two hours late. Drug dealers are never on time. He knocked, she knocked, Layne's partner yanked open the door, and the suspect came flying inside.

My partner threw him on the floor and jumped on top of him. If he was carrying a gun, we weren't going to give him any opportunity to get to it. But then I looked up—and there was another guy standing in the open doorway. I looked at him, he looked at me, his eyes got wider and wider, then he turned and took off running down the stairs.

I took three or four steps and leaped on his back. Both of us tumbled all the way down the stairs to the landing. It was like we were fighting in a cowboy movie, except we weren't stuntmen and those stairs weren't props. It really hurt. When we hit the ground, he ended up right on top of me.

I was in real pain, and I couldn't fight right then, so I pulled my gun and put it to his head, "You motherf—er," I told him. "You move and I'll blow your brains out."

That really must have scared him—because he pissed all over me. Now I was hurt and pissed on. "Oh man," I said. "You filthy bastard."

"I couldn't help it, man. You scared me."

I ruptured a disk in that fight.

Another time when we were searching for a guy in a cheesy trailer, I fell through the floor and tore my ACL and MCL. Then another time we went to a fugitive's address and found his son, who was an escaped prisoner, hiding there. He was twenty-four years old and muscled up, and we had one hell of a brawl. He kicked me in the knee that had been operated on, so surgeons had to do the operation again. In that case I brought charges against him for assaulting a federal officer. He refused to plead, so it actually went to trial. While I was testifying his defense lawyer tried to convince the jury that I hadn't really been badly hurt. "Does your knee still hurt?" he asked me sarcastically.

"Yes, sir, it does," I responded.

"I see, and would you tell us when it hurts worst?"

I looked right at the jury and said firmly, "It hurts me most when I'm in church on my knees praying." The judge was laughing so hard he had to hide his face behind a law book.

Years ago, deputies had a lot more leeway and much less supervision when they made arrests, and basically they did whatever was necessary to get the job done. "In those days it was like the wild wild west," remembers Donald Ward.

The only rule was do whatever you had to do to survive. Once my partner and I saw a drug deal going down and chased this guy out of a vacant building. This was a big guy, 6'4" at least, and the next thing I know my partner was on his back hitting him over the head with a jack, a wooden nightstick. That finally brought him down. It took us some time to drag him back inside the building. Then we realized if we took him in, with all the paperwork we would have to do, we were going to be late for what was called a "racket," a promotion party. We figured, well, this guy only had one deck of heroin and he'd learned his lesson. So we picked up a towel and handed it to him, "Put this on your head, you'll be good," and we left. That's how my partner became known forever as Jackman. In those days you could get away with things like that. It was a very different organization. But we didn't have a choice. A lot of times there was only two of us, and we were outnumbered.

In those days a lot of deputies relied on the overtime they could earn to pay their bills. Ward and his partner were picking up what they thought was some easy overtime on a Saturday afternoon when they decided to go pick up a guy on an IRS warrant. He had been in prison, and while serving his time he had been part of a group filing phony W-2 forms and claiming a refund. People wanted by the IRS tended to be white-collar criminals who rarely put up any kind of resistance; it turned out this guy was not one of them.

It definitely started well. When we got to his apartment, he was half asleep. But suddenly he woke up and started swinging. My partner jumped on his back, but this guy didn't slow down at all. He was like a running back carrying my partner to the goal line, which apparently was the front door. I jumped on him and put a choke hold on him, and the three of us started moving slowly backward into the room. Finally I yanked him down; we landed on the couch—and then we broke through the wall. Literally, we put a big hole in the wall. But we managed to get him subdued and cuffed.

We got him downstairs and as we started putting him in the car he wedged his foot in the corner of the door and pushed back. This was long before we had sprays or Tasers; we just had grit and muscle. We fought to get him into the car; when we got him settled, he tried to head butt me, and we ended up brawling in the car. It was one long endless fight from his bed to the prison, and we both just got too tired to keep going. It didn't end as much as run out of steam.

When we got him to the cellblock, I looked at his record and saw that he had been in Vietnam at the same time I had been there. I asked him, "What are you fighting me for? It's just an IRS thing. I was over there same time as you, man. You got to chill out, we can fight all day."

He said, "You know what I'd really like? I'd like an egg sandwich." That's it? An egg sandwich? We agreed that if I got him an egg sandwich he wouldn't give us any more problems. I got him his egg sandwich and that was it. He was easy. But about a year and a half later, I happened to be at the MCC, and I saw him in the distance mopping the floor.

He recognized me immediately. He tapped the guy he was working with on the shoulder and pointed at me, "See that guy? That's my AO." His arresting officer. He continued, "Whoa, him and me had some f—ing fight. He's a tough guy." Then he shook his head and said with true admiration, "That's my favorite arresting officer of all time."

Women will fight too. Fugitives often use women to carry guns or money for them, to get them drugs and provide a safe house, and sometimes to get between them and being arrested. So deputies often have to deal with them. James Benjamin explains,

I don't think people really understand how difficult it is to subdue an angry woman. In some cases you're not just taking her husband or boyfriend away, you're taking her source of cash, sometimes her drugs and protection on the street. In that world, when he's gone she becomes vulnerable. So she's going to fight for him. A 5'5", 110-pound woman with high heels and long fingernails is a dangerous weapon. If she starts fighting, there is a real chance the deputy is going to get hurt. Women will bite, scratch, and kick, and they will keep going until you can get the cuffs on them.

A Lexington, Kentucky, task force burst into a house just before dawn and found the fugitive they were hunting in bed with his girlfriend. Both of them were naked. They placed him under arrest and began running an NCIC check on her. Meanwhile, they permitted her to go into another room to get dressed and get some pants for her husband—instead she went out the back window and took off. By the time NCIC responded with the fact that there was a warrant for her too, she was gone.

Some of the fights literally are life-and-death battles. When deputies Geoff Shank and Ed Sloan went to an apartment to arrest a fugitive, they found him there with his two brothers. "It was only the two of us," Shank remembers.

I went in the front door, Ed was watching the back. As our guy came down the stairs, I told him, "Take it easy, it's all good," and cuffed the guy up. That was when one of his brothers hit me in the face with a table leg. It caused me to bite down on my tongue really hard, and I started bleeding. Then they started pummeling me, and I can remember thinking, *I'm not going to let this freakin' piece of dirt end me here in this crappy-ass apartment.* Just as I was about to push myself up, Ed comes bursting through the back door and we were able to take care of business. Next thing I knew I was out front leaning against a tree, bleeding badly from my mouth. "I'm okay," I told Ed, just before I collapsed. I ended up having surgery to get the damage fixed, but I lost a little bit of my tongue.

Not surprisingly, one of the most difficult things a deputy has to do before making an arrest is make certain the right person is being arrested. When dealing with literally hundreds and even thousands of fugitives, unless they are as big as the Monster or have an easily identifiable characteristic, like an obvious birthmark or a missing hand, it is possible to make a mistake. At times deputies have to identity a subject from photographs that are several years old. That can be tough enough, but fugitives often try to change their appearance, cutting their hair or letting it grow longer, dyeing it another color, cutting off or growing facial hair, even gaining or losing weight. Deputies can't rely on an ID because fugitives will either have false IDs or none at all. As Mike Pizzi admits,

We've definitely had identity issues. I taught all my young deputies how to use the fingerprint classification number. It's a twenty-digit numerical descriptive that starts with your right thumb and ends with your left pinkie and appears on FBI feeds or rap sheets. For example, if the right thumb has the letters AA, it means the individual has a plain arch-type finger-print. So if you look at the suspect's thumb and he has a loop or anything other than a plain arch, which is easy to read, then it isn't your guy. It isn't perfect and it may not lead to a conclusive identification, but it does help eliminate suspects.

For example, late one Friday afternoon I got a phone call from a cop in California informing me he had just caught a prison escapee we were looking for. *Okay, great,* I thought. I asked him to go on his computer and bring up the wanted flyer that was on our database. "You see something that says FPC on there?" He did. "Read it to me, please?" The last ten digits were XXXXXXXXXX. "Okay," I said. "Lemme ask you this, is the guy you're holding in the cage missing his left hand?" No. "Is he missing any fingers on his left hand?" No. I told him, "Then you got the wrong guy." There was a long pause and then he said to me, "Who the f—k are you, Charlie Chan?"

Tattoos and scars also can be invaluable in making an identification. No matter how much an individual changes his facial appearance, in almost all cases evidence of their tattoos will still be there. Different groups have different symbols. Members of the Mexican Mafia, for example, will have E-M-E tattooed on their forearm. One of the first identifiers deputies look for is a distinguishable or unique tattoo. On December 13, 2000, for example, seven inmates of the maximum-security Connally Unit near Kenedy, Texas, staged the largest breakout in that state's history. They overpowered prison workers and took their clothes, broke into the prison armory and stole weapons, then made their getaway in a prison truck. They lay low for almost two weeks, but on Christmas Eve, police officer Aubrey Hawkins interrupted them while they were holding up a sporting goods store in Irving, Texas. They shot him eleven times—when he was on the ground, they lifted up his vest and shot him in the chest—then ran over his body with an SUV. It was more of an execution than a murder.

The inmates escaped with forty guns and plenty of ammunition. By then law enforcement agencies from around the country had joined the search for the Texas 7. Bill Sorukas was working out of the command post in Huntsville, Texas, the headquarters for the Texas Correctional System. "After they had murdered a police officer, this became a nationwide hunt. We were getting hundreds of tips every day," he says.

Jimmy Bankston adds,

It was totally crazy. The phones never stopped ringing. With the national media attention, unbelievably crazy people were calling with bizarre stories. These calls were from everywhere and they really hindered our investigation. In addition to the usual crazies desperate for attention, we had people calling with literally felony false statements intended to obstruct our investigation; and unfortunately they sounded as real as any other calls. We couldn't possibly follow every lead so we had to determine which ones to investigate. Some of them were easy to eliminate because they were too crazy, but most of them had some element that sounded plausible in them. One question we asked every caller was to describe what these people looked like. The descriptions always were the same as the photographs being shown on TV.

Investigators were able to put together little pieces of information to make a reasonable guess where the escapees might be headed, which gave them some idea which tips to take a little more seriously.

Sorukas was eating dinner on a Sunday night when he received a call.

It was from one of our people in Colorado. He told me that a guy who ran a trailer park in Woodland

Park, Colorado, was reporting that all seven of the escapees were living in a motor home there, claiming to be missionaries. We started asking about identifiers, what names they were using, what they looked like, what type of clothes they were wearing. Most of the answers were consistent with information readily available to the public—but then he told me that the informant claimed one of them had a teardrop tattoo outside his right eye. I had gone through all the files. I hadn't seen any reference in any of them to a teardrop tattoo.

"The reason we suspected it might be a good lead," said Bankston, "is because we already were looking in that area. We had intercepted calls from pay phones to family members from outside Denver, and a rash of police vehicles had been broken into and police radios and bulletproof vests had been stolen. If this same call had come from the Upper Michigan Peninsula, we wouldn't have followed up as quickly or as forcefully, but with the other information we had, this one made sense."

A member of the task force named Terry Cobb, of the Texas Department of Criminal Justice, began searching through every file, every local police report, every photograph and mug shot—until he finally found one photograph of George Rivas, the leader of the gang, which showed a teardrop tattoo just under his right eye. "The informant had told us something completely accurate that we hadn't known," says Sorukas. "That night the troops started rolling in. We had the Colorado Springs SWAT team, the FBI SWAT team; we knew the fugitives had the stolen weapons, so before going in we gathered all our resources."

Early the next morning, three of the suspects drove out of the trailer park in a Jeep Cherokee. They were trapped when they stopped at a gas station down the road. Two others had stayed in the RV—one of those men surrendered, and after a five-hour stand-off the other one killed himself. That left two of them on the run.

The tips kept coming. Jimmy Bankston got a call at the command center from a woman in Albuquerque, New Mexico, claiming the two fugitives had broken into her home and briefly held her hostage, then left, taking her cell phone with them.

We got up on the phone and found out it was being used in Overland, Kansas. There was no possible way they could have gotten to Kansas in that time frame. I knew it was bogus and told that to the FBI, but they put people on helicopters and got ready to go there. I told them they were wasting their time.

Finally this woman admitted she was lying; she actually wanted to know where her boyfriend was and if he was with another woman. That number was his cell phone. We ended up charging her with obstruction.

Then we got a tip that they were in a Holiday Inn in Colorado Springs. I was asked to verify that the phone they were using was somewhere in that area. Our Technical Operations people were able to confirm it. It was good, they were there.

The Holiday Inn was surrounded. After being permitted to appear in a TV interview, during which they denounced the Texas criminal justice system as being "as corrupt as we are," they surrendered. All six survivors were sentenced to death because of their participation in Officer Hawkins's murder. But Rivas's tattoo remained a key element of their capture.

In the past, before the availability of computers and other now-common devices, deputies would carry around thick photo albums containing pictures of the people they were pursuing. They would constantly be flipping through the pages of these books, memorizing all the information about each fugitive. Obviously some people were better at recognizing fugitives than others; they either had a natural ability to remember faces or they had developed their own system. One deputy, for example, would find a celebrity the fugitive resembled and use that to make a comparison: He's a fat Frank Sinatra. He's a stumpy Willie Mays.

The ability to make a DNA comparison has made the job of law enforcement a lot easier, although for the Marshals Service, because of the time it takes to process, it has only limited application. Most often DNA is used to show the presence of a suspect at a crime scene, and by the time the marshals get involved, that already has been done. For deputies, DNA testing is used on occasion to confirm or disprove identification. Deputies sometimes have trailed a person into a restaurant or coffee shop and retrieved the glass or cup he or she used to make a fingerprint or DNA match to their fugitive.

Obviously, the best way to make a positive ID is to have the suspect identify himself. Deputy Mike Moran uses a technique taught to him at the beginning of his career, "If I'm not sure I've got the right guy, I'll throw the wrong name at him. I'll go up to him and tell him, 'Richard Langsam, I've got a warrant for your arrest.' And every time the guy will smile and tell me, 'You got the wrong guy. I'm not Richard

Langsam. I'm Brian McLane!' Thank you very much, Brian McLane, you're under arrest."

Another deputy had only an old photograph to use for ID purposes when he spotted someone who could have been his fugitive on the street. He called the man over to the car and asked him to look at some pictures. He showed him six or seven mug shots and suddenly the suspect smiled and said, "Hey! That's me!" When the deputy placed him under arrest for parole violation, the man told him he couldn't do that because "you fooled me with self-incrimination."

Deputies will use any possible tool to make a positive ID. When Mike Bunk interviewed the ex-wife of a fugitive on the Marshals Service 15 Most Wanted list, she told him that he had a habit of making a strange noise with his lips. Then she did her imitation of it for him. When Bunk located a man he thought could be the fugitive, he sat down next to him at a bar as the man ate a sandwich and enjoyed a beer. And as soon as Bunk heard him make that sound, he arrested him. "And then I had to drive him up to Miami. It was a long drive, and the whole way up there he was in the backseat making that noise. Eventually he pleaded guilty to some of the charges, and when I ran into him, he asked me to do him a favor: he wanted me to send a copy of his 15 Most Wanted poster to his mother. I didn't know why he wanted that, but I sent it; maybe he just wanted to show his mother that he had been a success at his chosen profession."

Bob Leschorn shares another story about IDing fugitives.

A lot of times we got old cases from a local PD and would have to guess what a person would look like ten years after his mug shot was taken. One time we were searching for a Pittsburgh attorney and degenerate gambler named R. Mark Hunter, who was accused of offering a hit man $25,000 to kill his mother because she had sued him to force him to repay a $273,000 loan—with interest—that she'd made several years earlier. Hunter had been on the run for a while, and, as we later found out, he'd dropped sixty pounds, dyed his hair, and had some plastic surgery. Eventually we got a tip from an informant that he was paying people up in the Bronx to protect him. So we started looking there.

The informer told Leschorn that Hunter played cards in the same social club every night, but he wouldn't identify him. Leschorn went to the club. He looked at every person in there, trying to determine if his eye socket, which can't be changed, had the same shape as the man in the old photograph.

I couldn't pick him out, not until I noticed one guy ducking his head every time I looked his way. Every single time I looked at him he ducked his head or turned away. That was interesting.

We rousted him up off the table. He gave us his ID and asked us why we were busting his chops. I kept staring at him; there was a little similarity in his eye sockets, but other than that he didn't look anything like the person in the photograph. When I told him we needed to see additional ID, he said it was back in his hotel room. So we drove him to his hotel. I could see he was starting to get real shaky. On the way there I said to him, "Give it up, Mark. I know it's you."

"I don't know what you're talking about," he insisted.

We searched his hotel room and didn't come up with much, until I noticed a suitcase in a corner. There was a bus tag on it and I looked at it: Mark Hunter. It was his one mistake. He was stunned; he'd gone to such elaborate lengths to disguise himself, and as we took him in he just kept shaking his head and repeating, "I can't believe you guys got me. I can't believe you guys got me."

As would be expected, people react very differently when they're arrested. David O'Flaherty caught up with a bank robber who had violated his parole for the third time. When he was placed under arrest, he told O'Flaherty that the arrest wasn't legal because he knew his rights—he'd been arrested twice before for this crime so it had to be "triple jeopardization."

Bill Sorukas was working with a San Diego PD detective tracking a murder suspect when an informer alerted them that he was supposed to meet the fugitive at a local mall.

This was an especially bloody murder case, so obviously this guy was very violent. He was a local gangbanger, a tough kid. But when we arrested him, he didn't resist. This detective had the most amazing demeanor I'd ever seen; he could calm down anybody. He told the kid, "Look, I've got some bad news and I got some good news. What do you want first?"

The kid decided, "Give me the bad news first." The detective continued, "Okay, you know why you're being arrested. There was blood from two individuals in that room; the person that was killed, his blood was all over, and because a knife was involved the assailant's blood was there too and that matches your DNA. I'm seeing little wounds on you and so I'm figuring you were there and you're the guy who did this."

The kid dropped his head—he knew his situation—then he sighed and asked him to tell him the good news. The detective looked him right in the eye and told him, "Your cholesterol level is really good."

Many times deputies have to put on some sort of disguise or create a character to get close enough to a fugitive to make the arrest. Tony Burke, for example, carried an assortment of props in the back of his car, explaining,

I'm just a dumpy white guy with a shaved head and a goatee, so putting on a uniform enables me to pass for whoever I need to be. In my vehicle I kept a Domino's pizza shirt and a pizza box, a workman's belt with all the tools and tape measures hanging down, clipboards. There were several times when I put my gun inside the pizza box and knocked on the door. Sometimes they would open right up. But sometimes they wouldn't open it because they hadn't ordered a pizza. At those times I'd yell to them that the people who had ordered it screwed me and I was trying to get rid of it for half price. Half price? That door would open!

Because people still tend to think of law enforcement as primarily a man's job, female deputies like Geri Doody often could get close to fugitives without being detected. She remembers,

We were looking for a guy whose girlfriend had just given birth to their child and we figured he might try to visit her in the hospital, St. John's in Jamaica, Queens. We couldn't risk any type of confrontation in a hospital, but we needed to know if he was there. So I wandered into the mother's room pretending to be completely lost. The fugitive was sitting right next to the bed. I wished them luck with their new child and left. Then I let my partners know he was in the room. Vic Oboyski put on a doctor's shirt and hung a stethoscope around his neck, and when the fugitive walked out of the hospital's front door, he grabbed him. The guy couldn't understand why he was being arrested by a doctor. I remember he struggled because I got pushed against a wall and cracked a couple of ribs.

I played lost many times. I'd go into apartments pretending to be desperate to use their bathroom, or

I'd knock on the front door claiming I was the Avon lady or someone from the welfare department. As a white woman working in black neighborhoods I would be a teacher. Whatever I had to be to get close, that's what I became. Nobody would pay attention to me because I looked more like a social worker than a deputy marshal.

When Stephanie Creasy began her career in Utah, that office didn't emphasize warrants. As she explains,

Their idea of working warrants was to send me to the front door of a house pretending to be looking for a fictitious person. When the man who answered told me there was no such person at that address, I would say something like, "Oh well, you're cute, what's your name?" If it was the person we were looking for, I would flip my hair—that was the sign, flipping my hair—and my partners would come up and arrest the guy.

One night we had a warrant for a man who had raped a thirteen-year-old. He lived in an apartment building that was way back off the street. After I confirmed it was him, I flipped my hair—and nothing happened. So I did it again, and again. I was standing there flipping my hair like a crazy woman, and finally I heard them approaching. I yanked the screen door open, and one of the officers was able to grab him by the neck before he could slam the door. The deputy managed to pull the guy out of the house—and then the suspect pooped himself. He was so scared he went right in his pants. All of the guys had just gotten new cars so nobody wanted to bring him to the office. They stood there arguing for a while about who was going to bring him in. That was my introduction to warrants.

In a New England case, Deputy Wayne Warren was able to convince a fugitive that he was a woman. This young man was wanted for the rape of a twelve-year-old. After obtaining the suspect's cell-phone number, Warren began texting him, pretending to be a beautiful twenty-two-year-old woman.

I sent him a picture of a Hooters girl and convinced him it was me. He began texting all sorts of illicit things to me, and finally I asked him to send me a picture. The photograph he sent me showed him standing in front of a house with a lot of snow on the ground. We knew he was hiding somewhere in Maine, so I sent that picture to my counterparts up there. They had been to his parents' house and recognized it in the background. So we knew he had been there. The question was whether he was still there.

I told them to go sit on that house and let me know when they were in position. When they were in place, I sent the fugitive a text telling him, "I really want to see you. You look so good I want to see you without a shirt on in all that snow." So he went outside into his front yard, took off his shirt, and took the picture. When our people saw him do that, they moved right in and arrested him.

Although most undercover assignments are brief and end in a quick arrest, deputies have worked far more complex cases that lasted a considerable period of time and required a lot more than simply putting on a pizza deliveryman's shirt. One major case involved a woman known as Lilly Schmidt, who earned her reputation as one of New York's more successful scam artists. Lilly Schmidt was the name she used primarily, although she had forty different aliases and an uncanny ability to become any one of those characters. In the early 1990s, the apparently very attractive Bulgarian native and her partner, Leonard Steingard, were estimated to have scammed banks, foreign exchange firms, jewelers, and art galleries out of as much as nine million dollars. Their specialty was counterfeiting certified checks, which had enabled them to steal, among other objects, an original Claude Pissarro oil painting and a sable coat. They were an extraordinary couple: she actually had infiltrated the Pentagon, walking into a colonel's office and stealing his ID and security clearance, which she and Steingard then duplicated and used in their crimes. Steingard successfully duped FBI agents into believing he was working for the bureau as an informer. And when Schmidt had been arrested under one of her aliases, Steingard had bailed her out—with a counterfeit $30,000 certified check.

They usually would arrive at a shop in a limo, looking every dollar the part of a wealthy, fashionable couple. But the NYPD had circulated wanted posters, so when they began shopping at an exclusive store in Trump Tower, a former NYPD officer working as a security guard recognized them. The reign of the "Queen of Con Artists," as she had become known, was over. "Lilly was sent to Rikers Island," explains Bob Leschorn, "the hellhole of New York City. Deputy John Cuff arranged to have an undercover informant put in her cell with her. And eventually that paid off big time."

Lilly began planning her escape as soon as she was incarcerated. Because she had infiltrated the Pentagon, her case was considered a national security issue, so rather than being escorted to court by marshals, two very sharp NCIS investigators transported her back and forth. Lilly came up with a plan. She was going to hire a contract killer to murder those agents and steal their IDs, then walk her out of Rikers. That's when Bob Leschorn became a Mafia hit man. He recaps what happened.

John Cuff's informant had agreed to make the arrangements for Lilly. Lilly had offered to pay $300,000 for the murders. We needed an under-cover to go in and make the case. I had spent years working organized crime in New York so I knew how to talk it and walk it. I knew all the tricks. John posed as a captain in the Colombo crime family. He set the terms, she made the plan. The details she provided included a physical description of the agents, their automobile, the route they trav-eled from Rikers Island to federal court, the type of weapons they carried and potential places the killings could be carried out. Somehow she had found out that every morning these two special agents of the Department of Defense Criminal

Investigative Service, Kenneth Siegler and Kenneth Connaughton, stopped at a certain store to buy her the soda she had requested. She instructed the killer to shoot them both in the head, steal their credentials, then take her out of Rikers as if she was being escorted to court.

"The hook was in," Leschorn explains.

My job was to make her admit on tape that she had arranged these murders. We set up a controlled breakout. It was dangerous because the prison guards didn't know what we were doing. And we didn't know if she had made additional plans. She was alleged to have been involved in violent crime in Bulgaria, so we had to be alert to the possibility she was going to double-cross the hit man. It was a lot cheaper to hire some Bulgarian gangsters to kill me than pay me $300,000. We protected the planned "escape" route; we stationed deputies armed with machine guns at strategic points; we had the car wired, and the hotel room we were going to was wired and video cameras were in place. There wasn't one second that we weren't being watched and protected by deputies or that she wasn't being recorded.

The morning the hit was scheduled to take place I showed up at Rikers dressed like one of the agents, wearing his cross and his jewelry and carrying his credentials. I even had his kid's baby pictures in my wallet. When I walked in, she said, "Oh my God! Oh my God!" and knew that I'd done it. Playing my role, I whispered firmly to her, "Shut your f— ing mouth. Don't you say another f—ing word. It's done, yeah." She knew she had to be cool around the guards because a Mafia killer was walking her out of prison.

We went through three guard gates. Everything went perfectly and we were outside. She couldn't believe it. She was telling me that she loved me, that she wanted to work with me, that we were made to be a team; she could kill with a pen, I killed with a gun. We were going to be criminal super- stars. She was telling me her husband had to be killed because he was a rat; she wanted everybody to be killed. Then she demanded to know every detail about the killing of the two agents. She wouldn't stop talking.

I took her to the stash pad we had prepared at the hotel. According to her plan, she was going to pay me, then we were going to dye her hair and get her ready to be transported out of the country. But when we got there, she started making excuses about paying me, so I threatened to kill her too. Actually we had expected her to pay me with counterfeit money. One thing she knew was that I wasn't going to take her check.

She was absolutely elated, but I had to get her to say the words. As soon as she did, I gave the signal, and deputies suddenly broke down the door and burst into the room. They had to make it look good, so they arrested both of us. They held us at gunpoint, searched us both, found the .44 Magnum I was carrying, then cuffed us. She bought the whole act: as they took us away she was screaming to me, "I'm sorry, man. I'm sorry, man."

The next time Leschorn and Lilly saw each other was in Judge Kimba Wood's courtroom. Lilly Schmidt refused to believe Leschorn was a cop until the moment he walked into the courtroom to testify against her. She was sentenced to an additional thirty years without parole. She made one last effort to beat it, pleading insanity, but Judge Wood ruled against her, and she will spend most if not the rest of her life in prison.

One of the more complex—and sensitive—arrests that required a deputy to work undercover was that of neo-Nazi leader Hendrik Möbus in 2000. What made this arrest especially difficult was that eight years earlier, after almost a year and a half of failed negotiations, a team of six deputy marshals attempted to arrest a white separatist named Randy Weaver on ATF weapons charges at a place called Ruby Ridge. Weaver and his family had moved to a remote mountainous area of northern Idaho to await the Apocalypse. They lived there without running water or electricity. Although much has been written about what happened on that mountain during the eleven-day siege, the tragic result was that Weaver's wife, his fourteen-year-old son, and Deputy Marshal Bill Degan were all killed. The case has been written about numerous times and dramatized in movies and remains a dark moment in the history of the U.S. Marshals Service.

A year later ATF agents raided a complex in Waco, Texas, that was operated by a religious group known as the Branch Davidians to arrest their leader, David Koresh, and confiscate weapons supposedly hidden on the grounds. Koresh had learned that the raid was imminent and organized resistance. As a result, four ATF agents and six Branch Davidians were killed, and a standoff that eventually would last fifty-one days began. On April 19, 1993, an FBI assault on the complex resulted in the deaths of seventy-six men, women, and children when a massive fire destroyed the buildings in which they had taken shelter. In fact, the tragedy at Waco was a primary reason Timothy McVeigh gave for his murderous attack on the Alfred P. Murrah Federal Building in Oklahoma City. But following Ruby Ridge and Waco, law enforcement began developing new strategies for dealing with such confrontations. After those disasters, the last thing anyone wanted was more deaths from another large-scale assault.

That was the situation when an international warrant was issued for the arrest of Hendrik Möbus in 2000. As a sixteen-year-old living in Germany, Möbus and two members of his death metal band, Absurd, had tortured and murdered a fourteen-year-old high school class-mate who they claimed was a "race defiler." Sentenced to eight years in a juvenile facility, Möbus was released in 1998 and eventually became head of the German branch of a racist, neo-Nazi organization known as the Heathen Front. Several months after he was released from prison, the German government brought new charges against him for distribution of Nazi propaganda. He was sentenced to eighteen months in prison, but when faced with an additional five-year term, he decided to flee to America.

Möbus had gained international recognition among neo-Nazis for his "national socialist black metal music," and the white supremacist structure in America, headed by William Pierce, author of the *Turner Diaries*, welcomed him. After landing in Seattle and legally entering the country in December 1999, Möbus began moving across the nation, staying briefly with various white power groups. In March 2000, the German government issued an international arrest warrant and the Marshals Service began looking for Hendrik Möbus.

In cooperation with German law enforcement, deputies discovered he was communicating with associates in Germany over the Internet and tracked his IP to the headquarters of William Pierce's National Alliance, a presumably heavily guarded compound outside the small town of Hillsboro, West Virginia. The problem was how to get Möbus out of there without creating another confrontation. The Marshals Service put together what was essentially an A-team of top deputies who could work successfully in that type of rural setting. The team included deputies Jerry Lowery, Chris Dudley, Joe Parker, and Tony Burke, who actually had relatives living in that area and had grown up hunting in those woods.

The team moved into the area as quietly as possible. It was impossible to know who was cooperating with Pierce and his National Alliance, so the local police force was not informed they were coming. Instead, the team checked into a local hotel pretending to be

U.S. Forest Service employees. "It was a perfect place to put a compound if you really wanted privacy," Burke observes.

> It was so rural that our cell phones wouldn't work. The first thing we had to do was set up a working communications system. Hillsboro isn't too far from the National Radio Astronomy Observatory, which operates an extraordinary radio telescope, so it's not uncommon to see people driving around the area in weird trucks. We brought a domed cell-phone tracking vehicle with us, which could cruise around without raising suspicion. That enabled us to communicate with each other on satellite phones. But our radios would only work on certain frequencies, which could have been a serious problem. So whenever possible, Jerry Lowery was in the air, using his aircraft as a mobile receiver/transmitter for our radios. But Joe Parker and I found an abandoned silo and turned it into a very large receiver; we hid a big antenna inside it, which boosted our power and made it possible to talk to each other.

The initial objective was to simply gather as much intelligence as possible; the Marshals Service team needed to know how many people were in the compound, what life was like inside, and how they operated—and to confirm that Möbus actually was there. Doing that, Burke says,

meant fitting in as much as possible without attracting attention. So we became a group of good old boys. As we know, everybody's got needs; white supremacists or not. They're listening to heavy metal music, they're drinking somewhere, and they're looking for local white girls. We needed to find them. We found out what bar they hung out in and started going there. I put my cap on backward and a big old dip of Copenhagen in my cheek, and we ended up drinking with them. As far as they were concerned we were working for the forest department, a government agency, but basically we were okay. We drank with them; we laughed at their jokes. Eventually they got used to seeing us there. Whatever tests we had to pass, we passed them. Eventually we found out that they had a boardinghouse in the next town over, where, believe it or not, they met "purebred white women" who had come over from Germany to mate. Sometimes they would take them back to compound and then back to this boardinghouse.

Several days after the deputies moved into town, the FBI arrived. "They wanted our operation shut down, claiming it was a matter of national security," Burke remembers.

They told us they had been investigating this group for almost a year and a half and our presence could blow their whole operation. They finally had been able to get an informer inside the compound, so they wanted us to close down and get out of there. This argument went all the way to the top of the Justice Department. Eventually Attorney General Janet Reno gave her support to our investigation, and a meeting was arranged in Chris Dudley's hotel room to try to work out an arrangement.

That was quite a meeting. All the deputies were dressed to fit easily into the local area. The FBI agents were neatly dressed in pressed pants and Polo shirts. They were stern and stiff, and one of them was carrying a thick case file. Mike Earp, who was running our operation, calmed everybody down and suggested we might be able to help each other. We began laying out maps and talking about telephone systems and warrants, and I casually mentioned this boardinghouse where they went to meet their white women. One of the FBI agents stopped me and asked, "Where is this boarding-house?"

We were all surprised. Mike said, "Wait a minute. You guys have been here a year and a half, we've been here eight days, and you don't even know where these guys go to drink and get laid? You kidding me?" It got a little tense, and the agents left the room to go out into the hall to discuss the situation. And when they did, they left their file on the table. We started flipping through the pages and found a photograph of their informant. Mike stuck it down his shirt.

When they came back in and saw their case file opened, they looked like they were going to pass out. You don't understand, they said, this case involves national security. They had an informant telling them everything. And when they said that, Mike pulled the photo out from under his shirt and asked, "You mean this guy?" After a few seconds of stunned silence, we helped them put the case file back together. After that they were pretty cool throughout the rest of the operation.

The deputies laid out their plan, emphasizing that under no circumstances was this going to be another Waco. They were going to stay there as long as it took, but they were not going to storm the compound. Möbus had to come out eventually, but nobody knew what eventually meant. The deputies had established a very good surveillance of the perimeter. There was only one good road into and out of the compound. They had hidden vehicles in the woods about two miles from the place, covering them up with tree limbs. Then almost a mile away an observation post had been set up: deputies snuck into the woods one night and cut the tree line out to give the spotter a direct line of vision to the front door. There was one point at a bend in the road when cars had to slow down, which gave the spotter a clear four-second look. He literally could see the faces of the driver and the passengers and get a good read on the license plate.

Then, Burke remembers,

We waited. Finally, one morning everything we'd been doing paid off. We heard our spotter saying softly on our radio, "I think that's our guy coming out of the compound. There are three cars, he's getting into the third one . . ." Lowery was in the air relaying a clear signal to our command post. Seconds later the spotter confirmed Möbus's identity, "That's our guy. Third car. I'm going to stay on him." Lowery spotted their cars and kept us informed about exactly what they were doing.

After they drove past our position, we piled into the vehicles we'd hidden, black Suburbans, and took off after them. We stayed far enough back so they didn't know we were there, following Lowery's directions for at least twenty miles into the next town. When they pulled into the parking lot of a bar, we were ready to go.

We came up on both sides of his SUV just as they were opening the doors. One deputy grabbed the keys from the driver and threw them away, and when the driver started bucking, he knocked him back in the car. Two of our people grabbed Möbus. He was a little skinny guy, and when he started fighting, they slammed him against the car. As rapidly as possible we placed him under arrest, cuffed him, threw him in the back of the Suburban, and got out of there. The whole takedown probably took two minutes. It could not have gone any more smoothly. But to anybody watching, it probably looked like a kidnapping. We got out of there with him as fast as we could. We didn't know how the people in the compound would respond to this, and we wanted to get out of the area as quickly as possible. Before they could raise their own posse.

The deputies raced to a state police barracks that had a helipad; it was about twenty minutes away. A state trooper looking absolutely pristine, his uniform perfectly crisp, had been alerted to wait for them. When the team piled out of that Suburban looking like escapees from a bad cable TV show, he didn't know what to think or do. "Who are you guys?" he asked.

They flashed their badges, "U.S. Marshals." When the state police helicopter landed, they hustled Möbus out of the backseat and put him onto the chopper. That pristine trooper took in the whole scene and said with some awe in his voice, "This is like some movie shit."

Möbus eventually was deported to Germany where he began serving his sentence.

Like in the classic stings that reeled in hundreds of fugitives, sometimes getting close to a fugitive without spooking him requires setting up a whole scenario. In 1988, Steven Wolosky and Mark Gayer were accused by U.S. Customs and DEA of being ringleaders of a major international drug smuggling operation that had brought as much as four hundred tons of hashish and marijuana from Colombia and Thailand into Northern California. But before they could go to trial, their twenty-four-foot fishing boat was found floating half submerged in the Pacific Ocean. Officially, they were presumed to have drowned. Government investigators remained skeptical though; investigators discovered that the boat appeared to have been scuttled from the inside and its life preservers were missing, and Gayer's mother refused to hold a funeral for her son. So in 1992 a new indictment, adding a charge of conspiracy to avoid trial, was issued. Eleven other members of their drug operation were tried and convicted, but for the next decade there was no solid evidence that Wolosky or Gayer was still alive—although both men were listed on the Marshals Service 15 Most Wanted list. When Lenny DePaul captured another fugitive on the list, an accused drug smuggler named David Kaplan, in 2000, Kaplan immediately rolled over and began looking to make a deal, telling DePaul, "I had lunch with Steven Wolosky in Manhattan two weeks ago."

As DePaul explains,

Eventually we got Wolosky's cell-phone number from Kaplan. It was the first solid information we'd had in eleven years that he and Gayer were alive. At that time tracking technology was still five to eight minutes behind the originating call. We were able to figure out that Wolosky was living up in Manchester, New Hampshire, but because of that delay we couldn't pinpoint his exact location. And obviously he was living there under an alias. It was frustrating; we could see the phone going into Boston every day and then coming back to Manchester late in the afternoon. So we knew he was commuting.

There are three exits off the highway into Manchester and Wolosky had to be taking one of them. DePaul figured that if the marshals set up a roadblock, he would just keep going, and probably keep going until he was out of the area. So the deputy decided to stage a car breakdown at each exit, funneling the traffic into a single lane, which would enable officers to get a good look at each driver.

As DePaul described it,

It would be like putting a marshmallow in a piggy bank. About 3:30 in the afternoon we parked a car on each of the three exits, opened the hood, and had two undercovers peering into the engine while a uniformed police officer directed traffic into a single lane. We backed up traffic on all three exits, but by 5:15 we had to accept the fact that if he had been there, we'd missed him. It really was infuriating; I couldn't figure out how we could have missed him. And as I was standing there wondering about it, a commuter bus drove by. A bus. Sometimes reality just hits you. A bus. I said something about it to the local police officer who told me, "Yeah, that bus goes into Boston every day."

Of course it did. The bus terminal was ten minutes away. I told my partner to stay there and jumped into a police car, and the officer raced me to the depot. "I don't want you to be seen," I told him. "Drop me off and circle the block." I walked through the terminal and sat down on a bench. A newspaper was laying right next to me and I picked it up. Seconds after I got settled, the bus that I had seen coming off the highway came around a curve and stopped right in front of me, literally right in front of me. The door opened, and the third person to step off the bus was Steven Wolosky. I couldn't miss him; he was 6'6" and built well. I remember looking at him and thinking that I was looking at a guy no officer had seen in eleven years.

He walked into the depot. I wasn't prepared: I didn't have a radio, I didn't know where the uniformed officer had gone. I sat there watching as Wolosky went over to a pay phone and made a call. I started walking toward him. As I did I saw two uniformed police officers, and I signaled them

I needed assistance. I couldn't wait.

I went up behind Wolosky and grabbed his wrist. I twisted it behind his back and said firmly, "Steven, I'm a United States Marshal and you're under arrest."

His response was immediate. "I'm a peaceful man," he said. Wolosky was carrying three different driver's licenses when we arrested him. And like Kaplan, as soon as he was in custody he began cooperating with us.

Wolosky provided the information that allowed DePaul to track Wolosky's former partner, Mark Gayer, to a remote area outside Santa Fe. DePaul says,

Two weeks later I was lying on my stomach in a New Mexico field. It was a lot different than standing on a highway outside Boston. The house stood by itself in an area that provided very little cover. Several of us came in at night and lay down several hundred yards away, watching the house through binoculars. We were there for at least six hours, tumbleweed literally rolling right over us. A man came out of the house a few times but then turned around and went back inside. We couldn't positively ID him.

Eventually that man and a woman got in a car and drove away. We alerted a local policeman that this vehicle was coming and asked him to stop it for any reason, broken taillight, changing lanes without signaling—it didn't matter—we just wanted him to get a good close look at the driver. We showed him Gayer's picture and told him if the driver resembled this person he should give us a thumbs-up. This officer stopped him, and seconds later walked to the back of the car and gave us the thumbs-up. We moved in and made the arrest. After Wolosky had been arrested, maybe Gayer knew we were coming for him. But when I told him he was under arrest, he seemed resigned to it and offered no resistance.

Many arrests are quick and relatively simple, but occasionally an arrest has all the elements of a great movie. Few of them, though, can match the arrest of Italian terrorist Stefano Procopio for drama. The case began at 10:25 A.M. on August 2, 1980, when terrorists detonated a bomb inside the crowded waiting room of the Central Railway Station of Bologna, Italy. Eighty-five people died, and more than two hundred were seriously injured when the roof of the building collapsed on the waiting passengers. The Bologna Massacre, as it has become known, eventually was attributed to members of a neo-fascist terrorist organization, *Nuclei Armati Rivoluzionari,* whose members had quickly left Italy. One of these people, Stefano Procopio, supposedly followed a carefully planned escape route, ending up in a terrorist training camp in Lebanon. Eventually he got to France, where at some point he supposedly killed a law enforcement officer, then made his way to the United States. In May 1993, Italian authorities, who had issued a warrant for Procopio's arrest, were able to trace phone calls made by his mother to New York City. That's when U.S. Attorney Charlie Rose brought in the Marshals Service. The search for Stefano Procopio was assigned to Craig Caine, who remembers,

Charlie Rose and I started working on this thing. We did a reverse trap on Procopio's mother's phone and came up with two addresses, one in the Bronx and the other one right in the heart of Tribeca, directly across the street from Robert De Niro's very popular restaurant, Tribeca Grill.

This was a major operation; this guy was an international terrorist and we had no idea what he was doing in New York, what he was capable of doing and who else was with him. We went balls to the wall on this. I assembled a team of about thirty people to make this arrest; in addition to marshals, the team consisted of U.S. Customs, DEA, and NYPD. And then, just to make the situation a little more interesting, we decided to take him down on May 12, which turned out to be the same day President Clinton was coming to town. The president's helicopter was landing alongside the Westside Highway, not very far from the Tribeca location. When we contacted Secret Service to tell them about our plan, they supplied an assault team. They paid a lot of attention to this, and they did a lot more than they would normally do for a presidential visit. It probably was just a coincidence that an international terrorist was living within a mile of the helicopter landing point, but no one could be certain. The Secret Service deployed snipers on rooftops and stationed agents at sensitive positions.

We used De Niro's restaurant for surveillance. We didn't tell the management and staff exactly what we were doing, only that it was very important and we needed some room. We put several agents in there, a man and a woman were sitting near a window having lunch, other people were at the bar, and I believe we even had a deputy in a waiter's outfit. Tribeca Grill is on a one-way street, which we blocked off at one end. We still didn't know whether Procopio was in Tribeca or the Bronx, so we had a team up in the Bronx watching that address too. We didn't have to wait too long. We got a call from a deputy in the Bronx informing us that a woman driving a Jeep with Jersey plates had put a bunch of boxes in her car and was leaving the Bronx address. I told him to follow her, but keep plenty of distance between cars so she didn't get spooked. We didn't know who she was or where she was going, just that she had left the target address.

We tracked her all the way downtown, until she stopped right in front of the Tribeca building. I told everybody to stand down until we saw what she was doing. She just sat in the car for several minutes until a man fitting Procopio's description came out of the front door and starting helping her move the boxes. The people sitting in De Niro's place put a positive ID on him; that was our guy. We debated whether we should hit the location or wait to see what developed. We decided the safest thing was to get him while he was holding boxes in his hand. I got on the radio, "Every unit, converge on that vehicle. That's our perp."

The street just exploded into action. Cars started

rushing up and down the west side, they came from side streets, sirens, lights, people running out from cover and screaming at him, everybody wearing their raid jackets, weapons drawn, all converging on this car and this guy. There was nothing Procopio could do. Literally within seconds we had the cuffs on him.

And then, when I took a breath, I heard people clapping. I looked around and all these tourists were standing there applauding. It turned out they knew this was De Niro's restaurant, so they assumed this was a scene from a movie being filmed there. They wanted to know if they were going to see De Niro. When we told them this was a law enforcement operation, they didn't believe us for a quite a while.

That was the only time in my career that I got a standing ovation for making an arrest.

7

The Deadly Tradition

Derek Hotsinpiller didn't just know he wanted a career in law enforcement. He knew he wanted to work for the U.S. Marshals Service. And at 24, he was serving search warrants in his home state of West Virginia, an unusually young deputy in a profession that has many older agents.

Hotsinpiller was killed Wednesday in Elkins, W. Va., when a drug suspect opened fire on him and two other deputy marshals with a shotgun before they shot him dead, authorities said.

Jeffrey Carter, a spokesman for the Marshals Service ... described the job of a U.S. marshal as a "dangerous business" of chasing down fugitives that carries high risks ... "But this young man knew exactly what he wanted to do from a young age."

—Washington Post, *February 17, 2011*

A U.S. Marshal has died after being shot in the head during a St. Louis gun battle the Marshals Service said tonight. The marshal, 48-year-old Deputy John Perry, was one of a team trying to arrest a man on charges of drug possession and assaulting a law enforcement officer. A second marshal was wounded, along with a St. Louis city police officer.

"Our deputies and law enforcement partners face danger every day in the pursuit of justice for the citizens of this great nation," said Stacia Hylton, the director of the Marshals Service. "Our people and our partners are well trained and prepared, but it is impossible to predict when a wanted individual will make a fateful choice that results in the loss of life or injury."

—*ABC News, March 8, 2011*

When Jimmy Bankston was asked how often he had stood in front of a closed door wondering what—or who—was waiting on the other side, he replied simply, "Every time." Then he added,

You just never know if there's a guy standing there with a gun. Or ten guys with guns. You just don't know. You're going into somebody's kingdom. And most of time the reason you're there is going to change someone's life, and usually not for the better. Whoever is on the other side has had a lot of time to prepare for this moment. They know the whole layout. And we have no idea what's waiting there: it makes no difference how long you've done surveillance. We've watched places for months without seeing any movement, we've cut off the water and the electric—and when we went in multiple people were in there. You never, ever know.

Being a U.S. deputy marshal has always been an extremely dangerous job. In January 1794, Revolutionary War veteran Robert Forsyth, the U.S. marshal for the District of Georgia, took two deputies with him when he went to serve civil court papers on a man named Beverly Allen. Marshal Forsyth found Mr. Allen at the home of a Mrs. Dixon and asked him to kindly step outside. Apparently there was no challenge in his voice, but Allen and his brother William instead took refuge in a second-floor room. When Forsyth and his deputies approached that door, Beverly Allen fired through it, shooting Marshal Forsyth in the head, killing him instantly.

On that day Robert Forsyth became the first of the more than two hundred marshals who would be killed in the line of duty. There are few things more

dangerous than entering a home or building knowing that an individual with a criminal history might
be there waiting for you, an individual who has no
intention of going back to prison. Deputies may well
be the only law enforcement agents in the world who
routinely draw their weapons. As Bankston continued,
"Every time we go into a house we've got a weapon in
our hand. Absolutely, every time."

Robert Leschorn, reaching back in his memory
more than a decade, explains,

> For a long time we tried not to pull our guns unless
> it was a life-and-death situation. But when it's just
> you and your partner and you're at the front door
> and he's at the back door, and you've got a little
> radio that sometimes works and sometimes doesn't,
> and you're after a federal parolee who already
> knows he's going back to jail, and his mom is telling
> me he's not there but her eyes are telling me he's
> going to kill her if she doesn't lie, and you're sure
> he's in there ready to fight or shoot, you'd better
> have that gun and you'd better be ready to use it
> because that's all you got.
>
> We were issued a Smith and Wesson .38, and we
> also carried several keepers and speed loaders.
> I carried three speed loaders with eighteen extra

rounds and my handcuffs, and I always had a black-jack. In a really bad hit, we'd have a shotgun. Today we've got . . . my God, arsenals of stuff, and we use a completely different strategy. The days of two people doing the job alone are over. But that's the way we did this job for a long, long time.

Although the danger has existed since that first shooting, in fact the job got appreciably more dangerous as the Marshals Service role expanded, first when it was given the responsibility for arresting DEA fugitives, often meaning armed drug dealers, and then again in 2001, with the congressionally mandated creation of regional task forces. Until that time the marshals worked mostly federal warrants, but this growing role meant they were now going after violent felons wanted by state and local departments. That included a different type of fugitive: murderers, rapists, arsonists, and all violent criminals, including gang members who controlled the projects in urban areas.

No matter how many times a deputy has stood in front of a closed door, the feeling never changes. "I'm guessing I've been there close to a thousand times," says Mike Bunk. "If you're not scared, there's something wrong with you. You'd better be scared because you don't know what's on the other side. Your stomach gets in knots, your mouth gets a little dry. One case, I remember, we had arrested this man four times for parole violations without incident. The fifth time he opened the door with two guns in his hand. We were just lucky; we had him pinned against a door so he couldn't move, which allowed us to take control."

Bobby Sanchez agrees, "If your heart isn't beating fast when you hit a door, then it's time to get out. We are not going after guys who didn't pay their taxes."

And Lenny DePaul concurs:

You can only prepare so much, you can only be so tactically sound. I've stood outside ten thousand doors easy—we all have—not knowing what's on the other side of that door at four o'clock in the morning, but fully aware that it might be a person who has decided he is not going back to prison; maybe he's just committed a double homicide or burned down a trailer with kids in it, and he knows that shooting a deputy isn't going to make any difference in his outcome. It never gets easier; you can only be so smart. For one case we may interview a hundred people with the bad guy potentially being on the other side of that door every single time.

That one time he's there waiting is what we spend our time training for. Years ago we would simply have people raise their right hand and repeat the oath and they were deputy marshals. Now, before anyone goes into the field with us they have to go through our extensive training program. We do as much continuing training as any law enforcement agency in the world. In our program, essentially we teach people how to survive and, equally important, how to make sure the people on their right and left also survive. When we go up to a door now, we go with very well trained people using the best safety equipment available. I remember we put the ballistic shield into our training program in about 2003. A member of our task force, Detective Kennedy Murray from the Essex County, New Jersey, Sheriff's Department, who had recently completed the training, was leading a team going after twenty-one-year-old Niem Williams, a drug-dealing gangbanger wanted for the murder of the mother of two young children. Williams was believed to be at his mother's apartment. At about six o'clock in the morning, Detective Murray was in front holding his shield as he had been taught when his team got up to the door of that second-floor apartment. Murray loudly announced the team's presence and ordered Williams to surrender. Instead, four shots from a .40-caliber handgun ripped through that door. The first round hit the bulletproof glass window in the shield that Murray was looking through and spun him around, exposing his body; unfortunately, the second bullet hit him in the abdomen. But without properly using that shield, Murray would have been killed by that the first shot. He ended up undergoing surgery that lasted almost four hours, but he survived and returned to work.

Rather than going to prison Niem Williams shot and killed himself.

One of the great short stories in literature is "The Lady, or the Tiger?" which requires the reader to decide whether love or death is waiting behind a closed door. That's essentially the question deputies have to consider each time they approach a door and announce their presence. When that door begins to swing open, anything is possible—anything. Deputies have to be prepared to react. Their adrenaline is pumping, their minds are racing, their senses are fully engaged: without question, in those few seconds they are balancing on the edge. A team that included Lenny DePaul and the late Mike Hollander went to arrest a man known to possess and carry assault weapons. They knocked on the door and waited. During those seconds, deputies are exposed and vulnerable. Sometimes people on a higher floor literally will drop something on them, ranging from gallons of water to very hot spaghetti. So they don't like to just stand there too long. DePaul and Hollander knocked again, and this time the door suddenly opened. A man kicked it open and stepped out carrying something wrapped in a brown cloth in his arms. "Drop it!" Mike Hollander screamed at him, raising his weapon, "Drop it!" And in that instant DePaul realized the thing he was carrying was an infant. "Don't drop it," he yelled ever louder. "Don't drop it! Mikey, it's a baby!" The suspect was using the child to shield himself and was quickly arrested.

On occasion the man or woman answering the door will be naked or partially clothed. The general rule most deputies follow in that situation is, simply, don't look down. Ask your questions, then leave. Politely. And quickly.

But as has also happened too often through-out history, there are times when the response will be a bullet fired through the door. A team in Battle Creek, Michigan, went to an address to arrest a man on a murder warrant. When the deputies knocked and announced their presence, two shots came through the front door, both shots hitting a deputy in his bullet-proof vest. The team returned fire, wounding but not

killing the shooter, then took up positions surrounding the house. As a backup team approached the house
he fired again, this time hitting a SWAT team member
in the face. Eventually the deputies established phone
contact with the man, who continued to threaten them.
Finally, when he moved near the door again, a SWAT
team sniper killed him with a single shot.

As tense as those few seconds will be as a door slowly
swings open, an unopened door holds a much greater
threat. When the door isn't opened and there are no
sounds coming from inside, deputies have to figure
out if someone is in there or not. Marshals use a lot
of small tricks to make that determination. Sometimes,
for example, deputies stand outside the door loudly
discussing what to do and decide to leave a note and
depart. They write the note and stick it partially under
the door, then go down the stairs or get in the elevator
and appear to leave—leaving one man behind. Many
times, after a few minutes, that slip of paper is pulled in
from under the door. At that point the deputies return
and give whoever is inside the choice of opening the
door or having it blown off its hinges—warning that if
they are forced to break down the door, everyone inside
is going to be arrested.

Deputies also have some techniques they use to lure
people out of their homes or apartments. A deputy

might put on a gas company hard hat and go through a building knocking on every door to warn residents that there is a hazardous gas leak and that they have to get out of the building immediately. Other deputies have dressed as postmen and buzzed every apartment explaining that the mailboxes have been broken open and asking residents to come down to personally collect their mail.

If deputies have reason to believe the person they are tracking is inside, they have no choice, they are going in. They use a lot of different tools to break down or through a door, from simply convincing someone to open it to smashing it open—but the result is going to be the same: they are going through that door. When you're doing a hard hit, there is always what Jim Schield describes as "that pucker factor."

Generally, the two ways of going into any type of home or building are controlled entry and rapid entry. When making a controlled entry, according to James Benjamin,

We have a phrase: locate, locate, contain, and control. If we know our target is in the house and has a gun, we seal off the house, get all the neighbors out of harm's way, then try to talk him into letting the innocent people inside the building go and surrendering. We always begin by securing the perimeter so no one can get out or in. We don't want an innocent bystander accidentally walking into the scene. Many times, once we have surrounded a building, whether it's a house or a hotel, an empty warehouse or a shooting gallery, and we know the fugitive is inside, we make a phone call and tell them we're going to be there day and night until they come out of the door with their hands raised high in the air.

We had a violent individual trapped in a motel in San Marcos, Texas, for example. In Texas, motel room doors have to be secured by a chain lock and dead bolt. This was a metal door, so we couldn't just kick it in. It's what we refer to as a hard breach-in target. We could have gotten a key from the desk, but if he was awake and saw the dead bolt moving, he probably would take a defensive position. Was he armed? We didn't know. So rather than trying to breach a double-locked metal door, we placed a call into the room—"stiffing a call" is what we call it. About four o'clock in the morning we woke him up and told him, "This is the U.S. Marshals, take a look out your window, please."

We'd had the local SWAT team quietly bring up their armored vehicle and park it directly in front of his motel room window. We had police vehicles parked on either side of it. Armed men were in position. He looked out the window and decided, "I'm coming out. Let me get dressed."

"You have thirty seconds," we told him. "And when you come out, show us your hands."

The only time we want to make a rapid entry is when a life is in danger. At that point you can't wait. You just go. When making a rapid entry, the goal is to immediately dominate the entire house. The purpose is not to show how tough we are, but rather to deescalate the situation. It may look like chaos, but it's not. We have a methodical way of rapidly clearing a residence. We've practiced it countless times. The strategy is to be fast and forcible. What we're doing is flowing through the house very rapidly, securing every room, detaining and controlling every person we encounter. If someone gets in the way, we go over them or through them. Anyone who resists is put facedown on the floor with their hands cuffed behind them. When we know the bad guy is in there, we don't stop until he's cuffed up. Anybody who gets in the way is going to be detained and restrained. Only after the house and everyone in it is secured do we pick out the bad guy.

If it's possible to isolate the single most dangerous few seconds of the job, it's those few ticks of the clock after a team has burst through the front door. There are times it goes bad. Wendell Brock was pursuing the leader of a neighborhood street gang who was wanted on an ATF warrant out of Florida. He had served time for armed robbery and possession of drugs and weapons. Every other member of this gang had been arrested and most of them had been armed with assault rifles, AK-47s, TEC-9 pistols, and ballistic vests. No question this was a very dangerous individual. He was personally suspected of committing two murders and was involved in a third killing for which several members of his gang already had been convicted. As Brock explains, "One of his angry ex-girlfriends told Florida deputies he was up in Atlanta with another girl. They gave me her name and I checked with the utility companies and got the address of an apartment. I did surveillance on it for a while, but I didn't see him. So I decided we were going to hit the house. This was in late October, and the temperature was dropping just below freezing."

Brock's team consisted of about fifteen people. He briefed them, giving them the target's entire criminal history. He warned them that several other members of his gang had been armed when captured and reminded them that this individual had told his family in Florida that he was done running: when the cops caught up with him, it was going to be the last time. He did not intend to go back to jail.

Brock says,

That's a threat we do hear fairly often, and although most of the time the fugitive is not serious about it, we have to take it seriously every time. We don't have the luxury of being wrong once. Sometimes before you go in you have a gut feeling that this could be the one that really goes bad; I had that feeling in this case. The apartment was on the second floor and had stairs coming up the front and down the back. I put four guys in the back and I told them to be ready to run, fight, and shoot or do all three, because there was a likelihood this guy was going to try to run.

We hit it at three A.M.—we like to be the wake-up police. We could hear the TV through the door. We just knocked politely, no loud knock, but when we did, we heard the TV go off. We knocked again, a lot louder, this time yelling "Police! Police!" A few seconds later, I heard the rear perimeter team screaming at him to show his hands, show his hands, so I knew he was going out the back. I told my people to ram the door open and went racing down the stairs and got around back.

The entry team went in behind the man holding the shield. When I got around back, our target was standing on the rail of a little porch in front of the apartment, ready to jump. He had one arm through the sleeve of a big heavy coat, but his other arm was free. My people were yelling at him to show his hands, so I said to him loudly, but calmly, "This is the U.S. Marshals. You're not going anywhere. Be smart about this; there is nowhere for you to go, so give it up. Show us your hands, step backward off that rail onto the landing, and lie down."

We could see him considering his options. I assume he reached the conclusion that there weren't any. He backed off the rail onto the landing. At that point I fired a Taser at him, but one of my prongs hit the empty sleeve of his jacket, and the other one hit a slat on the balcony railing. At that point I holstered the Taser and came back out with my pistol.

The balcony was about eight feet long, with a closet at one end of it. The fugitive opened the closet door and reached into it. He had his back to the deputies so they held their fire, but every one of them was thinking the same thing: he was going to be coming out of there with a TEC-9 or an AK-47. At that same time the entry team had cleared the front rooms and posted up at the living room door, which led out to this balcony. This was all happening in split seconds. The entry team was screaming commands and the support team in the back was yelling commands at him to stand down, to stop moving. Instead, he stood up and he had something in his hand.

Brock will never forget what happened next:

It was real dark, but we had a lot of lights on him. He had a white tennis shoe in his hand. He had his hand stuck up inside it and there was something black hanging down from it. My immediate thought was that he had a pistol shoved up in that shoe and the black thing hanging down was the magazine. As he stood up he turned the shoe over, as if it was gang-style shooting like they do in the movies. He turned and said, "I ain't going back like that," pointed the shoe at our people standing in the doorway, and lunged toward them. He took half a step, and four of us opened up on him. We didn't miss. He died on that spot.

It was not a gun he was holding in his hand. It was a sock. A black sock. He had placed it there so we would do exactly what we did. The fact is, we all went home that night, or the next morning.

The Constitution is quite clear about when law enforcement is allowed to enter someone's home or, by extension, apartment or hotel room. "We aren't just storm troopers who force entry into people's homes," David O'Flaherty says quite firmly. "In every case we have done our homework and have a good reason to believe the person we want is inside." Whenever possible, deputies will get a warrant that allows them to enter the premises. Sometimes, though, that isn't possible—and there are legal remedies. James Benjamin and his partner, Texas Ranger Lance Coleman, received a call from the San Antonio PD that a wanted member of the Mexican Mafia was believed to be in the city. "They told us he might be staying in his girlfriend's house over on the west side and informed us that the house had steel burglar bars covering the doors and all the windows. That meant we probably were going to have to use a hydraulic spreader to breach the door. And then they casually mentioned that he probably had a gun."

The first thing the officers had to do was verify that he was actually at that address. The team consisted of four people: two marshals and two Texas Rangers. They did a couple of drive-bys. If the burglar bars on the door were closed and locked, it would take a little time to get into the house, which meant he would have time to get his weapon. If the burglar bars were open, the team could have quick access into the house. Benjamin remembers,

> We spotted his vehicle near the house, then we saw the burglar bar door was open, which meant we could knock down the wooden door easy. The San Antonio PD captain I spoke with told me to sit tight, that he could get their SWAT team there in a couple of hours. I explained to him, "Captain, your SWAT team might enter a house once or twice a month, this is what we do every day; we go after people with guns in houses."

There wasn't time to get a search warrant for that house. Here's the reality: the DEA will execute a search warrant and find drugs on the premises. But if the search warrant is thrown out, the drugs will be dismissed as inadmissible evidence. If deputies hit a house and find a fugitive, even without a warrant, the courts can't suppress the body of the fugitive. It's a complicated situation. During a hot pursuit, deputies may have to hit several houses quickly, making it impossible to get a warrant to cover each one.

Generally, as long as law enforcement officers have a valid reason to believe a fugitive is on the premises, the courts will allow it. In this instance the team didn't know when that barred door was going to close, but they were well aware that when it did, getting inside was going to become far more dangerous. They also knew the target's girlfriend was at work so he probably was in there alone. Benjamin continues,

> We had to make a decision right then and there: we knew he had a gun, we knew he was a heroin smuggler, we believed that there was some homicide in his background. But the deciding factor was how long it was going to take us to get into that house. When we saw the barred door was open, we knew we could kick in the wooden door so we made the decision to hit the house.
>
> We kicked open the door and completely surprised him. His gun was on the top of his dresser and he made a move toward it, but before he could get to it he was facedown on the floor, his hands cuffed behind him. It went down quickly and safely.

Today everything the marshals do has to be by the book, but in the old days it was possible to make up some of your own rules. Donald Ward remembers his team was going into a decrepit half-abandoned

building in New York's South Bronx to arrest a heroin
dealer in the early 1980s.

As I popped open the door a man said to me, "You
can't come in here. You don't have a warrant."

"You kidding me?" I responded. "Don't you
read the newspapers?" He asked me what I was
talking about. "Don't you know the Supreme Court
passed the obvious guilt doctrine?"

He didn't know anything about that, he said,
wondering, "What's that?"

"Pretty simple. If you got a warrant out on you,
you're obviously guilty. That gives me the right to
suspend your rights and search wherever I want
to in a limited space for a limited period of time. So
under the obvious guilt doctrine I am hereby sus-
pending your rights. I'm going to search this place."

He nodded. "Under those conditions you can
come in then."

We went in, looked around, and caught our guy.
We cuffed him and as we were leaving the first man
stopped me. "Marshal," he said. "Hey, Marshal."
When I asked him what he wanted, he told me,
"You forgot to reinstate my rights."

So I gave him the sign of the cross and said,
"Your constitutional rights are now reinstated. If

the NYPD shows up here, you tell them the United States Marshals gave you back your rights!"

Of the different methods that can be used to break into a house, the most prevalent is simple brute force: marshals just ram through the door as if they were opening the doors to a castle a thousand years ago. On just such an occasion Wendell Brock and his team knocked on a door and an unknown person inside yelled to them that he was opening it.

Obviously we didn't know what was going on inside, but we gave him several moments and nothing was happening. He kept telling us to wait, he was coming, wait, he was coming, but that door didn't move. We didn't know if that person talking to us was our target or what was going on inside, just that the longer we were standing out there exposed, the more dangerous it was becoming, and if he wasn't our target, the more time he was giving that individual to hide or run. Finally we rammed it open—and almost knocked the fugitive out of his wheelchair. We didn't know he had no legs; he was trying to open the door but having a hard time doing it. Fortunately, we just knocked him backward and he was fine.

Sometimes marshals will use a rabbit tool, a seventy-five-pound hand pump compression tool that can be wedged into the space between the door and the frame. Used mostly to open steel doors in projects, it literally will separate the door from the hinges. "We also use what is called a housing tool," according to Don Ward. "You put it in the door and pry it open. One time, though, I was working with a deputy who was about 6'8" and 280 pounds of muscle. We knew there were people inside an apartment—we heard them moving around—but they wouldn't open the door, so he literally got his hands on top of the door and started bending it. The people inside thought we had a monster with us and started screaming—and then they opened the door very quickly."

Some doors can't be opened with anything less than a stick of dynamite. Harry Layne ran across one of them in a project in Detroit.

It was a metal door with all kinds of locks on it. We tried several things, but we couldn't get through. We knew the guy was in there, and we wandered around trying to see what else we might come up with. Then we realized the apartment right next door was vacant and had been trashed. It looked like it had been used as a shooting gallery. Garbage was thrown all over the place, holes smashed in the walls, interior doors yanked off the hinges; it occurred to us that the only thing we couldn't do to that apartment was trash it worse than it already was—so if we couldn't get into the fugitive's apartment through the door, we decided to go through the wall. We literally smashed our way through the wall into his apartment, and when we got inside, we found him hiding in the bathtub and arrested him.

Deputy Mike Moran was part of a task force that faced another unbreakable door. By 2003, marshals had been tracking a fugitive named Eddie Mathis, who was on the 15 Most Wanted list, for more than six years. Mathis was wanted on a DEA warrant identifying him as coleader and brutal enforcer of a Long Island cocaine distribution ring; he was also implicated as the triggerman in a double homicide in which the killer used a MAC-10 machine gun with a silencer. Like so many career criminals, Mathis had kept on the move, and he had been spotted in at least five states. But when *America's Most Wanted* ran its fourth story about him in August 2003, authorities received a credible tip that his known associates were hiding out in Redford, Michigan. It was logical to assume that he was with them. Deputies from five different task forces, the Electronic Surveillance Unit, and local police officers converged on that suburb of Detroit. The DEA had warned that Mathis "carried firearms all the time, wore a bulletproof vest," and had told people he would not be taken alive.

Mike Moran remembers, "This chase lasted more than a week. We were close, but we weren't getting it done." In the middle of the manhunt, a massive power blackout hit the area, forcing the task force to suspend the search.

It was really frustrating. But finally we put him in a motel with a girl. We were able to verify that he was there. When we got there, though, we discovered that he was behind a very strong electric door. He heard us coming and closed it. There was no way we were getting through it. We were locked out. After a standoff, he let us know that he wasn't coming out but that he would release the female who was in there with him. He opened the door just enough for her to slip through. As soon as she got into the doorway we pulled her out—then managed to jam a ballistic shield inside the door. When a door opens, even that little bit, you can't hesitate. The team pushed the door open and got inside. He was waiting for us, holding a pistol, a 9 mm, and he fired at us. We returned his fire and it didn't end well for him.

He was still alive when they got him to a hospital, but he died there.

Deputies know that when they go through the door they have to be ready for absolutely any type of response. During their seventeen and a half weeks of training, Marshals Service recruits at the Federal Law Enforcement Training Center (FLETC), in Glynco, Georgia, are shown an extraordinarily horrific video of a 1998 robbery gone terribly bad. The surveillance video begins with two suspicious-looking men walking into a bakery in the town of Luquillo, on Puerto Rico's northeast coast. One of the men is Orlando Ramos, also known as Landy. The woman standing behind the counter has already triggered a silent alarm when Landy announces that this is a robbery and warns her, "If you call the cops, people are going to die." Seconds later a police car stops in front of the shop, its lights flashing. The woman explains that this is a routine stop, that the police officers stop by every night at this time for coffee and a bite to eat. As Sergeant Billy Colón-Crespo and Sergeant Ramón Ramirez-Castro arrive, Landy hides his gun under his arm, keeping his arms together as if covering his face.

The other robber takes a male hostage into the back of the store at gunpoint. The officers come into the shop and ask the clerk if everything is okay; she responds that it is. The officers then ask Landy the same question and he responds innocently, actually wiping his face with his T-shirt without revealing his weapon, no problem.

The second officer walks out of view and into the back room, where he obviously saw the hostage being held at gunpoint. The officer on camera moves immediately to assist his partner, turning his back to Landy, who is seen on this tape taking out his gun, pausing as if posing for the camera, then shooting the police officer in the back of his head at point-blank range. When the second officer comes out from the back, Landy raises his gun and fires at him. The gun misfires, and the officer raises his hands in surrender. Without hesitating, Landy cocks the weapon again and at point-blank range shoots him. The officer falls to the ground. Standing over him, Landy brutally executes him. Then the killer and his partner walk out of the bakery, without harming the clerk.

Landy actually was one of the prisoners who later escaped from White Bear penitentiary and was recaptured by a task force including Bobby Sanchez.

Every Marshals Service recruit sees this video and the message is unforgettable: even if you believe a person is unarmed, never, ever, under any circumstances turn your back on that person. The moment a deputy stops thinking of another individual as a potential threat, that person becomes far more dangerous.

That video is in every deputy's mind each time he or she walks into a room. Joe Lobue will never forget the night he was working with a DEA team at 3:30 in the morning.

> We were going after a bad guy, and we had been warned he had guns. We went into an apartment that was completely dark. It was pitch-black in there. I was the shotgun man. A DEA agent holding the ballistic shield was directly in front of me, and we were going down a hallway with closed doors on either side. The only light was coming from the shield. Suddenly a guy jumped out in front of us holding a baseball bat. I don't know why I didn't pull the trigger, but I didn't. We got him down, and it wasn't even the guy we were there to arrest. He was a family member, he said, and he didn't know who we were. Why he didn't hear us yelling "Police" I couldn't figure out; I was just so pleased I hadn't pulled the trigger.
>
> It isn't just me. You really never know when someone is going to pull the trigger. We were looking for a

fugitive named Maxwell Bogle, who'd earned his reputation as the enforcer for a Jamaican gang known as the Shower Posse. They were called that because they were known to use Uzis to create a shower of bullets. Bogle would break into the homes of people who owed drug money to his gang, brutalize them, and even kidnap their children until they paid their debt. In one home invasion, he raped a fifteen-year-old girl. After skipping $100,000 bail he was convicted in absentia and sentenced to sixty-eight years in prison. He also was a suspect in a block party gunfight that resulted in one person being killed and seven others wounded. He was definitely a Top 15, described as "armed, extremely dangerous and one of the most sought after criminals in the United States."

Lobue was working with the New York/New Jersey High Intensity Drug Trafficking Area Task Force when they received information Bogle was in an apartment in Crown Heights, Brooklyn. At the takedown, the well-armed Lobue was holding the shotgun.

We made a rapid entry, surprising him. He jumped out onto the fire escape holding a handgun. People were yelling, "Gun! Gun! Gun!" I saw the gun in his hand and I thought, this could be the time. We

were screaming at him, "Put it down! Put it down!"
There was that split second of indecision when it
could have gone either way. He made his choice: he
threw down his gun. We were screaming at him to
put up his hands, put 'em up, put 'em up, but he
wouldn't do it. He just glared at us. We were
behind the ballistic shield, and we just kept moving
toward him, just kept moving. Suddenly we all
bum-rushed him and knocked him to the ground.
People were scrambling, but until we had the cuffs
on him and his weapon in our possession I don't
think anyone took a deep breath.

"What you want to do as soon as you go through
that door is establish control," explains Don Ward.

One night we were going into a shooting gallery
looking for a dealer. Three of us were standing outside the door, holding our weapons. I signaled to
the others, then pushed open the door. Just as I did
a junkie started coming out. My momentum was
pushing me forward, so I grabbed hold of the guy
and literally put my gun in his mouth.

His eyes just opened, and he vomited all over my
gun. This junkie threw up all over my gun.
I dragged him over to the sink, dumped the bullets

out, and then made him wash my gun and dry it off. With all the diseases that were going around at that time, no way I was going to touch it.

Every deputy dreads finding children inside an apartment. When interviewing potential Marshals Service recruits, Lenny DePaul would set up the following scenario, "You burst into an apartment and the person you're chasing runs into a back room. You follow him and find him hiding in a bedroom. As you're holding him at gunpoint, the closet door opens and a ten-year-old is standing there pointing a .357 at you. What do you do?"

If recruits responded that they would have no choice, they would fire at the child, DePaul would ask them, "Then the next day how are you going to deal with the story on the front page of the *New York Times* reading 'Deputy Shoots 10-Year-Old Holding a Water Pistol'?" And if recruits hesitated and admitted they didn't know what they would do, DePaul or his partner on the interviewing team would leap up screaming, "Then what are you going to say to the widow and children of your partner who got killed because you hesitated?"

As DePaul acknowledges, there is no correct answer. "It's almost a helpless situation," says Jerry

Lowery, who has had to deal with it in his career. "You really have no idea what the bad guy's going to do and worse, you don't know what the child will do. Time gets suspended in those few seconds."

Donald Ward and his team went into the Brooklyn apartment of a Rastafarian fugitive who wasn't home—but his young children were there with a babysitter.

We secured them in a room and then searched the place but didn't find much of anything. When I walked back into the bedroom, his son, who was probably about eight, looked at my gun and told me, "My daddy has a few of them in the house."

Oh? "Would you show me where they are?" I asked.

He shook his head. "I can't."

I thought about it for a few seconds, then suggested, "Okay, but suppose I swore you in and made you a real deputy?"

He liked that, nodding and telling me, "Yeah, but I want to get paid."

We made a deal. "I'll swear you in as a deputy and then I'm going to give you a dollar for each one of these that you find." I had him raise his right hand, and I swore him in as a junior deputy marshal—with compensation.

He took us through the apartment, and we found six guns. After we'd packed them up, he told me, "He also has some bags with stuff in it that he hides." This kid was clearly an entrepreneur. Okay, I told him I would pay him a bonus to show me where those bags were hidden. He took us around the apartment and showed us where there was something like fifteen pounds of marijuana in bags. And as we were getting ready to leave, this kid came up to me and reminded me, "You forgot to pay me." I had to pay him $10. As we were walking out the front door, I saw a guy bopping down the street and he looked up and saw us—and took off. We knew who that was. We got in our car and raced after him, cutting him off, and we arrested him.

To deputies, at least, dogs are not as big a problem as children. While dogs can be very dangerous, especially pit bulls and other potentially ferocious dogs, deputies usually can push them into another room and close the door behind them. There have been confrontations though, and if the dog can't be controlled, it will be shot. Most of the time people don't want to see their animal killed so they take charge. "When they're just barking at us we try to ignore them," explains Mike Moran. "There are guys who will use pepper spray; that usually takes care of them." But dogs do get shot and killed.

Chuck Kupferer and his partner, John Wetmore, were trying to catch a bank robber who they were told was hiding in a house in an L.A. ghetto. Kupferer recounts what happened.

As we hit the house a sniper took a couple of shots at us. He didn't come close, and we never found him. We tried to shoot back but that was useless. My partner was on the front door and I went around back. We planned to hit the front and back doors at the same time. When I got around back, I went over the fence and as soon as I hit the ground a huge German shepherd came racing around the side of the house—and he was looking at me as if I was on the menu. I got on the radio and I sort of yelled to my partner, "Give me some help back here, John. I got a dog here that's got me cornered." I didn't move, and John came around and tossed me a can of mace. I sprayed that dog, hit him right in the nose. The dog dug a furrow about twenty feet long through the backyard getting away from me. I went right back over the fence. There was nobody home at that address.

Many times deputies break down a door and find an empty apartment. It happens. The information might be good, but the timing is bad. A few seconds can make all the difference. At least several times in their careers most deputies have burst into a house or apartment to find still-warm food or coffee on the dining room table, or a still-warm mattress. "One time we thought for sure the fugitive was in an apartment," Mike Bunk recalls.

We heard some movement going on, but when we broke down the door, there was nobody there. Only after we'd rammed through the door did we discover the walls were so thin we were actually hearing the people who lived upstairs. But we couldn't leave the apartment without a front door; when we hit the wrong place, the Marshals Service is responsible for securing it and eventually paying for repairs.

I was the one who made the decision to break down the door, so I was the man who had to wait there until we could get a maintenance company there to secure it. I was sitting out front in my car when another car pulled up and I realized our bad guy was sitting in the passenger seat. I walked over to the car and I asked him, "Are you so-and-so?" Yeah, he said; he had no idea what was going on, but clearly he was upset that somebody had broken down his front door—although admittedly he was not as upset as he became when I introduced myself and arrested him. We sat in my car until backup arrived and took him into custody, but even then I still had to wait there until the premises could be secured.

There also are times when the information is incorrect and deputies hit the wrong place. Lenny DePaul remembers busting into an apartment with a heavily armed team while looking for a major drug trafficker.

We flowed through the apartment and I opened up the bathroom door and I will never, ever forget what I saw: a woman, who had to weigh four hundred pounds, sitting there. I didn't even realize she was sitting on the toilet. Instead of being upset that six men had smashed into her apartment, she looked at me and said, "You know, this is the third time this month that this has happened. We been living here six months." She said it matter-of-factly without any anger. Obviously the drug dealer had been living there before.

There wasn't much we could do. I told my people, "Okay, we'll be leaving now," and we got out of there.

It isn't just the front and back entrances that present a problem; it's every closed door inside. The doors to every room and every closet have to be opened, and a fugitive may be hiding behind any one of them. Corey Britt was searching a home in Laredo, Texas, when he heard movement in the bathroom. He ordered whoever was inside to open the door. That person did not respond. Britt started beating on the door, then stepped back. The door openly slowly—and a frightened child was standing there.

Few people in this world are more experienced at conducting a thorough search of any type of premises than deputy marshals. Conducting a complete search literally can be a matter of life and death. So during training, a substantial amount of time is spent teaching deputies how to search as if their lives depend on it. The general rule about where people will hide is, forget all the rules. They will hide everywhere. They will squeeze into spaces that seem impossible for a human being to fit into. They will carve out space where no space exists. They will be up in the ceiling, under the floorboards, in the cabinets, behind the furniture. They will be in the dishwasher and the clothes dryer, they will hide in a clothing hamper, under a desk, inside big stereo speakers. One man was caught hiding inside a TV set from which all the parts except the screen had been removed. A search must be slow, methodical, and thorough.

Although a search might seem like a fascinating game of hide-and-seek, deputies are dangerously exposed when searching premises. "There are times," Tony Schilling says, "that I've walked past the same spot three times, four times without seeing the person hiding in there. They are in places you would never expect, and, in some cases, if he had a gun and wanted to shoot, I never would have seen it coming. We try to be smart, we try to be methodical, use good tactics, but there is only so much you can do to protect yourself and the people you're with."

The rest is fate. Before joining the Marshals Service, Wendell Brock began his career as a deputy sheriff. He recalls how the lessons he learned during training may have later saved his life:

In training we had an exercise in which we had to clear a house. I looked under the sink and then closed the cabinet door and started walking away—as I did the door popped open and the instructor said clearly, "Bang." "But I looked in there," I pleaded. "You looked," he agreed, "but you didn't do it good."

I made up my mind right there: whatever I do in my career, wherever I end up, I am looking good everywhere.

And in my career I did look good. I've crawled on my belly the whole length of a house, clearing spiderwebs until we were able to determine our guy wasn't hiding behind ductwork. I found one guy completely naked curled up inside a dishwasher. One time we knocked on a door and the people let us inside and we searched all over for a man we believed to be there, but we couldn't find him—until I opened the refrigerator and found him squashed in there. During those few minutes it took for his people to open the door, they were emptying the refrigerator, throwing stuff in the pantry where we wouldn't see it, and hiding him in there. That was a case in which we definitely had him cold.

Most deputies easily will search more than a thousand premises during their career, ranging from mansions to hellholes. They'll be in the penthouse of a luxury building or under a lean-to in a dump. John Bolen will never forget "going into a shack in eastern Kentucky to talk to the sister of the fugitive. I had to start by taking a rooster off the kitchen table and setting it on the ground. I've also been in a lot of places in that part of the country with dirt floors. They may have video games and satellite dishes, but the floors are dirt."

Conversely, Geri Doody spent her career in New York, which often took her to the projects.

We'd go into apartments where there would be a baby sitting on the floor with roaches crawling over it. I always said that if anything happened to me it would be because of a baby; you just want to grab it and run out of there. We were in places so hot you couldn't breathe and so cold your hands and feet would freeze. In the summer, apartments without air-conditioning would feel hotter than incubators; in the winter, people who didn't have heat would turn on their gas ovens and close all the windows and we'd have to run to open the windows. Sometimes it was the odors that made it impossible to breathe. I remember going into a house without working plumbing in the middle of winter; the bathtub was half filled with human excrement, roaches were everywhere, and the person inside was just about frozen to death. That turned out to be a rescue rather than an arrest.

Among the wisdom veterans pass along to younger deputies is that when you go into one of those types of places, never lean against the wall because you don't know if it can support you; and never sit down because you don't know what you're going to get up with. There are things deputies encounter on the job that they definitely do not want to transport home. Sometimes deputies have to crawl through the muck under a house or the mud in the woods. Generally most marshals like to say that there are only two types of conditions: too hot or too cold.

They end up in these types of places because in many instances they are pursuing people who can't stay in one place too long, who can't plant any roots, who survive from day to day, crime to crime, high to high. These people are rarely upstanding citizens. "My first duty station was in Philadelphia," says Thomas Smith.

They gave me the warrant on a heroin junkie. So we had to look for him in these row houses in a real crappy part of the city. These places had no electricity, no running water, but people lived there. I went into this one place and all these junkies were lying around mostly out of it; blankets were hanging between them that I had to keep pushing aside. I wanted to burn my clothes when I left there. I decided it wasn't worth getting TB looking for that guy. So I took that warrant and put it on the bottom of the pile. This wasn't a crime of violence, and I figured if he was living in one of those places, he was going to end up with a toe tag anyway.

Deputies don't often encounter the best-dressed people either. Or sometimes just dressed people. When the wake-up police hit a house at five A.M., the people inside are often partially dressed or even naked. And surprisingly, a lot of people will answer the door in their underwear. "I can't begin to figure out how many people I've arrested in their underwear," says Stephanie Creasy. "They always want us to let them put their clothes on. I tell them straight out, 'You ride like you hide. If you'd come out like a man, we'd treat you that way, but you get what you've earned.'" Even when deputies do permit someone to put on some clothes, they usually watch them. There's a good reason for that. At one point deputies in Florida arrested a very embarrassed naked man, who begged to be permitted to go into the bathroom and get dressed. Before allowing him to do that, a deputy searched the bathroom—and found the .357 the man had hidden under a tissue box cover.

Sometimes though, deputies do have to permit people to get dressed or change clothes. While on vacation Wayne Warren was riding along with officers from the local Virginia police department where he'd started his own law enforcement career. They were serving a warrant on a woman wanted for breaking into cars to steal Christmas presents. Although the team knew she was at home, no one answered the door.

Then they discovered a rear window was unlocked. Warren recalls,

We decided to make our entry that way. I have a distinctive, low voice, which helped me when I was a police officer working on the street by myself; I've always believed the way I carry myself dictates how an event will end. So as we were moving slowly through the house clearing rooms, I was shouting over and over in my deepest and most authoritative voice, "Police! U.S. Marshals! Step out! Show us your hands!" Finally we get to the front and we heard a woman scream, "Please don't shoot. Please don't shoot. We're here." Two people stepped out with their hands raised. As we took them into custody, we smelled something really unpleasant. I took the woman aside and said to her, "Look, I don't want to embarrass you, but my partner says he smells something kind of bad. I was just wondering did you end up going to the bathroom?"

She looked at me and said, "Heck yeah, I did. When I heard your voice going through my house you scared the living shit out of me."

I kept a straight face—from a slight distance. "No problem. We're going to take you back into the house and let you get cleaned up." But I told her we couldn't let her close the door all the way.

The fact is, as Vic Oboyski says, speaking for every deputy marshal,

There are things you see in this job that you will never forget. Never. On one case, we went to pick up a guy who had a history of violence, so we took a shotgun and other weapons with us. I banged on the door, and a big lady holding a baby answered it and told us, "I haven't seen that son of a bitch." She gave us permission to search the place. I'm a big guy, 6'3", and I was wearing a heavy bulletproof vest, and on top of that I had on a big raid jacket. I had my 9 mm on my side, and I was wearing jeans and boots. I walked into one room and two little kids were lying there on a mattress on the floor, all covered up. One of the kids—he had to be about eight years old—said, "Excuse me, mister. What time is it?"

I looked at my watch and told him it was almost seven A.M. And he said, "Oh, I got to get ready for school." Then he pulled off the blanket and he was completely dressed. I felt sick. I remember thinking, What is this kid's image of law enforcement?

We had been polite, we didn't try to control the place, but that does happen and it's warranted when there is the potential for resistance. This kid got up and put water on his face while his mother fixed him what they had. The first thing I did when I got home that night was hug both of my kids.

By searching enough of these places deputies eventually learn how to expect the completely unexpected. Lenny DePaul shares an example.

We were in a house very early one morning. We knew the person we were looking for had to be there, but if he was, we couldn't find him. I've been in crawlspaces; I've seen fake ceilings and fake walls; I've found people wrapped around the pipes under the sink—but this guy wasn't there. We were standing around in the living room trying to figure out exactly how we intended to proceed when for whatever reason one of our people opened up a curtain. Sunlight streamed into the room at a perfect angle and lit up the inside of a built-in stereo system that was covered with a dark glass door— and I saw a leg. He was inside a cubicle. If he'd had a gun, we would have all been dead. We'd walked past him a hundred times. I turned my back to the cabinet and signaled to one of my partners, he's behind me in the stereo. And he kept asking, "What? What?" I just continued mouthing the words, "Behind me in the stereo." Finally we casually went over there; when I opened the door, he saw six guns pointed right at him.

Robert Leschorn will never forget the fugitive he discovered hiding inside a refrigerator.

It was on Ralph Avenue, in Brooklyn. This guy was facing nine years for robbing a post office while on parole. My informer guaranteed me that he was in that house, but we couldn't find him. His mother and brother were there and they insisted he was gone, that we were wasting our time. I had two people with me, and we tore up that apartment. I told one of my people to watch the front and put the other guy on the back while I searched the kitchen again. There were two refrigerators, I noticed. That interested me. One of them was disconnected and the shelves had been taken out and what did I find when I opened the door. The mutt. After I had him cuffed, he said to me, "Admit it, I almost got ya, man. That's my newest invention, the empty refrigerator! It gets 'em every time!"

As far as being creative about finding places to hide, according to Phillip Matthews,

If you imagine it, we've found people hiding there. We've pulled them out of attics, under air conditioner vents, out from under vehicles and out of doghouses. We've found them hiding inside cabinets and outside in trash dumpsters and storage sheds. We had to search one house five times, five times, because we couldn't find the target and my informant kept telling me to go back, he's definitely there. This guy had never burned me, so I believed him. Finally I walked down a hallway that was covered with a rug. I lifted up the rug and found a trapdoor. We popped the trapdoor open and there he was, hiding under the house.

Once, I remember, we went to a residence to bring in a little person who had violated provisions of his supervised release. Supervised release is the federal version of parole; after you finish your sentence, you're still under control of the court and can be put back in prison. This little person saw us coming and he took off. He went out the back, and by the time we got there, he had disappeared. We looked everywhere, but we couldn't find him. At times like that you wonder if people actually can disappear. This man's small size made him even more difficult to find. Finally one of our people turned over a wheelbarrow way in the back and there he was. He had flipped over a wheelbarrow and was crunched up beneath it.

Actually, trapdoors are not especially unusual. Dave Dimmitt was with a team that believed a fugitive was hiding in a double-wide trailer home in Omaha, Nebraska.

One thing we always try to do before going into a building is try to figure out as much as possible what it's going to look like inside. How many rooms, how is it divided. We went to this place very early in the morning and the fugitive's girlfriend answered the door wearing a sheer negligee. He wasn't there, she told us; she didn't know where he was. After doing this long enough, you learn to read body language, and we knew by her actions that he was there. She gave us permission to search the place, but we couldn't find him. Then somebody on the team found a trapdoor under a carpet in their bedroom. The problem was that none of us were small enough to fit through it. We went outside and a deputy sheriff lifted a sheet of the aluminum skirt surrounding the entire bottom of the trailer and spotted our guy under there.

We surrounded the trailer and emptied canisters of pepper spray into the area under it. Eventually we heard someone banging against one of the aluminum panels. We lifted it and pulled him out. He was buck-ass naked—except for one sock. He was wearing one sock. Before slipping through the trapdoor he had taken the time to put on one sock, although we never found out why.

Trailers are essentially metal shells. The walls are sheets of aluminum. So it would seem that a trailer would offer only a limited number of places for someone to hide. As Tony Schilling points out,

You can't hide inside a wall because there are no walls, everything is built in and bolted to the frame so there is no space between them, but we've encountered some pretty ingenious hiding places. We searched a trailer one time looking for three armed robbers, a couple and another woman. We turned that place upside down and inside out but these people were not there. The woman who was home finally told us they were at another place about twenty minutes away. I left two deputies with this lady to make sure she didn't call anybody then we headed there.

The team arrested a man and woman at the other residence. After they were cuffed, the woman said, "Well, since you got this address you must have arrested so-and-so." Schilling shook his head and admitted she wasn't there. "No, no," the woman insisted, "she's there. I know she gave us up. I'm telling you, she's hiding behind the oven."

Schilling personally had searched that oven.

I'd opened it up and looked inside. "It's right up against the wall," I said. "There's no way anyone could fit behind there. No way."

"She's there," she said. "Trust me. It's our hiding spot."

Okay. I called a deputy I'd left there and asked him where he was at that moment. "We're in the kitchen with this lady," he said.

"Here's what I want you to do. I want you to open the oven and yell into it."

"C'mon, you're kidding, right?"

"I'm totally serious. Just open it up and yell in it. That's where she's hiding." He opened it up and yelled into it that she should come on out, that we knew she was in there—and a few seconds later, the oven began moving away from the wall. They had carved out a hiding place behind a working oven in a trailer. None of us had ever seen anything quite like that before. But if there's empty space, fugitives will find it.

At times fugitives manage to squeeze into places so small that they have difficulty getting out. Corey Britt discovered a man wedged so tightly behind a hot water heater in a basement that it was almost impossible to move him. Deputies sprayed the surrounding surfaces with a silicone substance, but all that did was make the floor so slippery that when they tried again to pull him out, it was as if they were trying to run on ice. "It wasn't funny at that moment; we had an unrestrained violent fugitive in a place we couldn't get to, and we couldn't move him. Finally he decided he needed to get out and together we managed to get him out and into our handcuffs."

During a search, everybody's nerves are taut; there are times when a deputy lifts a lid, pulls back a curtain, or opens a closet door—to find someone staring right back at him. Mike Bunk once lifted a pile of dirty clothing on the floor of a closet, for example, and uncovered a fugitive curled up in it. And David O'Flaherty was nonchalantly flipping through the clothes hanging in a fugitive's crowded closet, going through his shirts and pants—and eyes. The target had put his arms through a piece of clothing and was hanging there without moving. As O'Flaherty says, "Suddenly and completely unexpectedly, two beady eyes are looking right back at me. It definitely did trigger that pucker effect."

One time Geri Doody was searching a bathroom for a crack dealer. She says,

The shower curtain was pulled all the way open. It was a thin little strip of plastic against a wall. Normally I wouldn't have even moved it—I didn't think anybody could be skinny enough to hide behind there—but when I did, the guy was standing there looking right at me. I had my gun out so he didn't move. I was so surprised, I screamed—and then kept screaming for assistance. The fugitive actually tried to calm me down, telling me, "Lady, please stop screaming. It's like hide-and-seek, I was hiding and you found me."

People who know there is a warrant out on them spend a lot of time preparing for the day the marshals show up. One fugitive had cut a hole in the back of his closet wall that enabled him to escape into the closet of the vacant apartment next door. Although he successfully managed to get out of his apartment, he was caught when he went out into the hallway to get out of the building. Another suspect cut a hole in the wall behind a couch leading into the adjoining apartment, then pushed the couch up against the wall. Only after deputies moved the couch away from the wall did they discover how he had managed to escape. Fugitives often hide under or even inside furniture. As Doody explains, "We'd often go into a place and there'd be nobody there but when we touched the mattress it was warm, so we knew he was there somewhere. It wasn't unusual to find people hiding under the bed—some deputies would tickle their toes until they came out. We routinely flip over mattresses. One time we felt the mattress and it seemed unusually lumpy—so we took the bed apart and found the fugitive lying between the mattress and the bedspring."

Other deputies have found fugitives hiding inside the box spring, having previously removed the springs from a small section. One team found a man curled up under a blanket in a crib, his baby playing on top of him.

It's not unusual for deputies to find individuals scrunched up under the clothes in a pullout drawer, although one fugitive improved on that. David

O'Flaherty had been assured by an informant that a fugitive was in an apartment on the ninth floor of a Brooklyn project, but his team couldn't find him.

> The fugitive's wife or girlfriend was there with two kids. I asked a little girl, "Where's Daddy?" Needless to say, that did not make the mother happy, so she started screaming and cursing at us. I had a deputy escort the mother out and again asked the little girl where her father was hiding. And this time she said, "Daddy's in the drawer." Daddy's in the drawer? What drawer? I asked, and she pointed to a back bedroom. The only furniture in this room was a little wooden dresser. When we tried to open a drawer, we discovered it was a fake front; he had taken the drawers out and put a fake front on it. Daddy actually was inside the drawer, curled up in a fetal position.

An obvious clue deputies follow when searching a residence is to identify those places that residents don't want them to search. Obviously there is a reason people don't want you looking in certain places. Deputies looking for a Peruvian fugitive in Miami had good information he was hiding in an apartment. The family insisted he was not there and did everything possible to disrupt the search. There was one door that they tried to protect; they refused to open it. Deputies had to bust it down. It was a storage room filled with cardboard boxes—and scrunched up inside one of those cardboard boxes was the suspect.

In another case, Harry Layne was working in Kingston, Jamaica, with a Jamaican task force looking for a killer who had fled New York.

Informants gave us the address of a house where he might be. There were several people there, but he wasn't one of them. We searched the place but didn't find the guy. There was a small locked trunk by the foot of a bed. When we asked them to open it, they told us they didn't have a key. They definitely did not want us opening it, but we looked at it and decided it was too small for anyone to fit inside anyway, so we left it alone.

I guess these people thought we would just leave when we finished our search, but instead we took them with us to the station where we spent several hours interviewing them. We got nothing from them and we finally released them. Several hours later we were notified by the police that a body had been found in the street a block away from that house. Initially we assumed the people we'd questioned had found this guy and didn't want any trouble so they killed him. We were wrong. The body was wrapped in a sheet and eventually we learned what had happened: when we approached the house, they'd squeezed him into that trunk and locked it. By the time they came back from being interrogated, he had suffocated. They didn't know how to get rid of the body so they just tossed him in the gutter.

One of the most popular places fugitives like to hide is in a ceiling or attic. Vic Oboyski was told by an informant that a Jamaican drug crew, which included several individuals with outstanding murder and drug sale warrants, was using three mostly abandoned storefronts on Nostrand Avenue in Brooklyn as its headquarters. Oboyski's team got three search warrants and crashed the stores. "Eventually we took down the whole block," Oboyski says.

We locked up nineteen people. One of the places we went into supposedly was a dry cleaning store, but they only had two or three shirts covered in plastic hanging there—and no people. As we were standing around we heard some noise overhead; somebody was moving around in the ceiling. It was a suspended soft-fiber tile ceiling. We stood still and silent and just listened; something definitely was going on up there. Finally one of our guys grabbed a broom and hit the ceiling—and a man with long dreadlocks fell out of it. There were five or six of us, and we grabbed whatever sticks we could find and started punching into the ceiling—and it started raining Jamaicans. Four people fell out of there onto the floor and we arrested each of them.

After we cleared the place, we found the ladder that they used to climb up into the ceiling when anyone was coming. We also found several unloaded guns hidden up there, including a MAC-10 and an AK-47, as well as a quantity of drugs.

When the late Chris Dudley was a young deputy, he and his partners were searching a home in Atlanta for a fugitive. Eventually they went up into the attic where, according to Chris Dudley,

We saw the tops of two tennis shoes poking up out of the insulation. We went over there and tapped him on the knee. He sat up and grabbed my partner, then started wrestling with him. They were there, then he was gone: he fell through the ceiling, landed on a couch in the living room, bounced off, and hit the floor. A second later my partner fell through the same hole, hit the couch, and, boom, landed on top of him. I just watched them—and then I fell through right after them. I hit the couch and popped off. The three of us were jumbled up fighting on the ground—while a veteran deputy just stood over on the side of the room, watching all this and just shaking his head in disbelief.

Tony Schilling was fortunate to be covering the outside perimeter of a house during a raid on a counterfeiter. It was a two-story house, he remembers, with very thin walls.

As I ran along the side of the house I could hear people inside moving around. Then I distinctly heard the sound of attic stairs dropping down and hitting a hard floor. That's an unmistakable sound; I radioed the guys going in the door that somebody had just gone up into the attic. They responded that there was only one person, a female, in the house. "I heard two voices," I insisted. "I'm telling you, somebody's up in the attic."

My partner and I stayed outside while they searched the whole house, from the basement to the attic. Then suddenly all the windows opened and seconds later our guys were hanging out of them, snot dripping out of their noses. I had no idea what was going on. A few minutes later I found out that one of our people had confirmed that the bad guy was in the attic—and got the great idea that the best way to get him to come out of there was to saturate the entire attic with pepper spray. It turned out to be not such a great idea: you may spray it up into the air, but it's going to come down, and in this case it came down on the deputies in the house, not one of whom was wearing a mask. One of the guys leaning out the window said to me, "He's not coming out."

"No kidding," I said. "He's probably better protected than you." When the spray finally settled, they decided they were going to go up in the attic and Tase him. Using a ballistic shield, they went up into the attic. I was on the radio, and they spotted him dug down under the insulation. They began moving toward him with the Taser when all of a sudden he disappeared. They couldn't find him. There was a lot of chatter on the radio with everybody looking for him. Then one of our people downstairs said he'd found him: he had fallen through the ceiling into a back room, where he was lying helpless on the floor. But apparently he'd hidden his stash in that attic because inside that back room it was raining counterfeit money. Bills were just fluttering through the air.

They got the cuffs on him before he could get up. Usually I really didn't like being on the perimeter, out of the action, but I had never been so happy to be outside in my career.

8

The Running Game

Before this and after this, Marshal Williams and
Farmer Daly, and Ed Burns and three or four
others, told us at different times of threats made
to kill us, by Ike Clanton, Frank McLowry, Tom
McLowry, Joe Hill and John Ringgold. I knew that
all these men were desperate and dangerous, cattle
thieves, robbers and murderers. . . . I heard Behan
say to Virgil Earp, "For God's sake don't go down
there or you will get murdered." Virgil replied,
"I am going to disarm them"—he, Virgil Earp,
being in the lead . . . .

Virgil said, "Throw up your hands. I have come to
disarm you." Billy Clanton and Frank McLowry had
their hands on their six-shooters. Virgil said, "Hold
I don't mean that; I have come to disarm you."

They—Billy Clanton and Frank McLowry—
commenced to draw their pistols, at the same time
Tom McLowry threw his hand to his right hip
and jumped behind a horse. I had my pistol in my
overcoat pocket where I had put it when Behan told
us he had disarmed the other party. When I saw
Billy and Frank draw their pistols I drew my pistol.
Billy Clanton leveled his pistol at me but I did not
aim at him. I knew that Frank McLowry had the
reputation of being a good shot and a dangerous
man, and I aimed at Frank McLowry. The
two first shots which were fired were fired by
Billy Clanton and myself; he shot at me, and I shot
at Frank McLowry. I do not know which shot was
first; we fired almost together.

The fight then became general. . . . My first shot
struck Frank McLowry in the belly. He staggered
off on the sidewalk but first fired one shot at me. . . .
I never drew my pistol or made a motion to shoot
until after Billy Clanton and Frank McLowry drew
their pistols. . . . When Billy Clanton and Frank
McLowry drew their pistols I knew it was a fight
for life, and I drew and fired in defense of my own
life and the lives of my brothers and Doc Holliday.

—*Statement of Wyatt Earp in the inquest into events
at the O.K. Corral, November 16, 1881*

S ome people hide, others run, and a few stand and fight. Even veteran marshals can't predict who's going to surrender, who's going to run, or who's going to start shooting. Logic doesn't apply. Sometimes people who have only minor charges pending against them will try to go out a rear door or window or go for their weapon while others who are fully aware they are going back to prison for life will give up without resistance.

Deputies have no way of knowing, which is why before going into a building, they create a well-armed perimeter around the outside. But when an individual is determined to make a break for it, few things will stop him—even great height. "In an urban situation nothing surprises you," says Robert Leschorn.

> In an old three- or four-story brownstone, people will run up the stairs or up the fire escape to the roof and then you have to play jump the roofs. That's a fun game, because you can get killed really easy. There is usually some space between the roofs and the bandit's been jumping it for ten years. On occasion while they're running from you they'll do a Peter Pan, which means they missed and they get to fly.

I had that happen twice, and both of them became paraplegics. We don't jump. We're satisfied to fight another day.

Just as some fugitives work out places to hide, others plan elaborate escape routes. Lenny DePaul's team was tipped off that a man wanted for a homicide was in his mother's twelfth-floor apartment.

When we banged on the door at five A.M., a female voice responded, "Wait just a minute, I'm coming." When she continued to stall, we had a pretty good idea he was there. A few seconds after we hit the door, a man in his underwear came running up the stairs from a lower floor and told us that a guy was going down the side of the building on a rope. I went into a bedroom and there was a rope tied to the radiator going out the window. I put one of my guys in the elevator, and we took off running down twelve flights of steps.

The elevator got stuck, and the deputy inside happened to be claustrophobic so he started scream-ing. There was nothing we could do to help him. When we got downstairs, the fugitive was gone— but the rope was still swinging back and forth at about the fourth-floor level, maybe forty feet off the ground. At first I guessed he must have gone through a window into an apartment on that floor, but as I walked closer to the building I saw footprints in mud and a lot of blood where he had landed. He'd left a trail in his own blood. We found him sitting against the wall of the next building, broken bones sticking out of his legs.

It turned out to be one of the worst escape plans ever.

As we found out, he had planned this getaway a long time ago. His girlfriend lived on the seventh floor and he kept a rope in her apartment so if or when the police or his enemies came for him he could go out the window. When he stayed with his mother on the twelfth floor, he was always careful to bring his rope with him, just in case. That night, for whatever reasons, he was staying with his mother—and until he reached the end of his rope on the fourth floor it never occurred to him that his seven-story rope would not reach the ground from the twelfth story. The papers the next morning were headlined, accurately, FUGITIVE RUNS OUT OF ROPE.

Some fugitives successfully make it when they run, at least temporarily. Geoff Shank recalls the day he and

Russ Norman, Ed Sloan, and Bill Bonk were going out to Prince George's County, Maryland, to arrest a parole violator.

There are people who don't think parole violation is serious, that it's a minor offense, but what it really means is that this guy is a professional criminal. It means he knows his way around the system and had to have reasons to violate. He knows the deal, and when the marshals come for him, he isn't going to stick around.

He was in an apartment on the fourth floor of a building. When we knocked on the door, we heard a ruckus inside—people were moving around—but we were thinking, fourth floor? No way this guy is going to jump. We kicked in the door and went inside. The glass door leading out to the balcony was open, and the curtain was blowing. We went out to the balcony and looked over the side—and our target was rappelling down to the ground from balcony to balcony. He fell onto the grass and took off. The chase was on.

We chased him through the apartment complex, but he ran inside another building. He could have been anywhere, but we knew he had a cousin who lived on the first floor so we went to speak to her.

While she was telling me she hadn't heard from him and didn't know where he was she was indicating with her eyes that I should look over on the side. I did and saw two dirty socks sticking out from under the bed. While my partner continued to talk to her I went into the bedroom and suddenly grabbed both feet and yanked him out from under there. That was our guy, who had busted his knee in his escape attempt.

But as Shank knows from his own experience, often these attempts end a lot more painfully. He went to an apartment in the tough southeast section of Washington with team members on the D.C. Drug Fugitive Task Force. The suspect was believed to be on the fifth floor. The team established a perimeter and went to the front door. Shank called the phone number they had for the fugitive—who answered. So they knew he was there. Seconds later the team member guarding the rear alerted everyone that the suspect had climbed out the window and was lowering himself to the ground. "Like Keystone Kops everybody turned around and went downstairs," Shank recalls.

We looked up and there was this guy holding on to a rope made from several sheets tied together, rappelling down the side of the building like Batman. He had on long johns and he stopped and looked down and spotted us. He had no place to go. He was just hanging there between floors.

We ran back inside. Bill Bonk was waiting by the front door and said, "I knew you'd be back. Let's go in there." So we went into the apartment, and in the bathroom we found his girlfriend desperately holding on to a sheet with all her strength, her feet pressed against the wall to give her some leverage. We did we always do, we identified ourselves as "Police." Instantly, she let go of the sheet and put up her hands. A second later we heard a thud, then a moan.

Bill stayed with the girl, and I ran downstairs. The ground was mud and dirt except for a strip of concrete sidewalk about three feet wide. Unfortunately, this guy had landed on the sidewalk. He hit the ground so hard he had busted his feet, broken his jaw, fractured his pelvis, separated his rib cage—and he was going back to prison.

Unfortunately, people do die while attempting to escape. After a New York stockbroker who had been indicted for a white-collar crime failed to show up for his trial, Joseph Lobue went to arrest him. He lived in a beautiful apartment on a high floor of a classic Upper East Side building. Lobue remembers,

> He had decided he wasn't going to jail, so when we went to his apartment, he refused to open the door. When he threatened to jump, we called NYPD Emergency Services to assist us. They put down netting over a lower balcony just in case he really did jump. When we hit the door, he took a running leap off the balcony—and completely missed the net. The next day there was a photo in the newspaper of my partner leaning over the balcony looking straight down to where the guy had hit the ground.

When fugitives run, deputies chase them. That aspect of the job hasn't changed in two hundred years. While the official U.S. Marshals Service policy strictly prohibits car chases, in the past they have happened. "What we try to do is follow people to hopefully keep them in sight," explains Bill Noble. "There are times when we may not be pursuing them, but we are following them." For example, in January 2007, members of the Southeast Regional Fugitive Task Force spotted Tywan Lamont Williams, who was wanted for a 1997 Durham, North Carolina, murder and other violations, outside Atlanta. When he saw the marshals, Williams raced off in his vehicle, and rather than endanger people by pursuing him the deputies let him get away. The next day though, they went to an address where supposedly he was staying; they sat there for more than eight hours but he never showed up. At about five o'clock in the afternoon, he was spotted again, this time at a gas station just up the road. "We responded to that gas station," remembers Wayne Warren.

We had four cars; I was driving the second car. He was at the farthest pump from the street. We weren't using lights or sirens, but as he walked from the gas pump to the store he stopped. Obviously he saw a convoy of four cars with tinted windows and knew exactly who we were. He was driving a Cadillac Escalade. He ran over to it and jumped into it.

The lead car tried to prevent him from pulling out by getting right next to him on the driver's side. I pulled my Dodge Durango up to his passenger side so we were running parallel to him and boxed him in. He put the Escalade in reverse and stepped on the accelerator. I put my vehicle in reverse and ran parallel with him through the parking lot to protect anyone else inside the station. As we were running parallel he tried to turn the back of his car and tore off my whole bumper. He put the Escalade in drive and tried to ram one of our other vehicles guarding the exit head-on. Then he backed up again and tried to get out another exit; I blocked him again and he smashed into my passenger side and tore off that whole side of my car. Then he pushed his way through me and got out of the parking lot into the street.

I'd lost my fender and about half the side of the car, but my Dodge just kept going; that's why I loved that car. He turned the wrong way onto a one-way service road, trying to make it to I-285. I knew all our rules, but I also knew his criminal history and what had happened in that parking lot, and I had no doubt innocent people were going to get hurt if we let him go. When he turned the corner to get on the interstate, he made a very wide turn onto the ramp so I decided I could pin him there. I turned and got inside his vehicle and he started ramming the left side of my car. That ramp is on a very steep embankment and he was trying to push me over the side. My tires were on the edge of the gravel trying to get traction. I fought him the whole way down the ramp. This was in the middle of rush hour, and traffic on the interstate was standing still. At the bottom of the embankment he continued trying to push me into stalled traffic. At that point I thought, *This is it, I've got to end this here and now.* I drew my service revolver and engaged the laser sight. I aimed through my passenger-side window at his tinted driver's-side window; I guessed where his head might be and fired two rounds.

I reassessed after firing those rounds, and within seconds his truck started going all over the road. I knew I'd probably hit him. I holstered up and used my vehicle to force him up against a concrete barrier. Then I bailed out of the car and took cover behind my driver's-side rear tire. Other deputies got ready to rush him but I yelled for them to stay back, shots had been fired.

Everybody took cover and we waited. There was no movement from inside his car. We got the ballistic shield and came up on him over the wall, from his passenger side. When they broke out the windows, they saw him lying between the seats, his legs caught underneath the wheel. For a long time he didn't respond at all, then he said, "I can't come out. I've been shot in my head." We pulled him out of the car; one shot had hit him on the side of the head and blown out his left eye. The other shot had grazed him under his cheek. He was rushed to the hospital and survived and is now serving a seventeen-year federal sentence.

Jimmy Bankston also found himself driving the wrong way in pursuit of a fugitive—but in his case the suspect was on a bicycle. Bankston's task force had been tracking a 15 Most Wanted fugitive named Mark Anthony Williams, who was wanted for murder, through four states until finally getting a good address for him in Durham, North Carolina. As the task force prepared to hit a house in a driving rainstorm, Bankston's experience told him Williams wasn't there.

"I don't know where he is," I told the other members of the task force, "but he's not in that house. He's probably over at the Winn-Dixie watching us hit this house." We drove over there to take a look for him and as we went past a little roach motel, we spotted him on a pay telephone. He spotted us; we were driving a Ford Expedition with the antennas on it and we were wearing bulletproof vests. It was pretty obvious we were the law. So he jumped on his bicycle and took off.

Meanwhile, two blocks away we had a SWAT team in an armored personal carrier hitting the house. I was screaming over the radio, "He's not

there. We're chasing him, he's on a yellow bicycle."
He headed into traffic on Route 1, so we took off
after him. It was pouring, the roads were slippery,
and we were sliding all over the place. Finally he
ditched the bike and took off on foot. We lost him
for a while and guessed he was hiding up in a tree.
We went around searching for him tree by tree—
and eventually we found him hiding in the front
part of a boat that was up on sawhorses, in the
equipment stowage compartment.

Jim Schield was also chasing a killer who was known to
make his getaway by driving against traffic on a highway.

My partner and I were staking out a hotel in downtown San Diego with another two-person team
when our target got into a car with three other men.
We didn't know who the other people were, but
he was a gang member and part of a smuggling
operation. He spotted us. Before we could stop the
car, he took off. We chased him right through old
town San Diego. It wasn't quite baby carriages flying
and driving through fruit stands like in the movies,
but it was right through the middle of a city. I wasn't
about to let him go because this was a homicide case.
They went through a residential area, the wrong

way down a one-way street and finally ended up
going southbound in the northbound lanes of I-5.
They didn't think we would follow them. We did.
We drove on the shoulder about a mile, and when
they realized we were not giving up, they bailed out
of their car. We ended up chasing them on foot; we
ran down into a ditch and caught up with two of
them. We found a gun in the car and human blood
in the trunk. We were able to take him off the street.

"As a manhunter, among the most important traits
you can possess is discipline," explains Jerry Lowery.
"You can't allow yourself to get lulled into complacency,
because then if something happens, it shocks you and
you don't respond very well. You don't think logically or
make good decisions." No one wants to drive into traffic
on a highway, that's a difficult decision to make, but on
rare occasions it just seems like the right thing to do.

Lowery and his team had tracked a fugitive to a
hotel in Atlanta and they were getting ready to make
the arrest when their target came out with a female and
got into a car.

He pulled out before we could stop him and went to
a stoplight. He was the third car at the light and we
thought the car in front of him was one of ours

because it looked like it. But when we came up behind him to block him in, he pushed that car out of the way and took off southbound in the northbound lanes. He smashed into three cars before he left the stoplight, then caused two or three more accidents on the roadway as cars scrambled to get out of the way. One of our people followed him onto the northbound lane, but the rest of us stayed in the southbound lane and paralleled him at high speeds. We stayed right with him until he cut off the main road and pulled his car behind a building and bailed out. We lost him, but we caught up with him later that night at a hotel and made the arrest.

I can tell you from my own experience, when you're in one of those chases, trust me, you really want to be the driver, not the passenger.

Not every chase takes place at high speeds, and sometimes they are not really chases. Mike Moran and his partner were staking out a hotel, watching a car that had been associated with their fugitive when a man came out and got into it. They couldn't determine if it was their target, so they decided to follow it.

We didn't want him to know we were following him, but when the car started making right turns and left turns and going around the block in circles without any obvious destination, I said forget it, this guy knows we're following him. They were doing a good job trying to shake us. So we decided to stop the car and see who was in it.

Turned out our suspect was in the car and we were able to make the arrest. But once we had him in custody I wanted to know when they had realized we were following them. I wanted to find out what gave us away. So I asked the driver, "When did you notice that we were following you?"

He shook his head. "I didn't have any idea you were behind me."

"Then why were you making all those turns trying to lose us?"

He said, "I wasn't. I'm not from around here. I was just lost."

In the Old West, posses would chase bandits all the way into their hideouts, where sometimes their outlaw gang was waiting to ambush them. In a similar fashion Bobby Sanchez tailed a fugitive into the hills of Puerto Rico.

We followed him all the way back into a small town. Up there people stick together and there have been instances where roads have been blocked to prevent people getting in or, like in this situation, out. When we came back, they had cars blocking the road and would not allow us to leave. There was two of us and at least ten of them. To be honest, you do get a little nervous in those situations. There wasn't much we could do if this thing escalated. I told the fugitive, who was cuffed in the back, "You know, if this goes bad it's only going to be worse for you." He understood that, and he was able to convince those people to move their cars out of the way.

The difference between big-screen car chases and real life is that nobody really gets hurt in movies; in real life the potential for a violent ending is always there. David O'Flaherty and his team had received information that a bank robber named Albertus Freeman, who had violated his parole, was seen in a project in the Mariner's Harbor section of Staten Island.

We used to have an undercover truck that was disguised to look like a telephone company truck; we'd actually used our own money to get it painted at Earl Scheib and put the correct logos on it. The telephone company wasn't happy about it, but we did it anyway. There were three of us in that van when we spotted our fugitive. He got into a station wagon with four other men and a woman. As they were driving toward us we pulled the van in front of them to block them. They stopped and we got out; we drew down on them—and as soon they realized what was going down, they took off. And as they did, somebody in the back of the station wagon stuck his arm out over the roof of the car and fired a shot at us. We returned fire, then got into the van, and took off in pursuit.

O'Flaherty's team chased them all the way through Staten Island. People watching probably wondered why a telephone company van was chasing a station wagon at high speed. Finally, the station wagon pulled into the parking lot of a bowling alley and the people inside scattered. O'Flaherty took off after Freeman, who ran down the side of the bowling alley and jumped up on a big fence. He was just about to get over the fence when two large dogs appeared on the other side and started jumping up trying to bite him. Freeman paused, trying to decide between prison and two vicious dogs. He climbed down and surrendered.

Some fugitives run—literally. They take off on foot, which means while they won't get very far very fast, potentially there are a lot of hiding places available to them. It's a lot easier to hide in an apartment building than on a highway. And deputies know when they chase a runner that they are facing the prospect of a fight—or a gun—at the end. Harry Layne had walked into a Washington, D.C., hardware store to get duplicate keys made when an alarm went off. A thief had broken into a truck parked behind the store and grabbed a toolbox. Layne, who took off after him, recounts what happened.

I saw a guy going over a ten-foot high fence with a toolbox in his hand. My partner was waiting in front and I yelled to him to follow me, I was going to chase the perp. I chased him for several blocks and saw him make a right turn into an alley. I paused a second to check out the situation before I made the same turn. Then I took out my gun and turned into the alley. He was standing there holding a hammer he'd taken out of the toolbox in his hand. He raised the hammer and started coming toward me. I identified myself, shouting, "Police. Drop that hammer. Drop it!" Maybe I cursed at him. He kept coming—then threw the hammer at my head. As I ducked I squeezed the trigger and let a round go. The hammer went sailing by my head, and my shot hit the ground by his leg. But the instant I fired he threw up his hands so fast I thought he might dislocate his shoulder. My partner came up and we got him down on the ground.

My team couldn't decide what was funnier, that I had been attacked with a hammer or that my shot had missed at close range.

During a chase, a weapon is indeed the great equalizer. Stephanie Creasy was working on a task force with an African American DEA agent when they got information that several members of a major drug organization had been seen in a black neighborhood.

My partner decided it would be better if he went down there with another black agent, but time was running out so we drove down there with another white male. We got to a stop sign and looked over to our right—and we recognized the suspects in the car right next to us. They rolled up the window and took off. We followed them—not at a high rate of speed—just following them. They were way ahead of us, and when we reached a sharp turn, we saw that they hadn't made it; they'd hit a telephone pole then bolted. The three of us drew our weapons and took off after them on foot. The guy I was chasing had a really good stretch ahead of me; he ran down a few streets and through a couple of alleys but then made the mistake of trying to hide underneath a car. I came up on him and . . .

When I first started on the job I thought I was going to be one of those police officers who never used a curse word. But during a training exercise at the academy I was playing the bad guy and another woman trainee was trailing me. At one point she yelled at me, "Stop. Please!" Afterward I asked her why she had been so polite. It turned out she hadn't; she hadn't said please, she told me, she had yelled, "Stop! Police!" That was when I learned that when you throw in a few f-bombs people will take you very seriously.

. . . I came up to our guy and I shouted at him, "Police! Get the f—k out of there with your f—ing hands where I can see them." Then I made the arrest. In every situation you have to make it clear that you are in charge and will do whatever you have to do. It's when they doubt you that problems start.

While in the Old West a chase might have lasted several days and taken deputies through all types of weather and terrain, a real chase now will not last long but may lead deputies through unexpected places.

Mike Moran had been tracking a Jamaican drug dealer through South Florida for more than six months when reliable information put the target in an apartment building. Moran and police officer Brent Biagi went to the location to take a look. As Moran explains it,

We decided to wait there until we had a few more people, but our guy came out of the building and got into a car. We rolled up on him, blocking him in, but we were a little too quick. He took off running. He came up on a big canal, probably forty yards across, and hesitated. We thought, we got him now, he's got nowhere to go. But he dived into the water and started swimming. I told Brent to go get us some help, that I was going after him.

The guy was wearing a tank top and gym shorts. It was obvious he wasn't armed, and I didn't want to swim with my handgun and other stuff I had on. I handed Brent my gun, jumped in, and started swimming. I got about halfway across when it suddenly occurred to me: *This is about the stupidest thing I've ever done. I'm going to drown.* My clothes were weighing me down and I was just swimming with my upper body.

I managed to struggle to the other side and climbed up on the bank. I had no idea where the guy went. I had no radio, no phone, no anything, and I was dripping wet. I cut through a backyard and I was really frustrated. All that and I'd lost him. But then I looked down and noticed wet footprints running all the way down the street. I just started laughing and realized finding him might not be that hard. At that point I heard sirens coming in—and a helicopter. Brent had called the sheriff's office and they were coming to help us out. I started tracking the wet footprints to the point where he turned and ran off in the grass. It looked like he was gone.

A sheriff's car was at the end of the block, and when the officer saw me, he started shaking his head and said, "You must be the stupid marshal that swam across the canal after the guy." I wonder what gave me away. Just then a call came over his radio that someone cutting through a backyard had been cornered by a dog. He was trapped there. That could only be one guy. I got in the car and we raced over to the address. It was our fugitive, and we were able to make the arrest. Later I was told by someone that this case was being taught at the academy—as an example of what not to do when chasing someone.

Jimmy Bankston was involved in a very Hollywood-style chase when he and his partner used a pager number to pinpoint a suspect in the women's clothing store where his girlfriend was working. The store was in an all-black neighborhood, and Bankston and his partner were both white.

We opened the door and spotted him instantly; he was way in the back, talking to a girl. As we started walking toward him he began moving very slowly in the other direction, watching us the whole time, trying to figure out who we were. Then, suddenly, it must have dawned on him because he took off, running through the store, throwing over the racks of women's clothes to try to slow us down. The women in the store started screaming. We took off after him, pushing the racks out of our way. Dresses were flying right in our face. He raced out through a side door into the crowded parking lot—then literally started running right over the cars, over the hoods, the roofs, and the trunks—and we stayed right behind him. We ran right over the cars with him, just a few steps behind. That was when my partner got the great idea of spraying mace at him.

It was quite a sight: Bankston and his partner were right behind the suspect. Bankston's partner was spraying mace in front of them—which they were running right into. Eventually the fugitive ran into an abandoned apartment complex and disappeared. Bankston called in the dogs, and several deputies searched that area until the suspect was found scrunched under a sink in a bathroom.

"After we made the arrest," Bankston recalled, "my partner asked me what we were thinking, running over cars instead of going around them? Then I asked him why he was spraying mace at the guy from behind. Neither one of us had a reasonable answer, but the truth is when you're involved in a chase, you just keep going."

Lenny DePaul's pursuit of fugitive David Kaplan may take the honor of being the slowest chase in the history of the Marshals Service. David Kaplan had been indicted in both New York and New Jersey for running a multimillion-dollar marijuana/hashish smuggling ring and was facing two life sentences if convicted. While he wasn't considered violent himself, he supposedly employed very dangerous people to collect drug debts. He had successfully evaded authorities for more than seven years when a cooperator told DePaul that Kaplan was going to be in New York City over the Mother's Day weekend to collect some money. "David Kaplan had been my top priority for a long time," DePaul says.

I used to dream about him. I'd wake up in the middle of the night wondering what his next move was going to be. Who was who in his zoo, where was he likely to show up next? It was incredibly frustrating.

I was at a Saturday afternoon wedding when I got word he was in town. I left the wedding and we started surveilling all the locations he was known to frequent when he was in the city. Our cooperator told us he was wearing a pair of white pants, a T-shirt, and a baseball cap. We spent the rest of the weekend looking for him, but we never spotted him. Finally about one A.M. Sunday night we decided to pack it in. It was time to go home.

DePaul was angry and exhausted. This was the most promising lead they'd had in several years and it had turned out to be a big nothing. He was driving up Third Avenue on his way to the Midtown Tunnel when he stopped at a light in the East Village. As he sat there waiting for the light to change, he glanced in his rearview mirror and noticed a guy wearing white pants, a T-shirt, and a baseball cap walking down the block. He was incredulous: *It couldn't be,* he thought. *No way.* He couldn't believe it. What were the odds he would run into the guy he had been chasing for seven years strolling down a New York street? This person was walking pretty fast and was carrying a briefcase under his arm. DePaul pulled over next to a fire hydrant and remembers, "I put my police sign on the dashboard and got out of my car. I didn't have anything on me; my gun, my badge, my handcuffs, everything was in the backseat, and I didn't have time to get it out. I started walking behind him, probably sixteen to seventeen car lengths back."

DePaul followed him for several blocks, not knowing for sure it was Kaplan. At one point that person turned around and looked directly at DePaul. When he did, DePaul leaned over and grabbed the handle of a car door as if he was getting into that car. To his amazement, the door was unlocked. So he opened it and got into the car. The man crossed the street and went into an all-night café. DePaul resumed his pursuit.

> I got out of the car, locking the door for the citizen, and crossed to the other side of the street. I looked through the window and didn't see him. I went inside and looked around, but I still didn't see him. I went over and stood in front of the locked men's room door, thinking he might be inside. The job had put me in a lot of different places, but standing outside a men's room door at two A.M. was a first.

I waited. When the door opened, I tensed a little; I wasn't sure what I was going to do if it was him, just react.

It wasn't Kaplan. "Excuse me," the man said and pushed by in the small hallway.

DePaul walked around another corner and spotted a pay phone tucked away in a little nook. And talking on that phone was the man he had been tailing.

He was leaning on a wooden shelf, talking on the phone. His back was to me so I still couldn't determine if it was Kaplan. I backed out of the place and onto the street. As I did two NYPD rookies were strolling down the block. It was obvious they were just out of the academy because they were walking a beat at two A.M. and their trousers were perfectly creased. I stopped them and told them who I was. I didn't have any credentials; the only thing I had on me was Kaplan's wanted poster. I explained to them, "This is who I am, this is the man I'm looking for, and if it's him, you guys are going to be heroes. If it isn't, then we all go on our merry way." One of them asked me, "Who you with again?"

"Just back me up," I told them. I went back inside and looked over my shoulder. One of them

was on his radio, so I knew it was just a matter of time before the cavalry arrived. I walked up behind the man, who was just hanging up the phone. From behind, I grabbed his wrist and twisted it hard behind his back. He spun around—and the blood ran out of my body. It was him. It was the guy I'd been chasing for seven years, and finally, finally, I was looking right at him. "David Kaplan," I said. "I'm a U.S. marshal and you're under arrest."
He said, "I'm sick of running."

And I said, "And I'm sick of chasing you." With that the NYPD came through the front door. Kaplan immediately produced fake ID, but I knew I had him. After seven years, I knew I had him. We took him in, and after three days, he realized it was smart for him to talk to me. Through him we made several other high-profile arrests.

On rare and terrible occasions, it is the deputy who is being chased. One of the most horrendous crimes in DEA history was the kidnapping, torture, and murder of Agent Kiki Camarena by a Mexican drug cartel. More than anything else, the DEA wanted desperately to bring Camarena's killers to justice. DEA agent Don Ferrarone had come over to the Marshals Service as acting head of the International Branch

Enforcement Division. Ferrarone and Tony Perez put together a team. "Our target was Rene Martin Verdugo-Urquidez," Perez says, "who was a high-ranking member of the Rafael Caro-Quintero drug ring, and supposedly he was there when Camarena and his pilot were tortured and killed. Verdugo, incidentally, is a Spanish word meaning 'he who tortures.'"

Perez and Ferrarone crossed the Mexican border and staked out Rene Martin Verdugo-Urquidez. They were working closely with officers from several Mexican law enforcement organizations who had the actual arrest authority. Their problem was that he was always protected by no less than ten heavily armed bodyguards. And as Perez knew, there also was reason to believe that at least some members of Mexican law enforcement were on the cartel's payroll. Through an informant Perez and Ferrarone learned that Verdugo-Urquidez was going to have a birthday party for his daughter in the town of San Felipe, which is in the Mexican state of Baja California, about 190 kilometers from the American border.

Perez intended to be at that party.

I have always believed that if you're in the right place at the right time doing the right thing, you can make your own luck. Dumb luck is when you drop a quarter in a slot machine and win; smart luck is what you make when you are out there building toward a goal and an opportunity presents itself. We were watching the party and, unbelievably, Verdugo-Urquidez came out of the party because they had run out of beer. So he and a driver, just the two of them, went to a local liquor store to fill up on beer. We had no idea what happened to his bodyguards and we didn't care. It was a beautiful situation for our purposes. Beautiful.

We got into our rented station wagons and followed them to the liquor store. We walked in right behind him. He was in the back of the freezer getting the coldest beer when I took him down. We hooded him and his driver and put them in the back of a station wagon. We dumped the driver a block away and took off. We knew it wasn't going to be that easy. We still had to make it back to the border.

The owners of the liquor store did not want to be involved. They immediately called local law enforcement to report a kidnapping. As Perez recalls,

Within minutes we were being chased by the Mexican Highway Patrol. They didn't know who we were, and we didn't know if we could trust them. They started shooting at us, trying to keep us from getting to the border. We had some very brave guys from the Mexican Federal Judicial Police protecting our back, and they held them off. Eventually we made it to the border fence near Yuma, Arizona. We were racing through ditches while the Federales did their best to slow down the Highway Patrol. Finally, somebody got word to the Highway Patrol to stop shooting. Meanwhile we abandoned our rental cars and threw all our gear—and our prisoner—over the fence onto American territory.

Our prisoner had pissed himself because he thought we were going to kill him, but the first thing we did when we got to the Yuma office was take photographs of him to prove that he hadn't been tortured in any way—except for the bruises he got when we threw him over the fence.

That capture had serious repercussions. The drug cartel immediately put out contracts to kill everyone they believed had assisted in Rene Martin Verdugo-Urquidez's capture. The Marshals Service had to act very quickly to get all its assets out of there. Within the next twenty-four hours, thirty-two people—the individuals who had assisted in the capture and their families—were brought out of Mexico and put in protective custody in the Marshals's Witness Protection Program. Eventually Verdugo-Urquidez was convicted and sentenced to 240 years and an additional life term in prison. A lot of legal issues were raised by this case and the subsequent kidnapping and capture of Humberto Alvarez Machain, who allegedly was also involved in Camarena's murder. After Verdugo-Urquidez's capture, DEA agents received permission from Mexican Judicial Police to search his residence and seized considerable evidence about his drug operation. His American lawyers tried to prevent this evidence from being used against him, citing the protections against unreasonable search and seizure granted by the Fourth Amendment. But eventually the United States Supreme Court ruled that this search in foreign territory was not prohibited by the Constitution.

In 1992, the Supreme Court overturned rulings from two lower courts and found in the case of Alvarez Machain that the United States could kidnap a criminal suspect from a foreign country and put that person on trial in a federal court. When Machain was tried he was acquitted and allowed to return to Mexico. This question was never raised in Verdugo-Urquidez's case because this operation was officially run by Mexican federal law enforcement officers, who literally put their hands on him, while the Marshals Service was there observing, and avoiding bullets—until they picked him up and threw him over the fence.

The thing that all deputy marshals live with every day, when standing in front of every door, when searching every attic or walking through woods, is the knowledge that the badges they are wearing make them targets. While in many ways they take pride in the history and tradition of the Marshals Service, they are members of a different type of crime-fighting organization, working in an increasingly violent world. Every deputy knows the story of Gordon Kahl, who in some ways may have ushered in the modern era of the Marshals Service.

Kahl was a founding member of an extremist tax-protesting group known as the Posse Comitatus, which refused to recognize the right of the federal government to levy taxes. After being convicted in 1976 of failing to file tax returns, he served eight months of a two-year sentence. Upon his release, he became active in the so-called township movement that refused to recognize the sovereignty of the federal govern-ment. On a Sunday night in February 1983 outside the town of Medina, North Dakota, U.S. Marshal Kenneth Muir, Deputy Marshal Bob Cheshire, several other deputies, and two deputy sheriffs set up a roadblock to arrest Kahl for a parole violation. Kahl was in a car with his wife, his son, and three other people when they approached the roadblock. Rather than surrendering, Kahl opened fire, killing Marshal Muir and Deputy Cheshire and wounding four other officers. The shootings were sudden and unexpected, and they marked the beginning of a new and violent era in American history, an era in which armed individuals too often decided to shoot it out with law enforcement.

A day later Chuck Kupferer arrived in Fargo, North Dakota, to begin a pursuit of Kahl that would last four months and stretch across ten midwestern states. This all took place at the time that the Marshals Service was taking over some of the FBI's fugitive apprehension responsibilities. As Kupferer remembers,

> Early on we arrested Kahl's wife, his son, and one of his nephews, but nobody could find him. We set up a joint FBI–Marshals Service Task Force; my FBI counterpart and I had a team of twenty-five deputy marshals and twenty-five FBI agents. Small farmers in that area had been badly hurt by several economic factors in the past decade, so that area was dotted with abandoned farmhouses, barns, and silos. Kahl could have been hiding out in any one of them. We must have searched at least fifty

abandoned farms in that region. Eventually we received a tip from a young woman whose father was associated with Kahl that he was hiding in what was essentially a bunker in Smithville, Arkansas. More than a hundred officers surrounded Kahl in this bunker. They were trying to talk him into surrendering when a local sheriff suddenly broke through the ring, crashed through a side door, and exchanged fire with him. The sheriff was killed, but no one will ever know if Kahl also died in that shooting or if he was killed in the ensuing gun battle.

I had flown in on a Coast Guard plane and got there just in time to see a local constable climb up on the top of this bunker and pour a can of gasoline down the stack into the fireplace. Fire just blew out that whole place. The local fire department wouldn't get close because they claimed bullets were being fired; I told them it wasn't bullets, it was cement blowing up. I'd seen that happen before.

That whole thing was a mess. Eventually Kahl's son and one of the other people who had been in that car when Muir and Cheshire were killed were convicted of murder.

If there had been any doubt before the Kahl case that the Marshals Service would fight fire by firing back, it ended on that farm in Arkansas. Whether searching a building or a house, walking through a forest, or pursuing someone, deputies always have their weapons out and ready. At one time deputies were permitted to carry pretty much any weapon they wanted as long as it met certain criteria. But currently every one is issued a Glock 22, a .40-caliber handgun, and is permitted to carry a backup of choice; in addition, marshals pursuing fugitives can carry a shotgun or an automatic rifle if they choose. The reality is that this is not a game of hide-and-seek; shots get fired and people are wounded or killed.

The actual Marshals Service's policy governing when deputies can fire is restrictive. Obviously self-defense is always acceptable. At one time deputies were permitted to shoot at fleeing felons who represented a danger to the community, but that has been somewhat modified, just like hot pursuits. In the end the decision comes down to the moment: when a life is in jeopardy, deputies don't hesitate.

Do I shoot or not? That's the toughest decision any law enforcement officer has to make. While deputies are well trained and face numerous shoot-or-not scenarios, the reality is that there is no way to train for all situations. Sometimes deputies have to make an instantaneous decision that may have monumental consequences—and there are no second chances.

In some situations the proper response is obvious, and there is no reason to hesitate. In March 2000, Jamil Abdullah Al-Amin, who earlier in his life had been known as Black Panther H. Rap Brown, shot two Fulton County, Georgia, sheriff's deputies, killing one and wounding the other, then took off. A four-day-long, massive manhunt finally managed to pinpoint his location near the town of White Hall, Alabama. Jerry Lowery was among the U.S. marshals involved in the search. "We had a probable location and we were on our way over there," as Lowery describes the scene. "But as we drove past the location, we spotted him sitting in a recess in a doorway at the back of the building eating cereal. He looked up and saw us just as we spotted him; we both knew who each of us was, so we swung the car around to get back to him; that's when he started shooting at us."

Al-Amin managed to escape into the woods. The FBI SWAT team put the dogs on his trail. He made a big arc back into the little town where he was arrested. He was wearing body armor when they caught up with him, and they found the 9 mm and a .223 rifle used to shoot the police officers nearby. Al-Amin will spend the rest of his life in Supermax in Colorado.

The history of the Marshals Service includes legendary tales of Old West shoot-outs, the most famous being

Wyatt Earp's legendary gunfight at the O.K. Corral. And while those showdowns are pretty much confined to history, in rare instances deputies still get involved in spectacular gunfights. For a long time the island of Jamaica was a safe haven for Jamaican nationals. Harry Layne explains,

Large-scale drug dealers, murderers, robbers, rapists—they were all there, and we knew they were there, but there was almost nothing we could do about it. So we came up with the idea of establishing a fugitive task force with the Jamaican Constabulary Force, which had never done anything like that. Officially we were there to train them in our techniques, but the best way to train them was to be in the street with them. There was no other way. These officers had tremendous courage, they had guts, but they lacked the equipment, training, and most everything else. Police officers literally had to share their guns, leaving them at the station when they went off duty so the next shift could use them. We brought these officers to the United States to our Special Operations Group training center in Louisiana, and we worked with them on the island. Fortunately we were allowed to carry guns in Jamaica, which is not true in many other places outside the States. I actually had to go for an interview to get a permit to carry, which required me to tell my entire background about from the time I was born. Jamaica has some of the strictest gun laws in the world; you can't buy a gun there, and there are no ammunition stores, but somehow every bad guy in Jamaica had at least one gun and plenty of ammo. Law enforcement was outgunned. It was all smuggled in.

At that time, being a police officer in Kingston, Jamaica was one of the most dangerous jobs imaginable. Kingston was the murder capital of the noncombatant world. And with all the drug money being passed around, some law enforcement officers couldn't be trusted. But Layne and other deputies carefully vetted the officers who became part of their team. Layne says, "We literally trusted them with our lives. We went out with them to most remote parts of the island, and we went into the inner-city ghettos, which they call yards. There was a lot of gunplay, a lot of shoot-outs, and a lot of scary moments. Those officers never let us down."

Gangs had divided parts of Kingston into fortified areas where the police were not welcome. Neighborhoods had names like the Concrete Jungle, Glock Corner, Tel Aviv. For good reason people living in these places knew they couldn't rely on the government, so they would go to their local strongman to settle disputes or to get whatever they needed. When the police ran into trouble in the yards they would call in the mobile reserve, their version of SWAT teams, and in those instances when the mobile reserve got in trouble or was outgunned, they would call in the army.

Things could escalate pretty quickly. At one point Layne and his team went into the yards in pursuit of a fugitive wanted on various drug charges. Layne remembers,

He wasn't coming out on his own. We were limited by the fact that we were there at that time in an advisory capacity. But the result of going after this fugitive was an all-out battle. Eventually it was estimated that more than twenty-five thousand rounds were fired. While officially we were not supposed to be involved in situations like this I think it's accurate to state that we were on the periphery of it. We were more than close enough to hear it.

As Layne recalls, there wasn't anything at all unusual about shots being fired. In one situation he and his Jamaican team had a house surrounded.

We had people in the front and the back and then we heard shots fired. We were yelling, "Who fired?

Who fired?" Nobody admitted it. Then all of a sudden a woman came running out of a second-story bedroom onto the balcony and jumped off, landing in the yard. She'd been shot and wounded. We went ahead and kicked the door open. One of our Jamaican people carried an Uzi; he pulled it out and got that house cleared. We arrested our bad guy and took this woman to the hospital, then went on our way. No questions, no answers; that's just the way some things ended up there.

Returning fire is never an issue. That's an easy decision to make: somebody shoots at you, shoot back. But when—and if—to fire the first shot is a much more complex question. This is the life-and-death decision dreaded by every law enforcement officer in the country. It is every officer's nightmare and there is no easy answer. Dave Dimmitt was working warrants in Omaha, Nebraska, when he received a call from one of his informants who was working in a ground-floor bodega below a fugitive's apartment. Someone was moving around in the upstairs apartment, the informant told him. "We went to the door," Dimmitt remembers.

I put my thumb over the eye-hole and knocked on the door. As he started opening it, he asked who it was and I told him, "Police!" He tried to slam the door, but I pushed back hard. I was winning the push battle, so he took off running down a hallway that led to a living room. In the living room he sort of dived behind a couch. We went right after him; one deputy was completely exposed in the center of the living room while myself and another deputy had partial cover. We were screaming at him, "Show us your hands! Show us your hands!" But he held up only one hand, his left hand. We didn't know if he was armed or not, and we always have to assume a weapon. But we didn't know, and there is a special type of hell that you go through when you shoot an unarmed person. Time gets suspended in those situations. We had a deputy exposed only a few feet from the fugitive. How long do you wait before you start shooting? Finally, slowly, he raised his other hand. We had him come out into the room and got the cuffs on him. Then we went around back of the couch—lying there on the carpet, under the couch, was his loaded revolver. In those few seconds he'd made his decision to live.

Often only pure luck prevents a shooting. A split second, less than a split second, can make all the difference. During Operation Gunsmoke, a joint task force operation between the Marshals Service and the NYPD designed to take guns off the streets, Lenny DePaul and NYPD Detective Bobby Bolson were coming over the Fifty-Ninth Street Bridge at five thirty on a rainy October afternoon. They were on their way home after a long day when they saw two kids walking across the street with their hoods up. As DePaul explains,

> Bobby looked at me and I knew what he was thinking. "Oh, c'mon, Bobby," I said, "we've been up since four A.M. Let's get out of here."
>
> "Now just hold on a minute," he said. We stopped at a light and these kids crossed directly in front of us. After being on the job long enough, you get a really good sense of who's up to something. I think Bobby and I were both tingling. So Bobby opened his door then slammed it closed. Boom! Those kids took off running. We put on the siren and chased them as far as we could, then we got out of the car and chased them on foot. When they split up, Bobby and I split up. My guy ran right through traffic and I stayed with him. I chased him for three blocks, four blocks. I was running across Third Avenue when a cab almost hit me; I jumped up on the hood and went right over it. I was about thirty feet behind this kid when he took a 9 mm out of his

waistband and tried to throw it down a sewer grate. Unbelievably, this gun bounced off the metal grate, hit the curb, and bounced back—right into my hand. A fully loaded 9 mm bounced into my hand, and I caught it without breaking stride. I jammed it in my coat pocket and kept going. Finally I got close enough and pounced on him. Cuffed him up. An auxiliary cop who had seen me chasing him and followed me, gave me a ride back to the car. We were six blocks away.

When DePaul got back, his partner was standing there shaking. "What happened?" DePaul asked.

"That f—ing kid," Bolson said. "I caught up with him and told him to put his hands up. When he did, he had a gun in his hand. I told him to drop it and he wouldn't. If he had turned on me, I would've killed him." He paused. "He's sixteen." Bolson was really shaken by how close he had come to having to shoot this kid.

"Mine's fourteen," DePaul said, showing him the 9 mm. They took both minors in. Two weeks later DePaul was alerted that another warrant had been issued for the kid he'd caught, so they followed it up. He had been bailed out by his grandparents because both of his parents had died of a drug overdose.

We went up to his grandmother's house, and when she opened the door, we walked into a kind of hell. I had never seen a filthier apartment. In every bedroom there was a naked baby no older than a few months just lying in feces and crying. The mothers were lying in the hallway. Bobby called Child Protective Services and they closed that place down.

The grandmother told me the fourteen-year-old was in jail. He had gone out and got himself another gun and held up a woman for her bag of groceries. The police saw it and arrested him. Bobby and I left that place thinking those kids don't have a chance—and how close we had come to shooting them.

The memory of that instant when a deputy has to make the decision to shoot or not will last a lifetime, often bringing with it overwhelming emotion. Like every other marshal, Tony Burke will never forget his closest call.

I wasn't quick to shoot, but I've shot people before. This one time we were chasing two guys with guns in Compton. They ran into an alley between two houses, a kind of no-man's-land. I came around the corner, and one of them had a gun in his hand, which he dropped immediately. The other guy had a gun in his waistband, and he was making his decision. "Don't do it," I told him, aiming right at him. "Don't go for it." When you've done this enough times, you can tell who's serious about it. This guy went for his weapon, but the look in his eyes told me he was doing it out of fear; there wasn't any "I'm gonna kill you, motherf—er" macho there. His reasoning didn't matter to me. I didn't have a choice. He grabbed the gun, and as I began to squeeze the trigger, an L.A. sheriff's deputy who had been chasing these people walked right in front of me. Right in front of me. In that instant, the guy made a better decision and put down his weapon. There is no question that deputy saved that guy's life, no question at all.

Fortunately, luck does work both ways. Geoff Shank and a team including James Brooks went to an apartment to arrest a 340-pound man who had violated his parole—by threatening to kill his parole officer. Shank explains what happened.

He was just a big, violent guy who had threatened to cut off his parole officer's head, so they sent us out to get him. Five of us were in his place, and he was lying on his bed. We could see the end of a gun sticking out from between the mattress and the box spring. We were trying to talk him in, but he wasn't interested. I will never know why I did this, but I told James, "Cover him with the shotgun, I'll run and get him." That turned out to be a very bad idea.

While Brooks kept the shotgun on the man, Geoff Shank went around to the other side of the bed. Suddenly, when the parole violator glanced at Brooks, Shank tackled him.

I got on top of him, but as I started to swing my baton, he slammed me in the side of my head with something and split my head open. Blood was flowing all over the place, but somehow I ended up getting control of him. Later I found out what had happened: He had grabbed the Glock from under the mattress and swung it around; there was nothing James could do to help me at that point; he couldn't fire the shotgun without hitting me. After bashing me in the face with his gun, he aimed it right at my head and pulled the trigger.

The hammer clicked. Nothing happened. The first round in the chamber was a .380 and the hammer had hit outside the firing pin. It was the wrong ammunition for that weapon. The hammer hit on the end of the cartridge. Every other cartridge in that gun was 9 mm. That was the only bullet that wouldn't have fired.

Much later that afternoon, Shank was sitting at his desk; the bleeding had stopped but Shank was laughing to himself when James Brooks walked over and flicked a .380 round on his desk. "He was going to kill you, dude," he said. "He pulled the trigger."

Shank eventually testified against this very large and dangerous man. His parole was revoked, and he was given an additional eight years in prison for the attack. Luck, or fate, that's all it was that saved Shank's life.

There is one more type of shooting that many law enforcement officers have witnessed—and they never forget them. Some people are serious about not going back to prison. Rather than be arrested, they kill themselves. Most law enforcement officers follow a simple rule: one shot means suicide, two shots means they are shooting at us. John Bolen once chased a fugitive into the woods. "When we heard a single gunshot, we thought it was fired at us so we took cover and waited. After several minutes of silence we followed him into the woods and searched but couldn't find him. We figured he had taken a shot at us to keep us at bay so he could escape and then had successfully gotten out of the woods. That wasn't true. A day later a hunter found his body; he'd killed himself."

No one can explain why people choose to take their own lives when they just as easily could fire—sometimes point-blank—at law enforcement officers. Fortunately for officers, they do make that choice. Frank Anderson will never forget the day in the late 1960s that he pursued a fugitive who had escaped from custody inside a courthouse, stole a weapon from a deputy sheriff, carjacked a vehicle, and took off.

> He had been in jail for robbery, but we knew that he had hung out with a group of folks from a certain part of town. So me and my partner went down there and started asking people if they had seen him. One person told us he had been there and run out when he saw us coming; he'd run out of the place and down an embankment. We walked out the back and looked down. It was a slope of about twenty-five feet and there were railroad tracks on top of it. As we were standing there, the guy fired a shot that went right past us. He was down there, hiding behind a clump of bushes. That's when we called for help.

Eventually more than fifty law enforcement officers responded, and they brought the canines with them. At that time Anderson was the only black deputy marshal and he remembers vividly one of those dogs looking at him—and jumping up. "I was getting ready to shoot him," he says. "The trainer stopped him." The handlers sent the dogs down—and then they called them back. Anderson's commanding officer was afraid that the fugitive might shoot the dogs, so he decided to send several men down the slope. As Anderson says,

> A lot of people declined to go down there. I thought it was my job. So six of us moved real carefully down that slope. When we were no more than ten feet away from the bush, he fired one shot. He could have fired at us, but instead he blew his brains out.
>
> After we got back up top, my commanding officer ordered me to go back down there and help carry him out of there. I told him, "You tell them coward sons of bitches they can go in there and carry him out because he can't hurt them now."
> And that's the way it happened.

The Marshals Service and the entire law enforcement community have changed drastically and forever since Frank Anderson became a deputy U.S. marshal in 1965. In many ways the U.S. Marshals Service is both the oldest and the newest law enforcement organization. Many of the duties assigned to the marshals by George Washington haven't changed very much; the U.S. Marshals Service remains the enforcement arm of the American legal system. The traditional tasks of policing and protecting the courts, transporting prisoners, and seizing and disposing of forfeited assets have been expanded to include the operation of the Witness Protection Program and the enforcement of the Adam Walsh Act, which involves tracking sex offenders. But recent changes in law enforcement strategy have resulted in more cooperation between federal agencies and local departments than ever before in history and fundamentally changed the organization.

There is a permanent criminal class in this country, continually moving across local and state borders without establishing roots, many of them surviving by committing more crimes. Tracking down these people, arresting them, and taking them off the streets has quietly become the primary function of the United States Marshals Service. "Most people still don't know too much about us," says Harry Layne, who joined the Marshals Service in 1979 and, after retiring officially, twenty-five years later returned to the organization as a contractor, a special deputy U.S. marshal.

During my career just about everything changed. Everything. Except one thing. What we do really isn't that complicated: Growing up I wanted to be just like my hero, the lawyer F. Lee Bailey. I wanted to defend the oppressed and the innocent and make sure everyone got justice. But when I was in law school, my older sister was attending Southern Connecticut College while working as a club singer to make some extra money. One night a guy followed her as she was walking home and attacked her and stabbed her seventeen times.

He wasn't difficult to find. He also cut himself in the struggle and left a blood trail in the snow that went to his girlfriend's apartment. He'd told his girlfriend he'd been attacked by a gang and that she should burn his bloody clothes, but she hadn't done it. He was arrested and convicted. But what bothered me is that he was convicted of second-degree murder because they couldn't prove the murder was committed during the commission of a felony, robbery, or rape. But what else would be his intention at that hour? Then I found out that there was an arrest warrant out on him in Boston for rape. If the Boston PD had done its job and arrested this guy, he wouldn't have been on the street to kill my sister. And the prosecuting side made me angry because I felt with more effort they could've proved first-degree murder. So he went to prison; I never wanted to know when he was getting out because I was afraid of what I might do. Eventually he did get out, and he reoffended and went back to prison and died in prison.

But it was that anger, that hurt, that led me to want to put bad guys in jail. I changed my career path. I've been doing it ever since. Putting bad guys in jail is what we all do, every day, and what we intend to keep on doing.

Acknowledgments

I would like to thank some of the many people who have helped me throughout my career, provided guidance and encouragement, and hoisted a beverage or two with me. I quickly realized that the number of people who have helped me along the way is staggering and I am so grateful and blessed.

To my two Sergeants at the Tallahassee Police Department: David Frisby and Tony Ash, thanks for not quitting on a young police officer and for teaching me the ropes.

I thank Louie McKinney, Tony Perez, and Bob Finan, my bosses in the Enforcement/Investigative Division for all their support, wisdom, and advice.

To my directors: the Honorable Judge K. Michael Moore, John Clark, and Stacia Hylton. Thank you for promoting me; I hope it wasn't the hardest decision you had to make.

To the guys I could sit back, watch, and learn from: Jerry Lowery, Harry Layne, Danny Stoltz, Don Ward, John "Spanky" Clark, Bobby Leschorn, Art Roderick, W. S. Robertson, Mike Moran, Jim Carney, and that great Texan John Moriarty.

I'd like to thank the FALCON commanders, who not only had to be away from their districts for months at a time, but worked twelve to sixteen hours a day running the most successful nationwide law enforcement operations in U.S. history! My sincere gratitude to Chief Deputies Brad Miller, Dave Dimmitt, Karen Simons, Dave Harlow, Bill Fallon, and Tommy Thompson.

My special thanks to the best senior staff anyone has ever had: Geoff Shank, Debra Jenkins, Michelle Arnold, Dave Harlow, and Joel Kirch. As hard as we worked, we laughed equally hard.

I'd like to recognize the Chiefs and all the men and women of the Technical Operations Group (TOG), who are the world's best technical surveillance manhunters. To them I say that by the end of my career I think I actually understood 85 to 90 percent of your briefings to me. First and foremost I stand in awe of Bill "Huf" Hufnagel, who was the designer and developer of the entire TOG unit, taking it from a one-man unit to what it is today. Many thanks and much appreciation to John Cuff, the late Bob Bouffard, Scott Samuels, Jimmy Bankston, Brian Maxwell, Joe Parker, Mike Moran, and Steve Prosser. I am so glad you all are on our side.

There is a special place in my heart for the regional Task Force Commanders because I know what it takes to bring multiple districts and dozens of agencies together to work in harmony, set egos aside, and get the job done. My hat is off to those who accepted the challenge and succeeded at the highest level: John Clark, Timmy Williams, Keith Booker, Buck Smith, Rob Fernandez, Lenny DePaul, Tom Hession, and Frank Chiumento.

I never learned more about people, law enforcement officers, or running a multi-agency task force than I did in Puerto Rico. We had cops who couldn't speak English and deputies who couldn't speak Spanish; we melded them together and in a short period of time they all spoke Police/*Policía* fluently! My heartfelt acknowledgment to my favorite task force in the world and to my amigos: Rolando Fuentes-Lopez, Juan Correa, Marcos Penalosa, Danny Alvarado, and Jose Pena. You welcomed me into your "Enchanted Island," your culture, and your homes and showed me that our differences meant nothing; we are all the same because we carry a badge and a gun and are honor bound by duty. *Mira Mira.*

I realize that there are so many other people who have helped me along the way, and if I've overlooked anyone it certainly isn't because I didn't appreciate you.

—MIKE EARP

My introduction to the men and women of the U.S. Marshals Service was made by my friend and agent, the inimitable, the unique, and the greatly missed Mickey Freiberg. Somewhere Mickey is still on the phone making deals.

I also would like to acknowledge the longtime friendship and assistance of arguably the greatest power punchball player in Wickshire School history, Jerry Stern.

I also would like to express my appreciation to Rich Soll, to whom I have long been able to turn for no-frills advice when things get a little hectic or confusing, and who has been there when I've needed him. Or not.

This is the first book I've done with editor Peter Hubbard, whose quiet encouragement, consistent enthusiasm, and fine pen have added immeasurably to the quality of this book, and I am grateful for his contributions.

I also greatly appreciate the fine work done by my agent, Objective Entertainment's Ian Kleinert, who has been there throughout this process.

It would not have been possible to write this book without the assistance of Casson Masters and his absolutely first-rate transcription service, Scribecorp. Anyone in need of rapid and accurate transcriptions could not possibly find a better service.

There is so much work that goes into a project like this; it required very long days and nights and completing it would not have been possible without the love and support of my wife, Laura Stevens Fisher. She is at the center of everything good that happens in my life, and in addition to loving her, I appreciate her. Oh, and I also appreciate Belle the small dog, who sat with me every single day as I worked on this.

Finally, when a writer begins a project, he never knows what he will take away at the end. In this instance, in addition to the extraordinary appreciation I've gained for the U.S. Marshals Service, I've been fortunate to have gained some wonderful friendships, especially that of Mike Earp, a legendary figure in the service's history and a man whose low-key demeanor can't disguise his amazing accomplishments, and Lenny and Ellie DePaul. Thank you, all of you.

—DAVID FISHER